W9-BGO-553

CALLED FOR FREEDOM

CALLED FOR FREEDOM

The Changing Context of Liberation Theology

José Comblin

Translated by Phillip Berryman

ORBIS BOOKS
Maryknoll, New York 10545

Third Printing, September 2001

The Catholic Foreign Mission Society of America (Maryknoll) recruits and trains people for overseas missionary service. Through Orbis Books, Maryknoll aims to foster the international dialogue that is essential to mission. The books published, however, reflect the opinions of their authors and are not meant to represent the official position of the society.

Manufactured in the United States of America.

Library of Congress Cataloging-in-Publication Data

Comblin, Joseph, 1923–
    [Cristãos rumo ao Século XXI. English]
    Called for freedom : the changing context of liberation theology /
José Comblin; translated by Phillip Berryman.
      p. cm.
    Includes index.
    ISBN 1-57075-173-0 (pbk.)
    1. Liberation theology. I. Title.
BT83.57.C65413   1998
230'.0464—dc21
                                                97-48999
                                                  CIP

CONTENTS

TRANSLATOR'S FOREWORD

"Father Comblin, what would you say is the church's biggest problem?"

The Belgian-born theologian Joseph Comblin was being interviewed in 1962, when expectations had been raised by the opening of Vatican Council II.

"Antibiotics," he answered.

Puzzlement—had they misunderstood his Spanish? Or had he misunderstood the question?

Antibiotics, he explained, because they keep bishops alive much longer today.

It was an eccentric reply from someone whose "ec-centricity" (being off-center) enables him to see things from a fresh perspective. The remark was not intended to ridicule bishops—indeed, Comblin has worked closely with progressive bishops in Chile and Brazil for decades—but to indicate the problem of a church being led by men who had come of age before the council. Likewise, he was suggesting that the church's problems are rooted as much in the stubbornness of reality as in doctrinal or theological concepts. Finally, such whimsy may have punctured a bit of the solemnity surrounding the Puebla meeting: the CELAM and Vatican forces combating liberation theology, the liberation theologians who had been pointedly excluded from the official conclave but were meeting "outside the walls," and perhaps the journalists themselves.

Like its author this book is eccentric and does not fit easily into any neat theological category: systematics, foundational, historical, or theological ethics. It is closest perhaps to pastoral or practical theology, inasmuch as it is concerned with what is to be done, but it is primarily a reflection on the emerging context and does not offer detailed practical conclusions, let alone a comprehensive program.

What Comblin says here is somewhat different from the general tenor of his Latin American colleagues who since 1990 have been saying something like this: "Contrary to the claims of our critics, the end of the communist world does not affect what we have been doing. Our commitment was never to Marxism but to the poor, and today's triumphant neoliberalism is aggravating poverty. Of course some rethinking is in order, but liberation theology is now more urgent than ever." Little such rethinking is in evidence, however; with some references to "globalization" and observations on emerging themes like ecology, Latin American theologians have largely reiterated familiar themes. As early as 1992, however, Comblin was speaking of the "ambiguity, uneasiness, and uncertainty" of the present and expressing the concerns he put into this book.[1]

His language is blunt, for example, "Liberation theology is at a standstill, first of all, because Catholic theology and Christian theology in general are at a standstill; nothing new is coming out." That will probably be news to both theologians and their students who feel overwhelmed by the seemingly unlimited fields that must be covered, and the up-for-grabs atmosphere of post-modernity. Yet it strikes me that the most important ideas of post-Vatican II theology were launched by, say, 1975, and since that time we have witnessed a tug-of-war between those seeking to pursue the conciliar directions further and "restorationists" seeking to rein them in. Comblin's unnuanced statement makes an important point, that we are far from the ferment of the Council and its immediate aftermath.

Another blunt observation: "Traditional peasants are destined to disappear in Brazil; young peasants are convinced of that." In 1965, when I went to work in Panama, close to half of Latin Americans could be called *campesinos*; today about 75% of Latin America is classified as urban and a high percentage live in large urban areas (four of the ten largest cities in the world are in Latin America). While the general pattern of urbanization is obvious, I am not aware of any scholars who assert that peasants are going to disappear. Comblin is facing the likelihood that he has devoted almost forty years of his life to a people whose way of life is vanishing.

He states that while leftist organizers and intellectuals were dreaming of revolution and saw popular organizations (unions, peasant cooperatives, etc.) as part of a larger revolutionary movement, the people did not share the organizers' grand visions, even though they might attend a rally or march in a demonstration. They were moving to the city where they have been forging history not by taking state power, but by slowly building houses (out of scrap plywood or cinder block), and organizing to meet their needs (water, electricity, schools, clinics, bus service). The big story of the past generation turns out to be not revolution, but the building of the city.

Yet where is this story reflected in Latin American theology (including many dozens of Orbis books)? Doesn't much theological and pastoral writing from and about Latin America tend to perpetuate the notion that the typical Latin American, even today, is a peasant?

Comblin makes blunt observations about other topics frequently discussed uncritically in the theological literature:

- the "irruption of the poor": certainly the issue of the poor has "broken into" the awareness of the church, but the poor are far from having achieved power, as they are the first to realize;
- *conscientización* (consciousness-raising): it has often meant that people learn to bandy about new terms but their actions are far from the rhetoric;

- Christian base communities: they arose not from the people but from pastoral agents, who saw in them both a new form of church and the promise of a new society. When such hopes were frustrated, pastoral agents often gave up on them.

What is new is not that such observations have been made—critics of liberation theology have made them for years—but that someone strongly identified with the Medellín spirit in Latin America should raise the questions. Comblin has the intellectual and moral courage to question his own life work and that of his generation.

I first met Joseph (in Latin America called "José" with either Spanish or Portuguese pronunciation) Comblin in 1968 when I studied at IPLA (Instituto Pastoral Latinoamericano) in Quito. He was then an object of controversy because a background paper he had written for the Brazilian bishops in preparation for the upcoming Medellín conference had been leaked to a major Brazilian paper. The portion of the document that drew fire was a section on revolution, then a topic very much in the air throughout the continent. Although his intention was simply to clarify for bishops what Latin American revolutions might entail, the document was presented as a call to arms—at the very time when the Brazilian military government was becoming more repressive. After several weeks of negotiations he was allowed to return to Brazil, but in 1972, as he was returning from his annual trip to Europe, he was denied re-entry. He then went to work in the diocese of Talca in southern Chile, and remained even after the 1973 coup, when many church people, especially those identified with "Christians for Socialism," were forced to leave.   By the late 1970s, he became persona non grata to the Chilean military regime, but by this time he was able to return to Brazil, where he worked in the diocese of Joao Pessoa, with Bishop Jose Maria Pires.

In person Comblin is no firebrand. Thick glasses, frequent blinking to the point of being a nervous tic, nondescript clothes, and slow deliberate speech still accented in Spanish and Portuguese after almost four decades, all reinforce an impression of professorial shyness. Juan Luis Segundo remarked good-naturedly that Comblin's personal demeanor belied an underlying aggressiveness. It was both a psychological interpretation and an expression of admiration. Comblin is perhaps most himself when presenting a lecture series or workshop. (Indeed, I suspect that this book originated in a series of presentations that he later committed to writing.)

During that period of enforced idleness in Quito, I recall Comblin spending time listening to and counseling a number of sisters and priests at IPLA. Like his Latin American theological colleagues, he does his teaching not primarily in universities but in short courses and workshops, and it is those encounters that pose the theological questions for him. Although it is a commonplace to claim that both sides learn in such dialogue, I think it is especially true for Comblin. This book is testimony to his openness to fresh questions.

My other recollection of that time was that he was continually reading and writing (the clacking of his manual typewriter echoed down the halls for hours on end). His reading, to judge from the bibliography here and elsewhere, is wide rather than exhaustive. "Always read the heterodox," he once remarked with a smile. He was talking about historical works, but the implication was that it is better to employ one's limited reading time with authors who will say the unexpected than to amass an unassailable bibliography on a narrow topic.

Comblin is willing to face unwelcome developments. In this book, for example, he several times notes that Latin American societies are emulating the rich world and particularly the United States, and that hence to understand where Latin America is heading one must study the United States. For that reason he pays attention to authors like Robert Reich and Peter Drucker. This is a harsh saying to those who have hoped for more than a generation that Latin America would emerge from "cultural dependency." Comblin is not advocating that Brazilians and Latin Americans relinquish attempts to forge their own culture; indeed, the need to do so is a major theme in this book. His characteristic approach, however, is to face squarely what is actually happening, as distasteful and disheartening as that might be, in order to ground possible initiatives in reality.

One reason why Comblin has received little attention from the theological world, outside of Latin America, is that many of his writings are on ostensibly non-theological matters: massive theologies of peace, the city, and revolution in French, and works done in Brazil on education and nationalism (all from the 1960s and 1970s).[2] Others are pastoral reflections, and yet others are scripture commentaries (his degree from Louvain is in scripture).[3] Comblin often comes up with quirky interpretations, as in a 1969 study of time, where after surveying secular theories, cyclical and progressive (Toynbee, Marx, etc.), and theologies (Cullmann, Teilhard de Chardin, etc.) he states that the biblical notion of time is to be found in the genealogies (Genesis, Matthew, Luke). The answer is at first startling (like "antibiotics") but he seriously means that the biblical authors really understand time in terms of human generations and that the overall direction is in God's hands. Since by temperament I am far more concerned about the horizon of my own lifespan than in any "Omega point" I found this quite congenial.[4]

This brings me back to a feature of many of Comblin's writings, a lack of concern for the judgement of the theological and scholarly world. The style in this book is colloquial to the edge of carelessness—the kind of remarks scholars themselves might make in conversation. The upshot is a kind of refreshing candor, as, for example, when he discusses the way the will of God is often presented as external to people and arbitrary. Like human beings, God is imagined to be affirming his own power "by humbling the freedom of his creature. . . . This is all blasphemy, but one that is constantly repeated. The church's documents themselves are not exempt from it" (e.g., a Vatican II document where superiors are said to "take God's place"). In such colloquial writing an emphatic point can be made quickly and almost in passing, but the underlying theological seriousness may not always be apparent.

Potential readers of this English translation may also be tempted to wonder what light the reflections of a Belgian theologian in Brazil can shed on the present predicament of the church elsewhere. At the very least, this book should speak to those who have been inspired by liberation theology and its associated pastoral work, whether in the form of base communities, or in the defense of human rights under military dictatorships in South and Central America, or currently in Chiapas.

I would argue, moreover, that the "ec-centricity" of this book, the fact that it is written from rural Brazil, may help us see our emerging world more clearly than the oversupply of images we receive from Washington and Hollywood. Comblin notes, for example, that the Latin American privileged are increasingly moving out of the cities to enclose themselves in their own enclaves where they do not have to encounter the poor around them. In "seceding" from the rest of society, they are imitating what they observe in the United States (gated communities) but they also stand in continuity with traditional Latin American class patterns. Comblin's reflections here may help us open our eyes to the growing "social apartheid" around us. Although his reflections on the theological and pastoral consequences are aimed primarily at Brazil and the rest of Latin America, I think they offer a useful triangulation effect.

Rather than a systematic reflection on liberation, this book is primarily an invitation. The author is aware that the world in which he has carried out his life work is passing. Now in his mid-seventies, Comblin is encouraging younger generations to take a fresh look at what is happening, by assessing critically the work of the recent past, and drawing on the long tradition of the church to imagine the tasks of a new generation. We can certainly learn from Comblin's often startling observations, but more importantly, we can be prodded to similarly reflect on our recent past, on our traditions, and on the challenges of a new moment.

—Phillip Berryman

PREFACE

In a recent article, Gustavo Gutiérrez wrote:

> A series of economic, political, and ecclesial events around the world, in Latin America, and in individual countries, lead one to think that the period when recent Latin American theological reflection was born is now coming to an end. These years have been stimulating and creative, yet tense and conflictive as well. Given the emerging new situations (the worsening of poverty and the end of certain political projects, for example), many earlier discussions do not respond to current challenges.
>
> All indications are that a different period is beginning. It is ever more necessary that all be involved in dealing with the enormous questions with which the reality of Latin America confronts us.[1]

These are wise words. From many places we are now hearing a call to evaluate the past phase and reflect on the emerging new situations.

Latin America has changed over the course of the past thirty years. From a situation of oppression it has gone to one of exclusion.[2] Population has doubled. Almost half of the population has migrated from the countryside to the city, but does not know how to deal with the city. A vast amount of wealth has been accumulated, but it has been concentrated in a privileged minority. A "First World" has been erected in islands of abundance and consumerism on the outskirts of the city, but the vast majority is looking for a way to survive in a parallel economy.

What does all of this mean? What are the signs of these new times?

Liberation is more pressing and yet it is further away. Thirty years ago everything seemed simple; now everything seems complicated.

This book is a modest contribution intended to stimulate other writers, especially younger people who look at things with a fresh eye. If, as Gutiérrez says, one stage of history has ended, we cannot blindly try to keep it going. It is time to pause, evaluate, and prepare for a new history.[3] The important thing is to understand, as far as possible, what is happening.

The church has changed. Thirty years ago the talk was of secularization, history, and incarnation into history. Today the talk tends in a spiritual direction. The church's concern was with rationalism; now it is with irrationalism. But the church is at the service of the world, and cannot withdraw from it. Liberation continues to be a challenge, now more than ever. Although it is less popular, theologians have a mission to remind us of this.

This book is intended for a broad public; it will not teach specialists anything new. It simply seeks to gather for a non-specialized public information that is spread throughout many more works that are more specialized and not readily available to non-professionals.

Hence, references are supplied for a few works but no complete bibliography is provided. Moreover, the topics are so broad that so brief an overview can only present some aspects of the issues discussed. Even so, we think that it can provide a useful introduction for anyone wishing to delve deeper into the present situation of the world and the church.

God willing, the author may one day take up the issues considered more profoundly and more substantially. In order to respond to the most urgent demands, this more modest work may at least (who knows?) awaken the desire to learn more about the topics considered here.

INTRODUCTION: FACTS

End of the Socialist Revolution

The most obvious fact today is that the great revolution that spans almost the entire twentieth century—the revolution that begins in 1917 in Russia and ends in 1989 with the fall of the Soviet Union—is over. Some observers believe that the twentieth century began in 1914 and ended in 1989. If that is so, we are already in the twenty-first century, because the great movements that are going to drive the twenty-first century are already center stage.

The disappearance of the Soviet Union has had a worldwide impact.[1] Indeed, the Soviet Union was in decline starting in the 1970s, and the Marxist ideology that guided it has lost all credibility throughout the world since 1973–75. The disappearance of the Soviet Union has brought in its train the end of the Warsaw Pact and regime changes in all countries of Eastern Europe, the splitting up of the Soviet Union itself and Yugoslavia into a large number of unstable Republics, profound changes in the socialist regimes in China, Vietnam, and even North Korea in Asia, and Cuba in the Americas, and the ruin of pro-Soviet regimes in Angola, Mozambique, and Guinea in Africa, the realignment of the Arab Middle East in dependence on the United States, and agreements between Israel and its neighbors, including the PLO (Palestine Liberation Organization).

The decline and fall of the Soviet Union have also had an impact on Latin America. They have had an impact on the way that redemocratization has taken place. Many were hoping that the military regimes were simply a parenthesis and that history would resume from the point at which the military regimes had interrupted it. They were hoping that a new democracy in Chile would be a continuation of Salvador Allende, that the fall of the military in Argentina would mean a return to the Peronism of the previous years, that democracy in Brazil would be the continuation of the trends that appeared between 1956 and 1964, and so forth. Nothing like that took place. The forces of the left have found themselves very much weakened. Moreover, the many movements said to be "national liberation" movements, and even those of guerrillas, have found themselves having to yield, and to enter into the new supposedly democratic systems or be left powerless. All left movements are going through a crisis of conscience; they find that they have no program, no specific objectives, and are very much divided.[2]

In Western Europe the end of the Soviet Union also led to a loss of cred-ibility in social democracy which is now on the defensive and has no prospects for the immediate future. The welfare state and state planning of the economy have been discredited. A vast socialist experiment has come to an end.

This does not mean that socialism has no future. Actual socialist tenden-cies are so deeply rooted in humankind that they will inevitably have to reap-pear. It will not be the same socialism, however; it will not be a repeat of 1917 and the experiences flowing from 1917. Conditions will be completely different, and people learn from experience. The same mistakes will reap-pear, but not with the same intensity or in the same manner.[3] In the mean-time, there is no way to imagine, even vaguely, what a new socialist experience might be like.

Decline of the Nation-State

Many signs indicate that the nation-states of Western Europe and North America are very much affected by the crisis.[4] States can no longer control financial speculation and protect national currency. They have a hard time resisting the pressures of the large multinationals to "liberalize" markets, in other words to hand them over to the control of large corporations, which are acting ever more independently.

States have lost control over "national culture" and are no longer able to maintain a national ideology (patriotism, etc.). Culture has become increas-ingly something produced industrially. Culture has entered the market, and the culture market is preeminently United States territory. The upshot is that the public school has been left without content and national education is a pure formula with nothing behind it. The school is now preparing not citi-zens but consumers for the large corporations, and perhaps some workers (there is no longer such a great need for workers).

Military service is no longer the great school of the nation, since armies have become professional. Politics has become a show, like TV game shows. Since power always stays in the same hands, elections have no more impact than games on TV. States no longer have enough money to finance ambitious projects. They are managing the present but are not preparing the future. Democratic governments try to please public opinion; they are slaves of opin-ion polls such as IBOPE (Brazilian Institute of Public Opinion and Statistics), and operate with one eye on the next elections. The democratic system has become hollow.

The crisis of the state is also noticeable in Latin America, to the point where one of the topics most discussed in politics is the "governability" of the nation.[5] Thus in Latin America redemocratization has coincided with a strong wave of depoliticization. Significantly, the only political issues that bring out crowds are demonstrations of rejection (in Brazil, the "Collor Out" cam-paign against corruption, the impeachment campaign, the campaign against corruption in congress); by contrast, the 1994 election campaign did not arouse people's passions.

Return to the Cultural

While the political is on the wane, the cultural is on the rise. This has been noticeable since the 1970s and is still increasing.

The return to the cultural is primarily a return to religion. Around the world we are witnessing a striking resurgence of the phenomenon of religion. It involves not only the great traditional religions, but also many heterodox manifestations of the religious spirit. It can be said that all the vast religious material of the past of all cultures is being renewed and taking on new life. In particular, all the expressions of the *gnosticism* that came from ancient Egypt or Mesopotamia and spread throughout the Roman empire are coming back in new forms.[6]

The major traditional institutions of Christianity are not benefitting much from this religious resurgence. By contrast, new churches are arising in Africa and Latin America. They are independent churches; in Latin America, most of them are pentecostal. It is significant that within the Catholic church it is the charismatic renewal that is growing most rapidly, although the Catholic hierarchy has not yet found a place for it.

The older generation, which some time ago became familiar with a "theology of secularization" and whose sight was obscured by the issues raised by Gogarten and by the early Harvey Cox, is puzzled and disconcerted by all this. They thought that religion was in crisis and that the move was to politics, and suddenly politics is in crisis and religion is the beneficiary!

It is not just religion that benefits from the return to the cultural. As the state declines, all groups that can be constituted around strong signs of identity come out stronger. With the state weakened, indigenous movements become stronger, and they are currently the strongest social movements. Black consciousness movements have all the doors open, as do Afro-American religions. All kinds of differences can serve as the basis for forming powerful groups that tend to become independent fiefdoms within the weakened state, which is resigned to tolerating it. Cultural universes are set up on the basis of a sport (each team has its tribe), a dance (tribes of rock, rap, reggae, and so forth), an oriental wisdom, a kind of alternative medicine, a type of therapy, and so forth. Fashions, diets, celebrations, clothes— anything can serve to classify today's inhabitants, who show little concern for their citizenship.[7]

The Technological Third Wave

The previous three phenomena are particularly rooted in this fourth one, the most important of them all because it has struck the blow that has impacted the rest.

This is not the place for describing the profound technological changes that have led to radical changes in the economic and in social relations in recent decades and are producing ever more extensive changes. These changes are well known and have been made accessible to all who are interested through many works of scholarly popularization intended for the broad public.[8]

The first industrial revolution based on technological discoveries was built on coal and steel. The second was based on petroleum and electricity. In the third revolution, which is now underway, the technological developments have to do primarily with information and communications techniques. This new stage has led to a radical change in the speed of technological inventions. Machines used to become obsolete in fifty years. Then came a time when machines could operate for twenty years. Today they are obsolete in three years. The pace of inventions is such that being ahead in innovation amounts to creating and dominating the market.

The upshot is that in the economy, for example, given the array of new products, selling is more basic than producing; controlling consumption is more important than controlling production. What difference would it make if workers could control production but had no control over consumption?

Ease of communication enables production to be decentralized, automation makes it possible to drastically reduce the number of workers in industry, banks, sales, and so forth. Production can be shifted more easily. There is no longer any such thing as a national economy; the whole economy is being globalized. At least this is the prevailing trend, and in a few years it will be a reality.

In social terms, the result is the breakdown of what used to be the working class, which is now on its way to being dissolved into a large number of different functions, just like what happened in earlier phases of industry that destroyed the traditional peasant classes. Henceforth, knowledge is more important than labor or raw materials; it is even more important than capital, because capital shifts to where knowledge is located.[9]

The crisis of socialism results mainly from this wave of new technologies, because the Soviet economy was unable to take advantage of it and was left behind by the three poles, namely the United States, Japan, and Western Europe. The Soviet elites were unwilling to remain in a backward economy and so they gave up. Similarly, the semi-directed economies of social democracy are now in crisis. Social democratic parties have either lost their leadership or have adopted the ideology of their adversaries.

The crisis of the nation-state is largely the result of changes in the economy; that is even more true in Latin America than in Europe. Huge economic conglomerates are demanding ever greater privileges and are ever less willing to contribute. The new ruling class feels no solidarity with the nation, and is alien to any "patriotism" or "nationalism." Commercialized and transnationalized culture devalues the nation-state. Entertainment culture reduces politics to an amusing game.

Finally, the renewal of religion and of culture in general results from the general depolitization of society. Daily life occupies the center of attention. Once overall identification with the nation and nationalism has been lost, people look for other identities and they find them in religion and in the wide variety of cultural factors.

Such are the facts, presented schematically, simply as a way of indicating the broad phenomena which are described in many easily available works. The aim of this work is not to describe the present situation of the world but simply to situate the challenges posed to Christians in today's world.

Many Christians who were familiar with the situation prior to 1964 hoped that the redemocratization of Brazil would be a revival of contact with the movements, objectives, and ideologies of that time. Many of those who experienced the military regime, and the church's struggles under the military regime, thought that the dreams which nourished that struggle would be realized with the return to democracy.[10] They hoped that an agrarian reform would be carried out, workers would participate in the life of the nation, wealth would be better distributed, and so forth. They thought that base communities would supply the predominant model in the church and could embody a church at the service of the people, by putting the preferential option for the poor into practice. None of this took place; they have been left perplexed.

In fact, we stand facing a new situation in which earlier models no longer apply. Now at the end of the twentieth century, which is already the beginning of the twenty-first century, the times call for invention and creation. We all sense that the political system is not working, and is becoming obsolete. The same is true of education and the organization of health care, of politics even more, and of the armed forces most of all. Economic life has entered a transition phase and no one knows where it will end. Labor is very much in flux. Cities are becoming unlivable.

The point is not to repudiate the past. Indeed, all the aspirations and struggles of the past will have to be transformed if they are to become effective.

The church has a limited role in changing the world, but that task can be effective and meaningful. It can effectively serve the coming of God's reign; it can also pass it by and miss its chance in history.

This book does not have great ambitions. The time has not yet come for comprehensive works. The aim here is simply to provide some reflections with a view to a new stage in Latin American Christian thought, keeping in mind the new facts and the direction that events are likely to take over the next few years.

1

THE CHURCH CONTEXT

Recent developments affecting the life of the Catholic church, such as the new evangelization, the option for the poor, liberation theology, the "new movements," and so forth, are not isolated events. They are part of a development whose origins can be traced to the transition between the pontificates of Pius IX and Leo XIII. An era of "new evangelization" began with Leo XIII; *Rerum Novarum* laid the foundations for an option for the poor that became explicit under John XXIII. Since then, however, several stages have occurred within that same process. It is well to be aware of how the process has unfolded.[1]

Evolution of the New Evangelization

Before Leo XIII

To the end of his pontificate, Pius IX adhered firmly to the line followed by his predecessors since Pius VI. This line consisted in giving a single answer to modernity as it was embodied in political and social revolutions, new philosophies, and the new incipient sciences: a categorical "no." With modernity there could be no dialogue or even listening: the Catholic church could only resist, denounce, and condemn. The church hoped that modern society would collapse under the weight of its errors and its crimes, and that the various peoples, having recognized their error, would repentantly return to the bosom of the church. The church confidently repeated the same gospel as ever, stating that it was the ancient and traditional gospel and that it could offer nothing new. The very expression "new evangelization" would have been suspect—as if it thereby entailed some concession to modern error.

Since the pope insisted on his temporal sovereignty over the papal states, he shared the cause of the European monarchs. The pope wanted to maintain or reconstitute the christendom that existed before the French revolution. The traditional gospel included the political order of christendom.

1

After 1870, however, despite the obstinacy of Pius IX, the more clear-sighted were aware that his position was becoming untenable, and they were preparing the shift that was to take place in the subsequent papacy. Nothing was to be gained by condemning—sheer condemnation would never make the world turn to the church. It was necessary to shift discourse, accept some fundamental themes of modernity, and enter into dialogue with modern society, because it was neither collapsing nor disappearing. On the contrary, it was obvious that the modern world was taking firm hold. Thus it was that Leo XIII began the discourse of the "new evangelization," thereby authorizing the clear-sighted minorities who were conscious of where society was going.[2]

The New Discourse of Leo XIII

We cannot claim that Leo XIII foresaw all the consequences of the decisions he made. Personally, he did not want drastic changes, and he still shared many of the prejudices of his contemporaries. Many still thought against the backdrop of christendom. Nevertheless, it is clear that Leo XIII wanted to speak to his contemporaries in a new way. He was willing to loosen the hold over many of the positions that his predecessors had defended.

His new discourse is contained in his political and social encyclicals. In a sense, he pioneered a new literary genre, the encyclical, which his predecessors had not used much. Leo XIII's new discourse was not foreign to the gospel: it spoke of the implications of the gospel in the temporal world, and in this domain it was an innovation because it broke the ties with the monarchies that formerly used to be regarded as "of divine right."

Leo XIII was quite aware that this was not simply a matter of making adaptations out of sheer political opportunism under the pressure of circumstances. For he sought changes in the philosophy of Christian schools, opened space for biblical and historical research, and encouraged dialogue with the new modern sciences. He wanted a complete opening to the modern world and was aware that the changes would have some effect on all portions of the Christian message, while of course preserving the entire deposit of Christian tradition.[3]

Leo XIII opened the doors to a new evangelization: the church must learn the language of modernity and present Christianity in a way that would not be a stumbling block to modern spirits. He was acknowledging that there was in modernity a certain rationality that could not be rejected.

Through his encyclicals Leo XIII changed the social and political aspects of Catholicism, beginning a new dialogue. They inspired or bolstered Catholic "parties," which ceased to be "conservative" parties seeking to save what could no longer be saved. The new "Catholic" parties, whose model was the Zentrum of the German empire, participated actively in states that were now secularized or on their way to secularization. They contributed toward the working out of a new society, ultimately leading to social democracy or the welfare state. Leo XIII's new evangelization provided the basis for a new Catholic praxis that lasted over a century.[4]

The Modernist Crisis

Leo XIII did not live long enough to see where the reforms he advocated were going in the field of ecclesiastical studies, especially in the areas of biblical exegesis, church history, and philosophy. Immediately after Leo XIII's death, Pius X had to deal with this question and he had no hesitation: he halted the movement and almost managed to stop the entire process set in motion by Leo XIII. All approaches to modernity that entered into conflict with any aspect of dogmatic theology or traditional morality were identified as "modernism" and rejected. Hundreds of theologians and philosophers were condemned or discreetly removed from teaching. A rigorous and merciless purge was carried out. Nor were new entries into the political and social world spared: the condemnation of Marc Sangnier and the Sillon was a warning to all. The social encyclicals came to a halt.[5]

So strong was the antimodernist reaction that its effects have lasted up to the present and were decisive in restraining Vatican II. Even so, after the death of Pius X, his successors returned to the line of the social encyclicals. The "new evangelization" continued in its social and political aspects, but it no longer had any dogmatic and moral effects. Neo-Thomism became the cement of the medieval edifice; it became "paleo-Thomism." Catholic philosophy was marginalized, suspect, and remained practically without influence in the wider world. Biblical exegesis was ultimately freed of its chains, but confined to a domain quite separate from dogmatic and moral theology. Biblical exegesis ran along its own track and had practically no influence on church structures. There was no further "new evangelization" in anything having to do with the deposit of medieval tradition.

The antimodernist reaction is the source of the separation between two sectors in Christianity, the social and political realm where it is possible to innovate, engage in dialogue with the modern world, and propose new ideas, and the theological and dogmatic realm in which one may not innovate, dialogue, or propose new ideas. This separation prevails to this day and has been one of the causes of the problems experienced by a number of those who were said to be liberation theologians.

Catholic Action

A generation later, it seemed that the political parties and the network of social institutions (cooperatives, worker and peasant associations, mutual aid associations, and so forth) that provided the bases for them, represented primarily the attitudes of the most traditional and least modern groups in society (peasants, craftspeople, traditional nobility, etc.). They were not the instrument for a "new evangelization" in the modern world. However, the church's presence in the modern classes (bourgeoisie, proletariat) was quite weak, and very weak in the cities and among intellectuals. Apostles of the new evangelization capable of giving a new direction to Catholic political and social forces could come only from these classes. Catholic Action was intended to recruit the active minorities that the church needed within the new classes and in the more dynamic sectors of society.

Under Pius X, Catholic Action could not become aware of the problem and the challenges that had to be assumed. The major impulse came from Pius XI who was able to discern the tools that could provide him with the needed resources. Pius XI felt that without Catholic Action the church would remain outside of the modern world. That is why Catholic Action was the great hope of the church for about forty years (from Pius XI to Vatican II). It was the active presence of the church in the world, the bearer of the new evangelization. It would provide completely dedicated individual apostles and people to guide Catholic parties and the network of Christian social organizations.[6]

Catholic Action evaporated after it was officially consecrated through the Council's decree on the laity. In fact the Catholic church had charged it with an impossible mission. It then became obvious that enthusiasm alone was not enough for evangelizing and converting the world. The apostles of Catholic Action discovered that there really was a wall between the church and the world and that they were not in a position to knock it down.[7]

The modern world rejected the authoritarian structure of the church, a structure embodied in, and symbolized by, the system extending from parish to diocese to Rome. The modern world no longer accepted clericalism in all its real and symbolic aspects. It expected a gospel other than the traditional catechism. But Catholic Action was strictly subordinated to the clerical system and anything dogmatic remained untouchable. The only modern part of its gospel was the political and social teachings of the encyclicals. The modern world wanted more. Catholic Action sensed that it had surrendered its weapons, or it went looking for its own paths by breaking its ties to the hierarchy,[8] but it was condemned to exile; it either died out or was reduced to tiny groups with no presence in the church. Significantly, in his recent encyclical on mission, John Paul II does not even mention Catholic Action.

The Worker-Priests and the "Nouvelle Théologie"

Around 1940 some more clear-sighted Catholics had recognized the obstacles over which Catholic Action was destined to stumble, namely, the clerical structure and traditional theological doctrine.

The worker-priests (Mission de France, Paris Mission, and other experiences at that time) decided to tackle the first problem. In prisoner-of-war camps in Germany they had discovered that the problem was the priest. The priest was not the solution (there were lots of priests); the priest was the problem. We can anticipate by saying that to this day the priest continues to be the problem rather than the solution, even though there is much talk today about more ordinations.

Pius XII saw clearly that the worker-priests were going to question the entire clerical model, a whole structure that had existed for fifteen centuries. He deflated the movement. In France at that time there were a thousand worker-priests, among 50,000 traditional priests in France and 400,000 around the world. They did not amount to a strong enough argument to show that the church wanted to begin a new phase, so the reply was simple: "You're the exception, but you don't represent your church." In any case, it was a minority that demonstrated the problem.[9]

At the same time, some theologians felt that there was a problem in theology. To begin with, the church could not forever hold onto a modern historical theology alongside a medieval dogmatic theology. Traditional theology was the most obvious obstacle, because Christian language was becoming ever more distant from the language of contemporary people. Seeing a danger here as well, Pius XII halted any effort to bring theology up to date by cutting the roots. Even though the theologians of that period were rehabilitated and some of them were even made cardinals at the end of their lives, the effect of Pius XII's action are felt even today. Because of what he did, Vatican II maintained so many ambiguities and held back from some fundamental options. Bringing theology up to date continues to be a problem in our own day.[10]

The new evangelization does not include a new face for the church nor any new theological expression. It is limited to the church's social doctrine and enshrines the separation between the two parts of the gospel. Vatican II notwithstanding, after the Council the new evangelization was further away from its objectives than ever. Vatican II promised a great deal but it did not change anything radically, and left the problem of evangelization just where it was.

Post-Vatican II Ecclesial Situation outside Europe

What was happening outside Europe throughout this period? How did the church respond to the challenge of evangelization? Actually, outside Europe the local churches tried to imitate what was happening in Europe as much as their means allowed, and they had the support of the Roman church.

After Vatican II, conditions were created for a flourishing of base communities (CEBs) in both Africa and Latin America—with the support of Medellín. [Eds. note: The historic meeting of the Latin American bishops in Medellín, Colombia, in 1968.] (We will have much to say about CEBs later on.) In the 1970s, many had the impression that now, at last, the new evangelization had found the tools that had been lacking: CEBs would be the prime agent of the hoped-for new evangelization. CEBs were thought to have overcome the two obstacles that impeded evangelization in Europe: the clerical structure and medieval theology. In Latin America, the CEBs would be the shape of a declericalized church. Instead of a medieval theology, they had liberation theology which could be intellectually attractive and provide guidance for effective action.[11]

The CEBs no doubt went much further than Catholic Action and anything previously existing for evangelization. If they have not fully achieved their objectives, it is largely because they have not been accepted by most dioceses and parishes in Latin America. There was almost always more declared support than real commitment. The impact on evangelization was always limited because they were not able to really overcome the obstacles already mentioned.

First, it has not been possible to overcome clericalism, because CEBs have remained predominantly subordinated to clerical control in their ideology, theology, mentality, structure, and in their everyday activity. Secondly, they continue to have two ideologies: a medieval dogmatic theology and a liberation theology for the social and political realm.

Of course, the role of CEBs goes beyond these observations on the new evangelization. We will later come back to consider them in other respects. However, at this point we may note that CEBs continue basically with the same problems experienced by Catholic Action.

When a Polish pope rose to the chair of Peter, everyone expected something new. The new pope could only bring new perspectives—and that was indeed the case. The pope brought the experience of the Polish working class which, armed with both its fidelity to traditional theology and the social doctrine of the church, and backed by the clergy, had been able to defeat modernity in its socialist form. The pope seems to think that the working class offers the contemporary world an exemplary evangelization.[12]

Indeed, John Paul II has invited all the churches to a new evangelization. He has returned to this topic that has been present since Leo XIII and given it a very special emphasis. He has exalted the clergy and been concerned to multiply it because for him the traditional clergy is clearly still the solution, not the problem. He has insisted more strictly on the traditional (medieval) theology, culminating in the publication of the new catechism, which is intended to provide the basis for Catholic teaching. He has again raised up the church's social doctrine, bringing it up to date and presenting it to Christians and to nations and peoples as the complete answer to the yearnings of people today.

It could be said that the pope has not paid much attention to the experience of the Western churches since Leo XIII. For him the Polish example was overwhelmingly conclusive. It could serve as the basis for a new evangelization of the world, without any of the changes proposed in the West.[13] The Polish working class existed only in Poland, however. Who might be the agent of the new evangelization in other countries, given the clerical structure, medieval theology, and the church's social teaching?

Certain movements have expressed the same convictions: Opus Dei, Communione e Liberazione, the Schönstatt movement, the Focolari movement, and so forth (especially the first two).[14] Such movements promised to re-evangelize and refashion a christendom with the very same means as those used in Poland. Certainly, those movements have been favored during this papacy, and the pope often looked at the world through their eyes.

We are now coming to the end of this pontificate, and we can say that the problems of the new evangelization in the Western world are still the same. The hoped-for response has not been forthcoming. Moreover, evangelization

in Eastern Europe is obviously problematic, and on other continents the traditional formulas have raised many questions, to the point where it is difficult to maintain this same methodology on all continents.

It is true that very strict orthodoxy has been established in all Catholic
institutions. Even so, Catholics have not been moved to remain faithful to
that orthodoxy. Increasingly, Catholics consult other religions and other
philosophies or forms of wisdom, and each individual secretly prepares his
or her "religious menu." Medieval theology is not reconquering the world.
The propositions of the faith are not questioned within the premises of the
church, but Catholics go looking for information outside their church.[15]

True, the number of priests is growing. But people today are not accepting the traditional style of the clergy: Catholics feel that they are treated like
children. This does not at all mean that the priests are not good. Individually
speaking, they are better than ever in history. Even if all priests were saints,
however, the problem would remain. The holiness of the priest does not
resolve the problem of clericalism.[16]

It is true that the church's social teaching has been updated with judge-
ment, knowledge, and prudence, but it does not win people over by itself.
No one is going to become a Catholic because of the church's social doctrine.
Capitalist society is not as easily destroyed as socialist society.[17]

The new evangelization continues to be an open problem, more acutely
now than a generation ago, because the world has been evolving while the
church was looking much more backward than forward. That is where the
new challenges that did not exist at the end of Vatican II now lie.

The Option for the Poor

Before John XXIII

We can say that until the fourteenth century the Western church continued
to give privileged attention to the poor, at least in intention. The struggle
between the pope and the empire often took the form of a struggle of the
poor against the rich, the defense of the free people in the cities against feu-
dalism. The struggle took place not only at the top, but in every fiefdom, city,
and parish. Parishes arose precisely in order to take ownership of the
churches and the goods of the church out of the hands of landowners. The
alliance between the popes of the thirteenth century and the mendicants is a
symbol of a certain option for the poor (with all the limitations flowing from
the fact that the clergy themselves became property owners in order to struggle against the property of the powerful).[18]

A split occurred in the early fourteenth century: Boniface VIII, the Avignon
popes, the alliance with the kings of France, the condemnation of the spiritual Franciscans, the trials in which a number were burned at the stake, and
finally the condemnations issued by John XXII, to the effect that Jesus was
not poor—all this led to a break.[19] After that, poverty and the issues of the

poor were absent from the activity and official thought of the church. Poverty was a concern of saints like Vincent de Paul or of certain religious who make a vow of poverty, but it was no longer a matter for the church.[20]

Concern for the poor reappeared in the late nineteenth century, as symbolized by the encyclical *Rerum Novarum* (1891), which dealt with the undeserved poverty of workers. Leo XIII took on the defense of the rights of workers. For the first time in several centuries, the pope addressed a particular class, the new poor who were proletarians in industry.[21]

A great deal of research and many reports, episcopal documents, and congresses on the dire situation of the workers helped prepare for *Rerum Novarum* within the church. From the beginnings of industry, voices of lay people and priests were raised to criticize the inhuman conditions of industrial labor. Since then, the critique of industrial poverty has been part of the preaching of the Catholic church.[22] Even so, it can be said that until the 1940s concern for the poor was not placed at the center of the issue of evangelization. Nor did it reach the point of calling into question the church's own way of life.[23] Here also the worker-priests took an important step when they made the "descent into hell" and discovered by experience the chasm separating the situation of the poor from that of the ecclesiastical world.[24]

John XXIII

John XXIII's gestures and his style had a greater impact than his writings and speeches. By his habit of emphasizing his own poor origins, his rejection of signs of power, his abandonment of claims of power, John XXIII encouraged another style, another way of living in the church. It was also he who first spoke of the "church of the poor," indicating that he wanted to make the church come down off its pedestal and go out to meet the poor and humble.[25] His short pontificate was enough to draw out a number of experiences and a number of theological or pastoral directions. They are expressed, for example, in short works like those of Gauthier and Congar at the time of the Council.[26]

All that was not enough to bring Vatican II to move clearly toward an option for the poor. The idea circulated widely behind the scenes at Vatican II but it did not prevail.[27] Even so, it was cultivated by a group of bishops from all continents who at the end of the Council committed themselves to promote a new episcopal style, one poorer and more committed to the causes of the poor.[28] The group is still continuing today. After the council this issue was taken up by the bishops of Latin America who prepared the Medellín conference within the Episcopal conference of Latin America (CELAM).

Medellín (1968)

What had not been possible at Vatican II happened at Medellín because of the intuition and perseverance of some bishops from various places in Latin America. The option for the poor was intended to indicate that the church was being changed to make it more welcome to the poor, and that it was choosing to focus on evangelization and to make the liberation of the poor a priority; in short, it was an option for changing this unjust society.[29] The issue of the poor thus became part of church discourse and has been there ever since. Reality does not always fit what is said, however.[30]

For a number of reasons, since Medellín there has been a very strong movement to reduce the scope of this option. The option was defined as "preferential," not "exclusive." Other options have emerged alongside it, such as the option for youth at Puebla [Eds. note: The meeting of the Latin American bishops in Puebla, Mexico, in 1979].[31]

The expression apparently sounded confusing to many, because the idea of evangelization is confusing. Many view evangelization as having two relatively independent parts: on the one hand, the gospel is a call to choose heaven and an invitation to go there, and on the other hand, the gospel is the expression of the social teaching. The first part, they say, is addressed to all, since the call to go to heaven is intended for everyone. With regard to the social aspect, there is a certain preference for the poor in the sense that the call to justice is more on the side of the poor. Thus, the option for the poor refers only to the second part of the gospel.

On the basis of these two gospels, it is very difficult to give meaning to the expression "option for the poor." The formula ends up being diluted, as indeed happens as it is often used. The option for the poor acquires its full and proper meaning, however, only within a unified notion of the gospel and of salvation.

In any case, Medellín had such an impact that the option for the poor took its place among those things that the universal church had to speak about. The issue can no longer be ignored or passed over.

Even civic bodies, politicians, and economists claim an option for the poor. Capitalism's own "theology" proclaims it and offers consistent capitalism as the only way of carrying out the option for the poor.[32] Such success arouses suspicion: there must be some confusion in interpreting the formula.

The Argument of the New Evangelization

The Argument of the Old Evangelization

truth

In the ages of christendom, evangelization was carried out in the name of truth. Christianity was announced to the peoples of christendom and to others more recently encountered as the only true religion established by the only true God. All were obliged to accept Christianity in its concrete form as it was presented because that was God's will. Not to accept Christianity and to refuse to be subject to the church was to rebel against God and to commit the most serious sin and thus to deserve eternal condemnation.

The line of argument said to be a preparation for faith consisted in proving that Christianity was the true religion, and that the Catholic church was the only church willed by God. Evangelization was based on truth, and it rejected out of hand any discussion that might take into account what was suited to the interlocutors and their interests, preferences, or objections. The evangelizer had to be convincing because he was speaking the truth and no one could question the truth. Truth requires submission in mind and action, and that is all there is to it. The evangelizer was to speak with all the assurance that came with the certainty of speaking the truth. In order to confirm this assurance one need not consult one's hearers, but simply consult the authority by whom one had been sent. With the certainty that their message coincided with the truth guarded by the magisterium, missionaries could proudly face any opposition and any resistance, even to the point of martyrdom.

The new evangelization presented by John Paul II is remarkably similar to the message of what used to be that of christendom. What is new about contemporary evangelization seems to be largely a matter of extrinsic circumstances, not affecting content in the least. Actually, one need only read the recently published *Catechism* to see that there are changes in content, even though they are not presented as such. The church is assumed to have always taught what it teaches now, and thus there is no change in the content of evangelization.

The pope was apparently influenced by his personal experience and by integralist movements, such as Opus Dei and Communione e Liberazione, with which he has identified himself on a number of occasions. To these movements, evangelization means proclaiming the "truth" with all its antimodern rigor, with the entire legacy of christendom. They happily repeat the challenge of the English integralist in the last century: *Creo quia absurdum*. They insistently refuse to make any concession to the modern world.[33]

If truth is still a matter of shaping a complete system as a tight package or the complete system that the integralists like to set up in opposition to the world, we can anticipate that it will not win over many people beyond the sectarian minorities that can be found in any religion, minorities for whom the love for truth is dangerously confused with the fear of exposing themselves to encountering others.[34]

Seeking New Arguments for a New Evangelization

The papacy of Leo XIII made possible the expression of new aspirations and critical observations on christendom and traditional evangelization. A new evangelization began to be articulated, one whose newness referred not only to external aspects but also to the content of the message. Its newness was to be deeper than what would be promoted a century later.

The need for a new evangelization of the modern world has been felt since that time. The newness ought to take into account two basic things. First, modern men and women would never agree to return to christendom taken as a whole. Second, critical studies have shown that the gospel of christendom was quite different from the early Christian gospel; a message so marked by a now surpassed stage of history could never again be presented as the gospel of Jesus Christ.[35]

In the first place, the entire emphasis on the personal subject proper to modernity had to be taken into account. It was also necessary to bear in mind the continuity between basic human dispositions and what Christianity was offering. At first the demands of the new evangelization appeared in the form of a dialectic between immanence and transcendence. Immanence had to do with the aspirations of subjects, and transcendence with the entirety of christendom presented as an indivisible whole, as the objectivity that had to be accepted.

Certain Christian philosophers, such as Blondel, Laberthonnière, and von Hügel, represented the need for the new evangelization in the contemporary world. This movement was abruptly cut off by the antimodernist repression of Pius X in the name of the rights of transcendence.

Forty years later the problem reemerged after a long silence. A new generation of theologians (the *nouvelle théologie* in France—Bouillard, de Lubac, Chenu, Congar—and Karl Rahner and his followers in Germany) once more raised the issue of the content of the new evangelization. The issue took the form of the dialectic of natural and supernatural, and showed the continuity between them.

This initiative was cut off by a new wave of repression under Pius XII. The pope was unwilling to accept any risk for the sake of an opening to a new evangelization. Evangelization would have to be the same as ever with all its medieval theology. The Roman theologians obviously saw clearly that in the efforts of the new theologians was the germ of a revision of the entire contents of medieval theology. To prevent that from happening, they decided to cut the problem at the root.

Although the condemned theologians went on to play an important role in Vatican II, the process was interrupted and the Council did not touch medieval theology except superficially. What was new about Vatican II was found in the Constitution on the Church in the Modern World. Something unprecedented happened: theologians previously condemned became leaders in the subsequent period. However, the process they had set in motion had been halted, and the legacy of christendom was only superficially changed.

After Vatican II, a new generation of theologians continues to present the requirements for the new evangelization of modernity. This generation has once more been condemned or viewed with suspicion: Hans Küng, Schillebeeckx, and with them the journal *Concilium*, and, recently, E. Drewermann. The issue continues to be that of updating the new evangelization for the aspirations of human beings as subjects. The new *Catechism of the Catholic Church* is the response to efforts toward a theology of the new evangelization.

The only aspect of Christianity that can be updated is the church's social doctrine, and that is likewise the only place where the aspirations of modern people can be taken into account. The gospel remains neatly split into two portions: the dogmatic portion, which continues to remain the same, and the political and social portion, which strives to keep up with changing times.

At the end of the nineteenth century, there opened a new front for challenging the traditional content of evangelization: on the basis of historical and literary scholarship, or on the basis of "criticism," as it was called at that time. Indeed, biblical exegesis and historical research gradually won certain rights, once the acute phase of the antimodernist crisis was over. Exegesis and historical theology have managed to respond to some extent to the traditional demands of the Protestant churches since the Reformation. Both biblical exegesis and historical theology have come to the conclusion that the Christian gospel is quite different from medieval theology and from the structural and intellectual legacy of christendom.

All the work in this direction has nonetheless been in vain. Exegesis and historical theology have gone on their way, but nothing new has happened. A number of their conclusions were assumed into the Council's texts but nothing actually changed. The only thing that has been accomplished is that two parallel theologies have been set up in the Catholic church: a biblical and historical theology that is ineffectual because it has no impact on the actual reality of the church, and a moral and dogmatic theology that tranquilly carries on with medieval theology, as though nothing has happened since then, and as though neither biblical exegesis nor history existed. Thus biblical and historical research have never been important for evangelization. For practical purposes, things go along the same as ever.

In the present papacy, a hundred years of attempts and proposals to reexamine evangelization have been dismissed and rejected as useless and dangerous, and the proposal for a new evangelization has been taken over by integralist movements that believe in resurrecting christendom and want nothing but medieval theology, as it was codified in the Council of Trent and sixteenth-century scholasticism. The new evangelization has to be the old one, the one traditional in christendom. It consists of a new proclamation of the "truth" in its objective medieval sense. That is why biblical and historical research have had no impact on the message presented. It is true that they appeared to some extent in the documents of Vatican II, but they have been neutralized, and in practice nothing has changed.

The social teaching itself has been left split into two parts: that which has to do with social justice is subject to evolution and renewal, but that which has to do with sexuality is even more rigidly set than in scholastic theology. That is where truth approaches integralism because no concession to "modern novelties" is allowed. The role of women remains within traditional patterns, far from the concessions won by contemporary feminism.

Why has this new evangelization thus far met with so little interest, given that sociological research shows that people are continually leaving the church? The integralists and the pope seem to assume that what is lacking is willingness on the part of pastoral agents: what is needed is conviction, energy, enthusiasm. They seem to assume that if scholastic theology were proclaimed more energetically, it would overwhelm resistance to it. They seem to assume that five hundred years of modernity do not require any change on the part of the church. The faith continues to be the same solid package of scholastic doctrines as ever.

After 1960, decolonization began to affect the Catholic church. The leadership of the recently emancipated nations was handed over to the local clergy—at least with regard to official positions, although not necessarily in financial organization. The term "inculturation" began to be heard. For more or less thirty years now, that inculturation is said to be a primary objective, or at least a first condition for evangelization. The pope and the Roman curia have adopted the vocabulary, but nothing more than that, because Catholic inculturation has very strict limits: nothing can be changed in the catechism, or canon law, or the liturgical books (except through a very complicated procedure in the case of the latter). Inculturation must accept the entire legacy of the christendom of Western Europe. Support cannot be sought in the Eastern tradition, not even in the oldest black African church, the Ethiopian church.

The pope points to Asia as the great challenge to mission in the next century, but he is assuming that Asia will one day accept the entire legacy of Western christendom. He does not explain why the missions in Asia have had such limited success after almost five hundred years of evangelization. It does not seem to occur to him that the rigidity of Catholic "truth" could bear some of the responsibility for that situation.

The New Catholic Pietism

The Catholic "truth" of scholastic christendom has never been able to arouse enthusiasm in the people. That is why medieval christendom emerged and why the "popular religion" that has been so studied during the last twenty-five years was developed. This popular religion is made of up saints who work miracles; they are honored in their shrines or through their images in the form of novenas, processions, and other celebrations. Some have suggested that popular religion could provide an entry point for liberation movements.[36]

Popular religion imported from medieval christendom has lasted longer in Latin America than in Europe. Even so, its destiny will be the same: it is inexorably condemned to disappear with urbanization and modernization. The main cause of the decline of popular religion in Latin America is television. Indeed, popular religion is in decline almost everywhere. It seems to survive better in Central America or among indigenous communities.[37] But this is simply a lag, since television is going to rapidly pour into every nook and cranny of the continent, providing shows that are much more interesting than all the saints' devotions combined.

Even now in the rural areas where popular religion is still managing to hold on among older people (but not among youth) it tends to be taken over by local politicians who turn it into rallies sponsored by the beer industry or other commercial interests. (In Brazil local saints' feasts are being transformed into a platform for great competition among the major brands of beer. Each brewery tries to wield control over the largest possible number of patron saints.) Under such conditions popular religion is immediately degraded.

In the nineteenth century and the first half of the twentieth century, Catholic integralism would not have been able to be triumphant had it not been accompanied by a renewal of popular piety. Indeed, in order to enable declining traditional religion to survive, the clergy stirred up a new pietism. They did so through devotion to the Sacred Heart of Jesus and devotions to Mary. The apparitions of Mary are the strongest element of the new popular pietism: Our Lady of Lourdes and Our Lady of Fatima are the most powerful, but there have been many others. Among them, and in the same spirit, the national Marian figures were retrieved.

Since the 1960s, however, devotional pietism centered on devotions to the Sacred Hearts of Jesus and Mary has also gone into decline. Today, they are still practiced by older generations, but young people are not familiar with them and give shrines another meaning. The language of such devotional piety is not in tune with the expression of the newer generations.

A huge vacuum has been created. The hollowing out of traditional pietisms has led to a flight of Catholics, who in large numbers have sought in the new Protestant churches what they do not find in Catholicism. Since the early Middle Ages, the Catholic church has always needed a parallel pietism, a parallel popular religion, even one promoted by the clergy, in order to be able to win over the popular masses. That was true of lay people as a whole, inasmuch as even the monarchs had the same faith as the people and paid no attention to the hierarchy's scholastic Catholicism.

Some would blame liberation theology and CEBs for the emptying of the churches and the flight to evangelical "sects" and new religions. If that were the case, such phenomena would be present in São Paulo but not in Rio de Janeiro, an archdiocese where neither liberation theology nor CEBs have ever enjoyed support. In fact, however, the phenomenon is stronger in Rio than in São Paulo. This phenomenon extends throughout Latin America, although with different nuances, in accordance with each region's tradition and its involvement in modernity. Moreover, liberation theology and CEBs have never touched more than 5% of the Catholic population, and so their presence or absence cannot explain the wider behavior.

What has happened has been the breakdown of the old forms of Catholic piety, that is, of what was really popular Catholicism, the Catholicism of the laity. The laity find nothing except official, scholastic Catholicism, the dry and hard objective "truth" with no soul or feelings, a lifeless official liturgy, dull preaching, and bureaucratized structures.

In fact, for thirty years, the clergy have become more and more bureaucratic; they have less and less contact with real people. Clerics pass their time in administration, in supposedly pastoral meetings that are really about administration and in celebrating sacramental rituals that are increasingly disconnected from community life.

Lay people feel abandoned: nothing has replaced devotion to the Sacred Heart and Marian devotion. There has been nothing else for religious emotion. The new priests are unaware that the theology they learned in the seminary has never converted anyone, and they provide nothing to the faithful who ask for bread and are given a stone. Their professors have neglected to tell them that since the origins of christendom there has been a dualism in Catholicism between two gospels: a scholastic gospel for the clergy and a pietistic, devotional gospel for lay people.[38]

The Catholic Charismatic Renewal appeared at precisely the moment when Catholics were anxiously expecting a new pietism to appear. Necessity did not create the movement, but necessity does explain the Charismatic Renewal's striking success: it offers bread to those who would otherwise only receive stones. We can calmly guarantee the Charismatic Renewal movement a great future until the time comes when some other form of popular pietism appears. For now it is filling a very large vacuum.[39] People say, "Now I've learned to pray, now I've learned to know Jesus; I've learned to adore and praise God." In the Charismatic Renewal Christianity becomes personal and offers means of religious expression to a desire for piety that was repressed for lack of means of expression. Millions of other Catholics have gone seeking the same thing in pentecostal Protestant churches: recognition of their subjectivity, the possibility of a religion in which lay people are valued and in which they can express themselves and be active.

The persistence of the pietisms of the past has maintained the illusion that the strength of the Catholic church derived from its constancy in defending objective "truth." That was a delusion because lay people have never known that truth, and did not regard it as very important. Catholicism gave them a parallel religion of emotions, feelings, and acknowledgment of their subjectivity. Once the church is left with only its catechism, its liturgy, and its structures, it is lost.

Today the Charismatic Renewal serves to restrain the flight toward other churches and to renew Catholic pietism. But there are serious limits to this solution. The gospel it proclaims and embodies becomes very subjective. Its connection to the true biblical and patristic tradition is quite tenuous. The emphasis placed on individual and group religious emotion is still a great weakness. The limitation common to all Catholic pietisms reemerges. Moreover, pietisms are limited to short-term actions; they do not form a people forging history. Indeed, the fact that the clergy continues to have christendom as a goal allows them no other alternative. The clergy stands in the way of acting in history; it is not the fault of the charismatics.

Thus we have a situation in which a relentless objectivism offered as a gospel by the clergy confronts a radical subjectivism, which is the gospel generally lived by lay people.

Could there not be some other alternative? Or does the new evangelization amount to expanding charismatic religious expressions and spreading the new Catholic pietism? Some think there is no alternative: it's this or nothing. Other possibilities should be examined, however. Despite the restrictions, it is quite possible that in practice over a generation the new evangelization will be the work of pietist movements oriented toward religious experience, but such a solution may not satisfy everyone. It may be that an alternative is possible, even if it is inevitably that of a minority.

The Tradition of "Christian Humanism"

We are using the somewhat obsolete expression "Christian humanism" to indicate that some contemporary options are rooted in the church's past and are not suspect novelties. Historians investigating the origins of Christian humanism have found precursors in the Middle Ages, especially in the Thomistic tradition, and they have also found roots in the Greek and Latin patristic age. Properly speaking, however, the phenomenon appears at the outset of modernity in the fifteenth and sixteenth centuries.

Christian humanism was the great victim of the struggle between the Reformation and the Counter-Reformation. In the Catholic church it was relegated to a secondary role between a dominant integralist objectivism and an almost universal pietist subjectivism. The "third way" was a minority that had a difficult time surviving between such powerful poles.[40]

A minority made up of some critical clergy and some religious lay people became convinced that it was possible to reconcile the aspirations of human beings with God's revelation. They believed that God's word and the desires of the human being could be reconciled in the gospel, and that such a reconciliation could take place objectively and subjectively. However, this reconciliation required that there be a critique of christendom and a return to the origins of Christianity, and it also required that the most basic human aspirations be investigated. They believed that the Gospel of Jesus ought to satisfy deep human desires as well. In the act of faith itself, Christians could accept God's word and find themselves.

The humanists had to struggle to survive in the face of the attacks of the post-Tridentine reaction—initially the Catholic integralism that seemed victorious in the seventeenth century. Later they also had to struggle against the spirit of the Enlightenment which leveled a radical critique at the churches. Nevertheless, there was a Christian Enlightenment in the eighteenth century and even in the early nineteenth century before it almost succumbed to the new integralism implemented by Pius IX. John Henry Newman managed to survive, but just barely, almost in isolation and squeezed between a self-congratulatory Roman integralism and an intensely emotional popular pietism that was intellectually empty.

Moving into the breach opened up by Leo XIII, a new Christian humanism appeared in the early twentieth century. Unlike previous humanism, this one was not individual, but was born political, namely in the form of Christian democracy.[41] Christian democracy was much more than a political party; it was a real evangelization. It sought to create a new model of society which would draw on the double inspiration of the gospel message and the aspirations of modern human beings. It sought to be a Christian way of being in the world and being involved in it. The founders of Christian democracy sought to engage in politics in order to be Christians. They believed that one could not be Christian without being engaged in politics, and that their involvement in politics would be the true evangelization of the twentieth century.

Christian democracy had to struggle to be accepted by the popes and bish-ops, and it was actually only accepted after 1944. Even so, conservative Catholics in Latin America continued to resist for a long time; in Chile it was accepted only on the eve of the 1960s. Christian democracy involves political parties, but also intellectual movements, Christian labor movements, and a broad range of associations, cooperatives, and economic and cultural movements. It was a humanist movement that was bourgeois in origin and inspiration, and was led by the Christian bourgeoisie which drew inspiration from the Enlightenment and modernity.

From a very early time, Christian democracy was challenged by socialism. The fact is that in both Latin and Germanic countries, socialism arose out of anticlerical—and often anti-Christian and anti-religious—liberalism. As of 1917 the Soviet model was seen as the concrete shape of socialism, and Christian democracy entered into the resistance struggle against communism, and by extension, against socialism.

Even so, the battle against communism could not wholly monopolize its attention. Over the course of a century in many situations there appeared the challenge of a working-class, proletarian, or popular Christian humanism. This was what was proposed by the Young Christian Workers (JOC) but also by a number of isolated initiatives.

Under various circumstances, Christian leftist groups sought to go beyond the class limits of Christian democracy. In practice, they found it difficult to maintain their identity and were recruited by communist movements or by socialist movements calling themselves Marxist, which were in practice atheist or completely secularized. Such was the case of *Jeunesse de l'Eglise* in France, right after World War II. Then came the exemplary case of Ação Popular in Brazil, which officially joined the Communist Party of Brazil (PC do B). There was also the case of the MAPU in Chile and numerous other less noteworthy cases in Latin America.

Vatican II took place during a period of optimism in the world, and hence it could take some positions that have distanced the church from the underlying historic pessimism so clearly criticized by John XXIII. In a way, with Vatican II and the Constitution on the Church in the Modern World, the church adopted, at least in theory, some of the basic postulates of the Christian humanist tradition. Nothing like that had ever happened before, and that position remains a clear sign.

Vatican II's Christian humanism reached its high point in Paul VI's speech on December 7, 1965. Some of the statements were very perceptive: "Has all this and everything else that we could say about the human value of the Council perhaps turned the mind of the church away toward the anthropocentric direction of modern culture? Turned away, no; turned, yes." "The Catholic religion and human life thereby reaffirm their alliance, their convergence in a single human reality: for humankind the Catholic religion is, in a way, the life of humankind." These expressions translate precisely the secular program of Christian humanism. Christian anthropocentrism was one of the favorite topics of Rahner and of his follower Metz. Humanistic theology finally flowed forth in Paul VI's final address. It was both a euphoric and a deceptive moment. Even so, in this manner, the "third way" of Christian humanism received its official credentials and gained credibility.

In the context of Vatican II it was possible to move beyond the barriers preventing dialogue with socialism. It became clear that anti-communism was not enough; it did not provide answers to all questions. Socialism was not simply the reality the Soviet world spread around the continents; it was also the affirmation of the humanity of the proletarians, the dependent class, the outcast. Was the Christian humanism of Christian democracy taking on the world of working people? It was not evident.

The question was ultimately raised in Latin America, Africa, and Asia in the form of "liberation theology." The encounter between the aspirations of peoples and the word of God had to be pursued in the Third World. The search for a symbiosis between faith and deep human aspirations would take place through the dominated and exploited Third World poor.

Liberation theologies took a decisive step because they broadened the perspectives of a "third way." Instead of Christian democracy's bourgeois humanism it sought roots in popular humanism. The alliance between the deep human aspirations of dependent peoples and Christian faith would be made among the poor of Latin America. Liberation theology and its corresponding forms of Christian praxis (base communities, etc.) stood within a long Christian tradition, but they were taking an important further step, one that obviously would not have been possible in Europe, given the priority there of anti-communism.

Indeed, liberation theology, base communities, and other movements in this same line have paid a high price for abandoning anti-communism as a priority. They have been to some extent banished from the church up to the present. Currently, one may speak of liberation theology in Europe or the United States, but one may not speak of it in Latin America without immediately being marginalized. Ten years after the well-known instruction from the Congregation for the Doctrine of the Faith, the effect has been devastating. In the year in which we are writing (1995) we are returning to a rigid polarization in Latin America: clerical integralism versus charismatic pietism—with almost nothing in between. The alternative of Christian humanism, so present at Vatican II, has been reduced to silence.

Even so, there are still reasons to believe that the future lies in this direction. An emotional experience of God cannot provide the basis for a lasting foundation. Objectivist integralism, in turn, nourishes a rejection that is growing. The present task is to build the third alternative.

A truly new evangelization needs to announce a gospel that is both God's voice and a human voice, God's word going out to meet the human word.

Conclusion

The Catholic church has assumed the challenge of a new evangelization within the old christendom since the French Revolution, two hundred years ago. Since then, the new evangelization has been carried out in accordance with three different orientations.

There has been and still is a new evangelization that consists in reaffirming the former christendom, in which there was only one gospel, a single message that included dogma, morality, the sacraments, and the entire organizational form of christendom. Christianity was medieval theology, straight from the Council of Trent, the traditional morality of feudal patriarchal society, the divine right of the Catholic kings, and the entire social structure of the Christian world. No one conceived of a distinction between a theological teaching and a social teaching. Thus, the conservative evangelization was a matter of calling all peoples to return to the former christendom. Of course that preaching reached the traditional social classes: peasants and aristocracy.

With Leo XIII a change took place in the church's message: on the one side was a "theological" preaching (dogma, morals, sacraments); on the other, the "social doctrine." From now on, evangelization included two portions, one theological, the other social. For conservatives, the purpose of the social doctrine was to restore an equivalent of christendom. Since it was impossible to restore the religious monopoly of the Catholic church and the privileges of the clergy, at least Catholics could use the means of secularized society at their disposal to defend or reconquer more advantageous conditions for the church and assure that the civil laws of secularized governments enshrined as many Christian demands as possible (struggle against divorce, income for clergy, etc.).

This new evangelization option was manifested in the stance of conservative parties in both Europe and Latin America. The hierarchy accepted or sought alliance with fascist regimes that offered it favorable conditions (Italy, Spain, Portugal, Poland, Croatia, Slovakia, Hungary, Austria, and so forth). That has been the option of Pius IX, Pius X, and to a great extent Pius XI, Pius XII, and John Paul II. Within this framework, evangelization required that the church recover control, or at least a deep influence over the dominant culture. This was and still is an evangelization with a strong, but not very explicit, political component.

The argument of this evangelization was the proclamation of the "truth," that is, the objective truths of a Catholicism expressed specifically in scholastic theology. In short, the "truth" consisted of what was in scholastic theology (which indeed was largely assumed by the Council of Trent).

Alongside this evangelization through objectivity, there has been an evangelization through subjectivity. This was the age of the expansion of the new pietism of devotions to the Sacred Heart and Our Lady (apparitions). This pietistic evangelization managed to shore up the fidelity of the traditional rural world and of the middle classes in the cities; the only ones left out were the bourgeoisie and the working classes, the new classes in modernity.

Finally, there has been, and still is, a "third way." For lack of a term canonized by historians it has been called "Christian humanism." After the French Revolution, some Catholics have found that it was impossible to convert the new social classes—the bourgeoisie or the working class—to the former christendom. It was necessary to approach the modern world, hear the demands of the new science, the new values, and the people's aspirations. They sought to inculturate Catholicism in the modern world. Throughout the nineteenth century they were isolated individuals. They sought to dialogue with both liberals and socialists. Examples include "Catholic liberalism," "social Catholicism," "religious socialism," the "democratic priests," and so forth.

Leo XIII provided a degree of opening for them, a freedom of expression that they did not have before. Approaches were made to all areas of modernity. Efforts were made to reformulate the gospel so as to make it understandable to those who had the modern spirit. Accepting the fact that ancient christendom was in ruins, Leo XIII permitted the expression of a liberal theology and a social teaching that ignored the old order of christendom. Two aspects of evangelization were thereby emphasized, one theological and the other social—there was no longer a christendom to unite these two aspects.

Pius X halted this development. First, by condemning modernism, he halted any kind of theological dialogue. Dogma was also paralyzed, since theology could not develop. The repercussions of the condemnation of modernism continue down to our own day. It prevented Vatican II from entering into theological matters (except, to some degree, in ecclesiology). Secondly, Pius X blocked any dialogue with socialism, opening the doors only to a liberalism frightened by the socialists, a semiconservative liberalism. Since that time, the church's social teaching has always swung more to the right than to the left—which was regarded as the threat of socialism, which was in turn identified with atheism.

Vatican II and the papacy of Paul VI sought to open the social doctrine to a dialogue with the modern world (*Quadragesima Adveniens*). Thus, they gave support to a "third way." Even so, throughout the entire twentieth century—despite Vatican II, John XXIII, and Paul VI—the "third way," the way of dialogue with the modern world and of inculturation into modernity, has never ceased being a minority position. Several times it has been very much repressed. To the present it has not been able to carry out a serious critical evaluation of scholastic theology and its dogmatic "objectivity." The suspicion of "modernism" is still very much alive. This third way has always sought to give the most favorable interpretation to the church's social doctrine.

Such is the *status quaestionis* now at the end of the twentieth century. From a historical standpoint, the issue of the new evangelization is conditioned; it does not start from scratch. There are three traditions of the new evangelization and all three are still alive. Currently, the pietist current seems to be strongest as a result of the charismatic movement and other movements oriented toward personal religiosity. It is in this context that we wish to place the new signs of the time that are going to condition further development and our present options.

2

THE GOSPEL OF FREEDOM

The preceding chapter has indicated two challenges to which the church has not responded sufficiently in recent centuries. The first is the separation of the gospel into two objects and of evangelization into two operations—how, or whether, they are connected remains in doubt. The second is the striving for a middle way between objectivist integralism and subjectivist pietism in presenting the gospel. One thing is certain: in order to evangelize effectively, the church must know what the gospel consists of—just what the gospel is—and whether there is one object or two, one gospel or two (i.e., one more important and the other less).

In this chapter we will attempt to examine the second of these challenges and take up once again the alternative that more moderate and peace-loving Christians have sought since the end of the Middle Ages. Is it possible to integrate human aspirations and God's revelation into the same gospel? We will seek to show that the Bible shows us the way, and that the gospel of freedom responds to the deepest human desires today and always. It is true that the gospel of freedom has often been hidden or obscured in the ages of christendom, but it has never been completely forgotten. It has always had its witnesses, even in the worst periods. The third alternative that we seek is present in the gospel and in the true tradition of the church.

The Gospel of Jesus Christ

As a rule, the texts of the magisterium dealing with evangelization do not define what is in the gospel. Do they perhaps presume that the content of the gospel is so obvious that they do not need to reiterate what it says? Or is the meaning perhaps so obvious that it does not even occur to them to state it? The likelihood is that for those who draw up those texts the gospel means all of Catholic teaching, that is, scholastic theology, the catechism of christendom.

In any case, a document as valuable and rich as *Evangelii Nuntiandi* does not say what comprises the gospel. The Santo Domingo document, the main section of which is devoted to the new evangelization, likewise does not explicitly say what the gospel is. Pope John Paul II multiplies appeals for a new evangelization, but neither does he say what the gospel is. It seems to be taken for granted that the gospel is the whole body of doctrine, virtually all of the formulas compiled in the famous manual of Denzinger.

By contrast, in the New Testament the gospel is always a simple formula that has an impact, the proclamation of a good that can be identified immediately. The oldest formulation is that of St. Paul, and the most vigorous expression of the Pauline gospel is found in the epistle to the Galatians. In a sense the epistle to the Romans is like a long exposition of the Pauline gospel. However, the epistle to the Romans takes up again, spells out, and defends the shorter expressions in the epistle to the Galatians, which is more vigorous and has more impact. It condenses Paul's gospel with greater clarity and more radically.[1]

It is clear that, for Paul, the gospel proclaims and brings about a break in the author's life. The gospel is the word that causes a break in one's life. The gospel contains the rejection of a way of life as it has been lived thus far, and the adoption of a new way of life.

Now Paul's gospel is the proclamation of freedom. He announces the move from a way of life characterized by slavery to a life lived in freedom. For Paul everything can be summed up in one word: freedom. This fundamental statement sheds light on everything in Christianity. Everything else flows into freedom, and only that which builds freedom is Christian. "For you were called for freedom, brothers" (Gal 5:13). "For freedom Christ set us free; so stand firm and do not submit again to the yoke of slavery" (Gal 5:1).

Paul takes the word "freedom" in a very broad sense that makes its scope radical. For him freedom is enough to indicate the entire distance between historic Judaism and the gospel of Jesus. Freedom is the feature that affects the entire way of being that characterizes a disciple of Jesus.

It would be useless to reduce the scope of freedom to certain Judaic practices that are henceforth obsolete. Indeed, the freedom of Jesus changes everything—all human relations—to the point where Paul can proclaim, "There is neither Jew nor Greek, there is neither slave nor free person, there is not male or female; for you are all one in Christ Jesus" (Gal 3:28). We are no longer God's slaves, but children. The child shares what is the father's and is an heir, virtually equal (Gal 4:1-7).

The proclamation of freedom does not proclaim it as something completed but as a calling.[2] All are called to freedom: called to accept freedom, which entails overcoming their fear of being free.

Freedom is undoubtedly what affects modern human beings at the deepest level. The desire for freedom is rooted in what is deepest in human beings and never disappears entirely, even though some persons destroy their own personality.

We cannot assume that the freedom of Paul is exactly the same as the freedom of modern men and women. Indeed, there is a great difference between the freedom defended by Paul and aspects that are proper to modern freedom. However, we cannot deny the deep convergence either. The gospel of freedom highlights better the historic continuity between Christianity and modern aspirations to freedom and the permanent relevance of the Christian message.

The freedom of Jesus Christ is a calling and a task. It is God's gift, and the Pauline name for the reign of God. Like every gift of God, it never reaches completion here on earth. However, it is the fundamental drive that guides the human quest, the human adventure, the tragedy of human life. It is a never-ending task, a promise never fulfilled, an objective never attained. Yet, without freedom life would be meaningless.

Freedom is utopia and reality combined: utopia because it is never found in its pure form, finished, and stable; reality because the pursuit of freedom is present in all human activity as that which gives it energy, value, and delight. That is why Paul defines freedom as vocation, call, and appeal. The call is so strong and so demanding that the Galatians cannot look back; they cannot return to a state of slavery that is lower than the state of freedom to which they have been raised.

Why is this gospel of freedom so little known among Catholics? We can be absolutely certain that if we asked Catholics what word best sums up what is essential about their Christianity, few would utter the word "freedom."

On the contrary, most believe that Christianity is above all else a law, an obligation, a duty. They experience their belonging to the Christian church as acceptance of a law. Many say, "I was born under the Catholic law and I want to die in it." For such persons, Christianity is a body of dogmas that the mind must accept even if one does not understand them, a set of moral precepts to which one must submit one's behavior even if one does not agree with them, and a set of ritual practices that must be observed even if one does not know what they mean. The characteristic feature of faith is precisely to accept without understanding or desiring. The mortification of one's intelligence and will has long been upheld as the fundamental Christian stance, and a sign of adoration of the one God. Many traditional Catholics have internalized this teaching. If that is the case, where is the good news? Many Catholics do not want to be missionaries, because they feel that their religion, far from being good news, is sad news and they do not have the courage to proclaim it.

But Paul's gospel is so poorly known by Catholics, it is not simply out of ignorance but because it has been systematically concealed.[3] Paul's message has been set aside and replaced by a law whose inspiration may owe more to the Old Testament than to the New.

In his last works, Juan Luis Segundo expresses his surprise over rediscovering Paul's gospel.[4] He wonders how it could have happened that ecclesiastical organization as a whole (catechesis, preaching, and liturgy) should have hidden what can be seen in the New Testament to be the center and soul of what is new about Christianity.

We may assume that the bishops of that period did not hide the gospel by a conscious choice. The deviation took place unconsciously as the result of a new social and cultural context. Within the framework of christendom, where hierarchy and people are separated by an abyss, freedom becomes incomprehensible, completely out of focus, because it no longer corresponds to a lived experience. Greek philosophy in turn is unfamiliar with freedom in its biblical sense, and does not know what to do with it. That is why scholastic theology has never known how to value or understand freedom.[5]

For the Greeks and the Roman empire, and for Eastern Byzantine and Western Germanic christendom, the highest value was "order" (order in the universe, society, and personal life). God establishes order on all levels, and God wants human beings to live within order. There is no room for freedom in the ideology of order—at the very most freedom means the freedom to obey and to submit to order. Thus, for centuries the only freedom claimed by christendom was the freedom to profess the Catholic religion, that is, freedom to obey the church as part of the order of the world.

After so many centuries of christendom, which was the heir of the Christian Roman empire, freedom has become so alien to Christians that many suspect that it is a weapon of the enemy and think freedom is a movement against God. For centuries, Christians have provided conservatives with their most faithful troops, and Christian parties have called themselves "conservative," so greatly was Christianity identified with the established order and freedom with hostility to religion.

In early Christianity, however, the supreme value was not order but freedom; and law was far from the last word. On the contrary, law was subordinate to freedom. It is understandable, however, that it is not easy to reverse a situation so deeply rooted in history. That is why Paul's gospel was to remain unknown for several generations. Many would be puzzled, wondering whether what Paul says is correct, or whether his text should not be understood to mean the opposite of what it says. Indeed, the content of his message continues to sound strange to many Christians ears.

Juan Luis Segundo is right in stressing that the churches very early adopted the Gospel of Matthew as their catechetical manual and that Paul's gospel was set aside to some extent.[6] It may be that the former was chosen because Matthew presents the gospel of Jesus as the "perfection" of the law of Moses. Thus, Matthew was able to present Christianity as a new law, thereby making it possible to introduce Christianity into the system of the "order of the world." That may have been how it came about. It may be that the community leaders understood Matthew in this fashion or chose it for this reason. Furthermore, the Gospel of Matthew seems to be the most didactic and most "complete" and that may have played an important role. Our concern here, however, is not to examine the historic facts.

In any case, if we examine it carefully we will see that the gospel according to Matthew is not in opposition to the gospel according to Paul—indeed, it supports it. Everything depends on how the "perfection" of the law is understood.

Matthew 5:17-19 is indeed puzzling. That puzzlement is for all Christians, not simply those promoting Paul's gospel. If Jesus' words were taken literally, they would support the teaching of the pharisees and the doctors of the law, and they make Jesus a radical proponent of the most closed form of Judaism of his time. Of course, these words have to be placed in the overall context of his preaching, and specifically they must be interpreted in the light of the words that Matthew places immediately afterwards (see Mt 5:20-48).

In this section, the basic word is "perfection" (v. 48), or "Unless your righteousness surpasses that of the scribes and Pharisees. . . ." (v. 20).

However, "perfection" and "surpassing" are clarified by the cases that Matthew has attached in vv. 21 and 47. There we find listed a series of behaviors representing the "perfection" of the law. What do the words of Jesus add to the words of Moses? Let us see what Moses said. In his law, Moses sought to lay down the rules by which the tribes of Israel could live together in a human manner. Now, living together peacefully demands that individuals limit their desire for vengeance, that they agree not to render justice by themselves, out of their own aggressiveness, but rather agree to submit their desire for justice to common rules which are the same for all.

Matthew so focusses his attention on the issue of vengeance and living together peacefully that five of the six antitheses in chapter 5 have to do with this matter while the sixth has to do with sexual desire. Moses summed up the whole law with the *lex talionis*—"eye for eye, tooth for tooth"; it is the rule of equality between offense and reparation or retribution. In effect, this rule puts constraints on natural aggressiveness.

But Jesus goes much further: he demands that all vengeance be abolished, and thereby changes the meaning of the law. Where the law sets limits to vengeance and thus enshrines it, Jesus places such limits that vengeance disappears. He changes social organization: from now on society is to be founded on the principle of forgiveness. The law of Jesus is forgiveness. Forgiveness makes the human subject entirely free: he or she becomes independent of the need for vengeance, free of any inner need. He or she is free vis-à-vis the one offending, who remains trapped in the offense that imposes a role, that of offender and wrongdoer. One who forgives is not obliged to anything; he or she has won freedom.

It is true that Matthew does not see all aspects of freedom nor does he give his gospel the same wide scope that we find in Paul. But it stands in the same line, in basic continuity with it. Jesus does not intend that forgiveness make people more subordinate to a law, more submissive and more dependent, but on the contrary, that people become more independent, more sure of themselves, and freer indeed than those who have offended them.

It is well known that the basic theme of the Gospel of Matthew is the forgiveness of sins. The God of Jesus is the God who forgives and teaches to forgive. He sends Jesus to forgive in his name.[7]

Forgiveness is plainly uppermost in Matthew. After the Our Father, the only petition commented upon is that of forgiveness (Mt 6:14-15). The Beatitudes, which seek to provide a portrait of the true disciple, all have to do with forgiveness: the "meek" are those who forgive, as are the "poor in spirit," those who "hunger and thirst for justice," those who "mourn," the "merciful," the "pure of heart," the "peacemakers," the "persecuted." What is common to all of them is forgiveness of offenses.

The gospel according to John radically merges with Paul's gospel of freedom. "The truth shall make you free," says Jesus in the Gospel according to John.[8] According to John, truth is in Jesus in the sense that Jesus is the manifestation of the Father's love, the presence of this love as call to love and gift of love. Jesus is also the presence of the only commandment, namely the commandment of love.

Sin does not merely mean not loving, but not making love the radical priority of one's life. Sin means putting one's trust in some other thing, even if it seems to be a way of communicating with God, such as the temple, the law, or worship. The ones called "Jews" in the fourth gospel are those who refuse love, and who thus reject Jesus and remain "slaves of sin" (8:34). One who does not make love the highest thing in life accepts the slavery of falsehood and even murder (8:37-44). Jesus frees because he opens to love (8:36).

If we go back to the gospel in the different expressions it received in the New Testament, we see that everything revolves around the issue of freedom. Such a gospel may shock many Christians, but it remains extremely relevant to today's world. It is good news for all human beings, and indeed for all known cultures. It does not clash with the aspirations of peoples. Even today such a gospel is seen as something new, as good news.

If Christianity had limited itself to this gospel it probably would have been much more widely accepted than are the churches that by profession are devoted to proclaiming it. Why such a gap between openness to the gospel and openness to the church?

It is obvious that over the centuries the church has added many things to the early gospel. In theory, these things are consistent with the early message and have developed alongside the original content. In principle, that could be the case, but in fact it is not. What was added has come to conceal, in the eyes of many, the core that it sought to spell out or illuminate; instead of illuminating, it has obscured the original message.

The official documents of the church never deny the message of freedom. Often, however, in catechisms, liturgies, and the documents of the magisterium, this message never appears. It remains silenced, and the upshot is that the people are unfamiliar with it, inasmuch as few are going to read the Pauline epistles seeking to discover there something that they have not learned in catechism or in theology.

Scholastic theology has placed the largest obstacle. Once it had taken up the concepts of Greek philosophy, there was no longer any room for speaking of freedom. Its idea of God was more conditioned by metaphors subjected to a process of philosophical reasoning, which in practice ended up being a reduction. If there have ever been periods when the Christian gospel suffered "reductionism" it was under scholastic theology. However, since the Middle Ages that has been where the magisterium put its trust as the source from which to draw its basic concepts. The message of freedom has either disappeared or has been enveloped in so many restrictions, precautions, and warnings that nothing of it has survived.

In fact, however, despite the silence in official teaching, the gospel message of freedom has never been entirely absent from the church. It has been preserved and transmitted by the "mystics" and by the mystical tradition. Unfortunately, the mystical tradition is little known in the church, and even less in Latin America. We have in mind not only the oblivion that has befallen many mystics who never wrote and about whom nothing has been written, especially mystics among the popular classes who make up by far the largest numbers. Such oblivion extends also to the mystics who wrote and were published.

During christendom the mystics were almost always considered suspicious, precisely because they did not feel bound by the official scholastic terminology. However, in them lies a Christian tradition which may be more worthwhile today than the scholastic theological tradition, which is so dependent on Greek categories.

One of the most pressing theological tasks would seem to be to resurrect the mystical tradition and give it its due. More building blocks for updating the Christian method and for a new evangelization would be found there than in the theological tradition. Indeed, if the theological tradition is almost exclusively male, the mystical tradition is predominantly female, and can provide deep and wide roots for another aspect of Christian teaching which is too dominated by theology.

In Latin America freedom [*liberdade*, *libertad*] and liberation have been regarded as opposed to one another for twenty-five years. Theologians or philosophers of liberation have mistrusted the idea of freedom and regarded it with suspicion. For them freedom or liberty seemed to be owned by liberalism (in the European sense). In Latin America liberalism is confused with the ideology of the traditional elites, among whom there was no real difference between conservatives and liberals. The roots of the question of freedom go back much further than modern liberalism, however. It is the basic theme of the Christian gospel, and it cannot be ignored in the effort to provide a basis for liberation theology.

At that time, some thought that it was possible simultaneously to proclaim a message of liberation in the social realm and a conservative traditional religion—the religion of christendom—in the religious realm. That effort has been shown to be an illusion (the same illusion as that of those who place their trust in religious fundamentalisms). Some think that they can use religious fundamentalism to tear down social or political barriers and then subsequently establish a free society. That is an illusion, because religious fundamentalisms establish dictatorships that eliminate room for any other alternative. A popular religion of domination by custom, subordination to rigid mental structures, and attachment to rites devoid of any content will not be capable of promoting social change toward greater justice and brother- and sisterhood.

Juan Luis Segundo discovered that there could be no theology of liberation without a liberation of theology.[9] Likewise we can say that liberation in society cannot take place in society without also taking place in the church, at least assuming that the liberation of society takes place *with* Christians and not against them (as has often occurred in the modern era).

The Christian Concept of Freedom

According to the Bible, freedom is more than a quality or attribute of the human being: it is humankind's very reason for being, the depth, the core, of all human existence. God made human beings—man and woman—to be free and in order that they might act with freedom. God willed to be in the presence of a free being like Godself.[10]

Indeed, human freedom comes from God's love. Scholastic theology was unable to appreciate human freedom because it was incapable of appreciating love as God's essence. For Greek philosophy, God was, above all, the foundation of order; God was part of this order (the unmoved prime mover). Hence, human beings achieved their destiny by occupying their place in the cosmic order: the raison d'être of human beings was their submission to the universal order established and moved by God.

In the Bible, however, everything is different because God is love. Love is not the basis for order, but disorder; love shatters every structure of order. Love is the basis for freedom, and hence for disorder. Sin is the consequence of God's love.

If God is love, God can only create out of love. But in order to love one must have an interlocutor, another being present to oneself. Only the other can be loved. God wanted to love, and so needed an other, but there was no other. In order to love, God wished to provide Godself with another, and hence made creation, whose end is the human being. A submissive and well-ordered creation was not truly an other whom God could love. God created in order to face a creature who could be loved and who could return love. God created freely, and in order to be loved, God needed an other who could also love freely.

In order to love, God needed to make human beings free. Hence human freedom is a condition of God's love. Human beings are God's other, made equal to God by their freedom. Before God, human beings are nothing in all respects except the one in which they resemble God: freedom. Of course this freedom is a gift of the creator God. Even so, through freedom humans can block divine action. They can reject God's love; they can frustrate God's love.

If love is the reason for the creation of the universe and of humankind, which is its arrival point, the supreme achievement is the act of love by human beings, the free response to God's love, the response that makes possible a true dialogue of love between God and human beings. Without dialogue there is no love; without reciprocity there is no love. Neither grace nor love is addressed to a rock or to a being who refuses to respond or is incapable of responding.

If God is love, creation's reason for being can only be free love, free acceptance by human beings. The world was made with the hope of arriving at
this point. However, the world can fail, and God's hope can be frustrated if
human beings so choose. Creation can succeed or fail; everything remains in
suspense because everything depends on the human freedom that God willed.
God was willing to risk failure so that the success would have some value.

The most complete and exact definition of God is found in the well-known
statement in the Revelation of John, often cited by Juan Luis Segundo,
"Behold, I stand at the door and knock. If anyone hears my voice and opens
the door, I will enter his house and dine with him, and he with me" (Rev
3:20). If no one opens, God accepts the defeat, knowing that creation has
failed. God has created a world that could fail.

The whole Bible is actually a narrative commentary in these matters. The
one who confused things was Aristotle with his metaphysics. Aristotle's God
was almighty, sovereign, unaffected, unchangeable, immovable, imprisoned
in himself and his perfection—unable to love. It was inconceivable that such
a God could love because there was no one who could be loved. Being order
itself, God could not really be free.

Hence, there was no way to ground human freedom. Human freedom
could be conceived only as a defect, a lack of the assurance of order. Freedom
was an imperfection of a being not yet established in order. There was no
way to give a positive meaning to freedom because there was no apparent
reason for it to exist. Freedom for what? To do what? Compared with the
perfect order of the stars, the earth, plants and animals, human freedom
looked like a sign of incompleteness.[11]

The Bible shows that human freedom is due to God's love. God needed
human freedom in order to love and be loved. And because of human freedom, God, who was all-powerful, became impotent vis-à-vis human freedom. God became able to fail and to suffer. God became patient, and learned
to hope, and to learn from disappointment. The fact is that there is no human
freedom if God is all-powerful. However, that should not lead to the conclusion that human freedom is sheer illusion or that God is illusion if freedom exists. Indeed, God has waived infinite power in order to depend on the
free human being. Love can freely surrender power, command, domination,
even order. All human love is like that, and is capable of such abandon—all
the more reason that God can surrender power so that freedom may exist.
That God is love and that the human calling is freedom are two aspects of
the same reality, two thrusts of a single movement.

It is of the essence of freedom that it is always in the process of self-con-
struction. God has not given human beings a freedom that is completed, all
set up—that would not make sense. God has given human beings the capability of winning their freedom, of becoming free by themselves.

Human beings can succeed or fail, they can build or destroy their freedom, they can want to win it or not. Refusal to accept the calling is sin. God
has made the world in such a way that sin is a possibility. Without human
freedom sin would be impossible; that is why it was so repugnant to the

Greeks to accept a freedom that could lead to evil. God has nonetheless created the possibility of sin, and hence does not step in to prevent sin.

At times the church has thought, as it did in the age of christendom, that its task consisted of preventing sin. By seeking to prevent sin, however, it can bring about the greater sin, namely the rejection of the message of love and of God's forgiveness.

Freedom is a task, a calling, the goal of human beings in their brief existence in this world. They have come here to win their true being. Freedom is not given—it is won. No one makes someone else free; one can only allow another to win his or her freedom.

Indeed the conquest of freedom is both individual and collective. All human beings are set within an ongoing development and a history, and are dependent on their situation to win freedom. Each can become free within this collective movement, however. There is no collective freedom of the human species; freedom is always personal. It can only exist, however, within an overall emancipation of the entire human race.

In some sense, we can say that the pursuit of freedom begins with the origins of the universe, inasmuch as from the outset there emerges a movement that will continually tend toward the final outcome of freedom. However evolution may be explained, whether through neo-Darwinism or in some other way, it has a direction. Everything is gradually creating conditions for the emergence of a free being. The probability was infinitesimal, but it happened. Once the phase of hominization begins, once the human species (and later true *homo sapiens*) appears, the conquest of freedom becomes immediate and direct. From that time on, freedom already exists in the pursuit of freedom. One who begins to seek freedom is already in some fashion performing the complete act of freedom. Hominization continues but humankind is already present. Freedom already exists even though it has to be unceasingly won, without stopping, without reaching limits.[12]

Of course freedom is never complete. It is limited by its history, limited by the possibilities of the body which has evolved out of the living world, limited by history which is irreversible. History is the basis for a culture which is the support for life, but it also sets boundaries. Present freedom cannot remake evolution or reshape history. Freedom starts out from a twofold biological and cultural inheritance. Within those limits, however, there is room for endless conquest. And on the other hand, from the beginning of the conquest of freedom by the representatives of *homo sapiens*, an act of complete freedom already exists: since then, human beings can choose and in that choice they already achieve their freedom. Modern humans are freer than Neanderthal people; and yet Neanderthals were able to make choices that were the fullness of freedom.

Freedom exists as a call. To accept the call to freedom is to respond positively to God's love, to make oneself able to be loved and to love. Response to God's love, which is the acceptance of the call to freedom, is what Paul calls "faith," John "love," and the synoptic gospels "conversion." In faith, God's love encounters the other who is being sought; the dialogue that justifies creation begins, and God's purpose is attained.

Human beings are earthly, bodily, fully a part of the material universe. Their freedom cannot be sought in an ideal, imaginary world, projected beyond this corporeal world. Once we learn to use words to designate things, we easily come to think that by playing with words we can invent another world that is better or more suited to us than this world that is so material and that puts up so much resistance to our desires.

The calling to freedom is the conquest of autonomy, of personalization in the world by taking advantage of the breaches that open up. Freedom cannot be won by a single act. Just as there is no revolution that changes a society completely, neither is there an act that can completely emancipate the totality of a person.

Freedom exists only within a wide variety of "freedoms," and each is the object of long, repetitive, wearisome conquest of operations: freedom from the domination of the physical nature of the unconscious, freedom from the many political and economic forces that proceed from a complex history of mutual relationships between individuals and groups, and so forth.[13] There is no leap, no option allowing access to a world where freedom is achieved; there is no passage from a realm of necessity to a realm of freedom.

It has always been tempting to believe that one can better practice love for God, faith, and response to the divine love away from this world than within it. Hence, the theme of flight from the world and the pursuit of paradise in the monastic life. One can apparently love more fully, and achieve freedom away from the material world.

This is all nothing but illusion. First, there is no place that is not within this world. It may be unaware of its relationship with the world (which is very dangerous) but it cannot live outside the world. One cannot "leave" the world. Secondly, our being is such that it can only act in the body and through the body, that is, in the realm of relationships between bodily beings. Our freedom exists in freedoms won in the midst of these multiple relationships with other human beings and with the whole of the material world.

In Christian tradition, it is a false and illusory mysticism that seeks to love God in a love that is disconnected from material contingencies, above the material world, through purely spiritual acts unconnected to this world and to one's brothers and sisters. An "ecstatic" life would be a false life. That is why there is so much insistence on love for neighbor as the concrete reality of love for God in the New Testament. There is no such thing as love for God on a plane situated above the material world: a freedom without material content is false. That would be the freedom of an empty option, choosing for the sake of choosing, an option for the sake of an option, similar to caricatures made of Rudolf Bultmann's idea of faith: faith which consists of opting for opting, with no definition, no object, no determination, an openness to everything—which looks very much like an option for nothing.

The call to freedom takes place in the trivial struggles of daily life in the midst of so many conditionings, so many needs, so many constraints, and so many dependencies. Freedom emerges out of so much inertia and resistance.

Not the least of resistances is that found in the person: fear of freedom, fear of having to choose and assume responsibilities, prejudice, timidity and insecurity.

Despite everything, freedom exists and the struggles for freedoms are never ending, even though the struggles or ideologies of "order" seem to remain unchanged. The struggles may be humble, almost out of sight, sometimes reduced to internal resistance, but they never cease. The calling to freedom has been placed by God and is the very definition of the human being.[14]

Freedom and Law

The opposition between law and freedom is basic to the Pauline message and is implicit in the entire New Testament. It is how Paul shows the newness of Jesus. It therefore lies at the center of any new evangelization. No matter how much one might want to reconcile them, law and freedom are in opposition. What is most new about the New Testament is that it points out this opposition. The newness is so scandalous that it continues to scandalize many church authorities up to our own day. "For freedom Christ set us free; so stand firm and do not submit again to the yoke of slavery" (Gal 5:1).

The law is slavery. This slavery refers not only to certain Jewish requirements, such as circumcision, that Christianity ended. The slavery of the law refers to the entire religious system that Paul lived as Jew and a Pharisee before his conversion.

The slavery lies not so much in the statement of the precepts or traditions of the law written in the Bible as in the overall conception of religion as submission to a law dictated by God from outside. The slavery consists in the system that proposes obedience to the law as supreme value. Such was the Judaic system. Such was also the system of Greek philosophy which proposed submission to order as a human ideal, and found its model in the universal order in which each being accepts and completely fits into the role to which it has been assigned. The complete subordination of the individual to the customs of the tribe also occurred in more primitive peoples. In all these systems the submission of the person was the supreme value and human freedom could have no other purpose but obedience.

Making the relationship to God a complete subordination was what Paul condemned as slavery; it was what Jesus had condemned. According to Paul, Jesus freed humankind from such a fate and called it to another destiny: freedom. And the goal of freedom was its own conquest. The purpose of freedom was to become freer. According to Paul, when Christianity entered the scene, there took place a decisive leap, one unique in human history, and whoever, like the Galatians, has taken this decisive step cannot go back without making a basic mistake.[15]

The opposition and contrast between law and freedom parallel the contrast and opposition between slave and child. "So you are no longer a slave but a child, and if a child then also an heir through God" (Gal 4:7).

Over the course of history, however, faced with the great newness of the New Testament gospel, church authorities have often been, and still are, afraid. They are afraid of losing the security provided by the traditional systems, the Judaic, Greek, or tribal system. Scholastic theology itself obscured the newness of the New Testament and expressed Christianity in the framework of the old systems: it made Christianity the definitive expression of an order, a law. The authorities could invoke the resources of theology for support.

They could not expurgate the scriptures; they could not undo what had been written. They sought, instead, to empty the content of the Pauline gospel and to reduce it to insignificance. They were afraid because freedom renders the future unforeseeable. They were afraid because freedom shakes the guarantees of order and tranquility. They were afraid because freedom opens the doors to disorder and sin. They believed, and still believe, that their mission is to prevent sin and assure social order—a mission that Jesus never claimed as his own.

This fear is expressed, for example, in the 1986 instruction *Libertatis Conscientia* (LC) of the Congregation for the Doctrine of the Faith. This instruction was intended to complete the warnings against liberation theology contained in the instruction *Libertatis Nuntius* published two years previously. The new document from the Congregation was to "highlight the main elements of Christian doctrine on freedom and liberation" (LC 2). On almost every page, however, the document exposes the terrible fear of freedom that dominates the unconscious of the authors, and probably a good part of their conscious mind as well.

By dispelling Paul's message through commentaries that completely undermine his meaning the Congregation simply ignores the central message of the New Testament.

Paul condemns the "slavery of the law," and for him the gospel frees the various peoples from that slavery. For the Congregation of the Faith, however, there is no such thing as slavery to the law, and hence there is no point to Christian liberation. For the Congregation slavery means a false impression on the part of sinful human beings. It believes that Paul intends to say that "to sinful humankind the law, which it cannot internalize, seems oppressive" (LC 54). For the Congregation, the law is not oppressive. In saying that the law is oppressive, Paul's intention must have been to say that it is not oppressive. But if that is what Paul meant, why didn't he say so?

For the Congregation the only oppressive aspect of the law is simply the false impression held by sinners. It is interesting that the Congregation sees the duty of human beings as "internalizing the law," not winning freedom. That is why the law "seems oppressive" to sinners, but not to the just, since it is not really oppressive. For the Congregation, the law is actually salvific, as it was for the Jewish authorities in Paul's time.

How to reconcile this doctrine with Paul's teaching when he states that "we were reduced to the condition of slaves" (Gal 4:3), and that those who live under the law are children of the slave Hagar (Gal 4:25)?

The fact is that for the Congregation freedom is not a good; it is an evil, a tremendous danger. The Congregation cannot reject freedom, which it claims to defend, but it disdains it, and cannot hide the fact that for the Congregation freedom is ultimately an absence in this direction—the Congregation follows the line of the Greek philosophers and scholastic theology.

The text reads, "God calls humankind to freedom. In each person there lives a desire to be free. And yet this desire almost always tends toward slavery and oppression. . . . In the human desire for freedom there is hidden the temptation to deny one's own nature" (LC 37). In the desire for freedom the Congregation suspects that there is always the temptation of wanting to be God, Adam's sin, the seduction of the serpent in paradise (37). If that were true, the gospel of Jesus would be reduced to nothing; it would be radically futile and vain. Freedom would be God's greatest mistake in creation.

The instruction *Libertatis Conscientia* brings nothing new, but stands in a long line of resistance to freedom. This resistance did not begin in the sixteenth century in the struggle against the then incipient modern age. It was at work throughout the entire Middle Ages in the resistance to the mystics and the mystical movements, precisely those who represented the Pauline and Johannine gospels in the church.

Section 54 stands in a long tradition and provides the most complete attempt to justify banishing the Pauline gospel and returning to the Judaic or Greek mentality, which was precisely what Paul was condemning. For its part, the new *Catechism of the Catholic Church* simply ignores Paul's gospel—a handier way to solve the problem.

Certainly, Paul does not mean that what was prohibited by the law is now allowed. Paul does not claim that killing, stealing, or committing adultery is of no importance. Taken in its material content, "the law is holy, and the commandment is holy and righteous and good" (Rom 7:12). But if the thief refrains from stealing only because there is a law prohibiting it, little is achieved beyond greater social order. Humankind was not created solely so that there would be social order. If all human beings were entirely subject to the law, that would achieve very little because the purpose of the human being is not to obey the law but to become free, that is, fully human, capable of acting out of love rather than fear. And the purpose of the church is not to assure public tranquility in order, but to proclaim the gospel of Jesus Christ. Moreover, there is no point in repeating the law because human beings are going to disobey it anyway. This so ardently yearned for obedience is not attained by the law.

St. Paul knows full well that the call to freedom can be undermined, that the name of freedom can be invoked to justify the opposite of freedom. "For you were called to freedom, brothers. But do not use this freedom as an opportunity for the flesh" (Gal 5:13). The flesh means the weaknesses of the human condition, fear, cowardice, the passions, unbridled desires. Paul knows that words can be debased. However, that possibility does not provide him with an excuse for destroying the very call to freedom and emptying it of content.

The instruction *Libertatis Conscientia* deserves special attention because it is presented as the church's positive response to the aspirations of humankind today. But the document is shot through with anxiety—anxiety over freedom. Every time freedom is mentioned, it is to speak about its abuses, to recommend prudence, or to impose limits or barriers. It cannot speak of freedom without immediately alluding to its dangers.

Why such fear and so much anxiety over freedom? Is it one more expression of resentment against a modernity that wrested control over society from the church? Is it simply an expression of the anxiety of all authorities over their subjects' desire for freedom? Is it fear that the freedom claimed in society will cause similar claims to be made in the church?

Authorities tend to receive any aspiration to freedom on the part of their subjects as a challenge, a questioning of authority in itself, and not simply of one decision or another.

Because of the way authority is exercised in the Catholic church, one explanation is that anxiety reaches levels not reached in other societies where there is some degree of dialogue between superiors and inferiors. In any case, the Congregation's instruction was an eloquent document that will be remembered because it helps explain many things in the ecclesiastical system.

It seems likely that the instruction still reflects the attitude of christendom, whose disappearance is not accepted. A significant portion of the hierarchy is not resigned to acknowledging the end of christendom and does not put aside the illusion of reconquering it. Indeed, all those groups and movements that set themselves the task of rebuilding it are welcomed with special appreciation (Opus Dei, Communione e Liberazione, Schönstatt, Sodalitium, Knights of Columbus, etc.).

In christendom, the clergy and hierarchy believe that they are invested with the mission of defending order in ideas, in the social structure, in moral behavior, and in the arrangement of time and space. Clergy and hierarchy believe that their task is to prevent sin: heresy, unbelief, immorality, and disobedience. The Inquisition was set up not only to combat sin but also to prevent it, to halt it in advance. The clergy believed that it could not rest until it had eliminated all sin from society; it anguished over sin. Countless writings from the age of christendom express this anxiety in the face of so many sins and so many sinners.

That was also Paul's anxiety before his conversion. Then came his enlightenment on the road to Damascus and Paul understood that his anguish had been in vain. The problem was not sin, for God forgives sin. The good news is that in the freedom acquired in Jesus, sin is defeated. There is no point in being concerned about sin; the important thing is to announce the good news of freedom in Christ. Only in the conquest of freedom can the human being be free of sin. Jesus has already resolved it: God forgives. In Jesus, sins are forgiven.

Let us return to *Libertatis Conscientia*. The instruction alludes to the countless warnings and condemnations of freedom by the magisterium in the course of the last few centuries. It says, "through its magisterium the church has raised its voice over the centuries to warn against aberrations. . . . With the passage of time . . . it is possible to do greater justice to the church's point of view" (LC 20).

Let us suppose that the church has been right and that history has confirmed its earlier anguished warnings. Solely for the sake of argument, let us imagine that in fact all movements for freedom have been a disaster, and that as the passage from the instruction says, every freedom movement has generated greater oppression and greater slavery. In any case, the price of this Cassandra role assumed by the church is obvious: the modern world has moved away from it—in Latin America as well. Because it was so discouraging to freedom movements, the church has aroused a massive, overwhelming rejection.

It is not helpful to hide the fact and make use of sociological or some other type of pseudo-analysis to explain the declining numbers of Catholics in the church and the flight to independent churches. Nor is it helpful to say that the problem is the shortage of priests or of places for worship. Even if there were ten times as many priests the problem would be the same. Most people stay away from the church not because of the distance, lack of communication, and so forth; they do not come to the church for the simple reason that they do not want to. They are not doing this out of religious ignorance, but because the church no longer interests them. They know that the church has always discouraged aspirations to freedom. Some heroic exceptions are not enough to undo the overall impression—except in some minorities who still retain hope (for how long?).

If the church was right in announcing the failure of freedom, the price paid for such clearsightedness has been very high. But it was not right. The history of recent centuries has not been simply the story of the failures of freedom. The various peoples do not feel that way about their history. Struggles for freedom have been hard, and full of trials. But humankind today does not feel defeated, and in particular it does not want to stop struggling for freedom because of partial failures in the past. If, instead of condemning, the church had aided liberation movements, its situation would be quite different today.

We have some very clear signs of this. During the time of military regimes in some countries, the hierarchy and most of the clergy clearly stood on the side of the struggle against oppression and paid the price for that option. We may cite, for example, the most outstanding case of all, that of the Vicariate of Solidarity in Chile. The church thereby built up a great deal of respect, trust, and appreciation among the people. All doors were open to it—many had formerly been closed. However, the church may lose the trust built up if it returns to performing its customary task as guardian of order in existing society.

Unfortunately, many signs in recent times, not just *Libertatis Conscientia*, indicate that the church has not given up this role of managing christendom. It believes it is called to denounce sin rather than to announce forgiveness, to teach the commandments instead of proclaiming the calling to freedom, to prevent disorder instead of launching human beings on the adventure of creating their own selves.

The Catholic church has acquired a reputation as an organization that defends moral order in the world. Its mission is seemingly a matter of combating adultery, abortion, birth control, drugs, street violence, and so forth. It seems to be a kind of huge World League for defending traditional moral values.

In fact, the numerous exhortations end up with no results. The number of sins does not seem to be declining as a result of such moral preaching. On the contrary, it seems that the more the church raises its voice to defend the moral order, the more it goes on losing members. Indeed, aspirations to freedom are no longer confined to a minority in the world as was the case up to 1960. With decolonization, urbanization, and the worldwide communications society, modern aspirations have become democratized. The masses themselves have now entered the movement for freedom in various ways.

It is true that the church is applauded by traditionalists who share its anguish over the risks of freedom. However, the new evangelization campaigns do not hit the target; the gospel is missing. Gospel spreading without the gospel produces no fruit.

The solution will mean surrendering the mission to run the world. Certainly society needs laws and police, prisons and punishments, rules and threats. But should this be the role of the church? Is that the mission taken on by Jesus? And who will go forth to announce the gospel of freedom? Just a few more or less marginalized mystics, as in medieval christendom?

At the center of the drama is the figure of the priest. Today, despite the appearances with which the church wishes to delude itself, the priestly problem is more serious than ever, because it gets at the very mission of the church, which is embodied today in the priest, inasmuch as he is historically placed at the center. Is the priest going to continue to be the guardian of the laws? Is he going to be the representative of the ecclesiastical police? Will he be the defender of the moral order, the person who judges and condemns? (That is how most people see him.) Or will he be the evangelizer, the promoter of evangelization, because he is the most conscious bearer of the gospel? Many priests lead a tormented life because they do not know how to choose or do not want to. Without a choice, however, there is no solution and no peace.

Freedom and Love

Freedom is a social reality; there is no freedom in solitude. Freedom is always such in relation to others. In Christianity this relation is that of love (*agape*, that is, charity, love, solidarity).

"You were called for freedom . . . serve one another through love" (Gal 5:13). Love is service of one another. How are we to understand this today? During the ages of christendom, most Christians identified love very much with spontaneous forms of solidarity. These forms of solidarity were not the object of personal options. They were imposed on all members of the human community without any questioning, more unconsciously than consciously, although the group always had sanctions available. Sanction was expulsion from the community, and expulsion meant death.

The basic and universal solidarity occurred in the family. Outside the family it was very difficult to survive except in a more or less abnormal situation as a soldier, prostitute, bandit, or beggar. Individuals received everything from the family and owed it everything. All their work was to serve the family, and they were entirely subordinate to it. The family was the condition for survival and the members accepted it, because they knew that without it they would not salvage their human dignity. The family demanded everything, total dedication of time, resources, and concern. Marriage was the most important decision because on it depended the future of the family; it was a family matter rather than a personal matter. People were taught that Christian love was primarily solidarity with one's family.[16]

In Europe this was the prevailing situation among the masses until 1914, and in some rural areas until 1945. In Latin America it was the situation of most people until the 1960s and 1970s. Under rapid urbanization, the family has been in retreat since then; even so, for many people the family is the greatest social force, the last refuge and the condition for survival; and family solidarity is still the highest value. Nevertheless, evolution toward modernity is rapid. The United States has modernized since the end of the Civil War, Europe has done so since 1914, and Latin America is now engaged in massive modernization.

The second solidarity is that of the tribe: those who live in the same territory, speak the same language, have the same customs, the same way of speaking, the same culture; they feel so much in solidarity that they are willing to die in warfare to defend their tribe. Tribes affirm themselves over against one another. All members of the tribe stand in solidarity and form a single front in battle against the neighboring tribe; they all sacrifice everything they have, including their lives, to defend their tribe ("My country, right or wrong!").

The third solidarity existed in the church or in christendom by way of the union of all Christian peoples, everyone who practiced the same religion. At that time, unity of culture was assumed by religion, and belonging to the Christian church was the strongest of bonds, capable sometimes of attaining a dedication and devotion stronger than that of family or tribe. The church awoke many vocations, and people sacrificed and devoted themselves to many works of solidarity.

For centuries love was practiced in the form of solidarity within the family, the homeland (the tribe), and the church, which were the three basic kinds of belonging. Initially, family, homeland, and christendom played a liberating role for the human personality. They made possible not only survival, but also a great deal of development. This system can be said to have reached its high point in the West in the thirteenth century. The very activity of family, homeland, and christendom, however, created higher aspirations in people, first in small elites, and then gradually in larger groups in societies. The three basic solidarities gradually began to act as repressive systems, impeding the further progress of the individual personality.

In the context of solidarity, love was obligatory and unavoidable. Little by little, the individual became a captive of this fate. The net result of love for family, homeland, and church was that everything was sacrificed for the good of these forms of solidarity. The individual was forced to suppress all individual aspiration in the name of love and solidarity. The drama of modernity has been to reconcile the experience of the conflict between love and freedom. Freedom and solidarity seemed to be in contradiction.

Modernity has signified the victory of individualism over solidarity and love as they were conceived in traditional civilizations. In other societies, solidarity was triumphant and individualism could not prevail; modernity did not take firm hold. The most obvious case is that of Islam. The Muslim peoples do not accept the emancipation of the individual and continue to impose the supremacy of collective solidarity on the family and on the Muslim peoples as a whole.

In Western society, individualism, which appears with humanism by the fifteenth century, unfolds gradually: more rapidly in the seventeenth century than in the sixteenth, more rapidly in the eighteenth century than in the seventeenth, more rapidly in the nineteenth century than in the eighteenth, and even more rapidly in the twentieth than in the nineteenth. As the twentieth century is coming to a close, it has reached such a point that it has expanded to the entire society of Europe and the Americas. Even so, individualism has become widespread only in recent years.

Individualism did not affect women until the second half of this century. Until that time, they remained within the structures of solidarity. Women sustained love, while men entered into the struggle for individual victory. Women continued sacrificing themselves in the family, the homeland, and the church, devoting all their energies to serving the community, the common good of family, homeland, and church. Even female education kept women away from the world of men, that is, the world of competition and individual struggle, thereby creating a separation that did not exist in the past of Western society or in other civilizations.

In the United States, the revolt against traditional submission and group solidarity began after World War II; in Europe it was after *Humanae Vitae*, and in Latin America in the 1980s.

Thus individualism has triumphed almost completely. It becomes difficult to talk about love and solidarity. Why does love have a bad reputation? Because the masters of suspicion, Marx, Nietzsche, and Freud, railed against it so much? Why has individualism triumphed so roundly? Probably, because love was lived as passivity and submission. The sacrifice of parents for children, and of all for the family, the sacrifice of all for their homeland or for the church was a quasi-necessity—it was not the object of reflection or reform. Such behaviors were obligatory. Anyone willing to question them would be excluded from society. There was a time when such forced dedication to the common good was accepted by all as a condition for survival. When the sense of urgency declined, some began to doubt and to live an individual life.

A mother was expected to sacrifice herself for her children without any limit, with no rest. She could not choose; her role was defined in advance. There was nothing to think about or choose. Society had decided everything, and its decision had been accepted by the unconscious. The eventual upshot was a resentment and rebellion against love. Freedom was sought as emancipation from the bonds of love.

Individualism first takes the form of the business enterprise, and the modern company has continued to evolve. Instead of working within the family, a person forms a company with no links to any family responsibility whatsoever. The company is based on the principle of individual property and it gradually comes to prevail and to eliminate the property of family, tribe or church (secularization of the property of the church and the nobility, that is, transforming them into individually owned companies). The company is an association of individual workers who receive an individual salary or wage. The woman is emancipated when she enters a company and receives her individual pay that allows her to have a life distinct from that of the family. There is no solidarity or love in the company; each one guards what is his or hers and competes with everyone else, striving to win. The company is a place of struggle (within the company and between companies).

Through individualism the nation gradually replaces the homeland, although for a long time—almost up to the second half of the twentieth century—the nation sought to appropriate for itself the attributes of the homeland in order to obtain support from the masses, who did not yet understand the nation and did not really participate in it.[17]

The nation is a society of rights. Mutual relations are defined by formal law. There is no solidarity between citizens beyond right—at least in theory. All are equal and enjoy the same rights, although in practice they do not have the same power to defend their rights. The nation is individualistic because it limits solidarity. None sacrifice themselves for the good of all. In principle all work together equally, and the good of the nation means the conditions whereby each may compete, struggle, and win within the framework of the law. Finally, in the place of christendom there has arisen the secularized structure of the United (or divided) Nations. In practice, however, the United Nations does not succeed in setting up a world body in which relationships are defined by right.

Actually, something remains of the family, especially in the world of the poor where the company does not absorb the individual entirely. Something remains of homeland and tribe—and their corresponding solidarity—more or less coinciding with nations, more in Europe and less in the Americas. Something remains of the church itself in the churches that have been divided and separated since the Reformation.

Nevertheless the problem of the contradiction between freedom and love has been posed by modernity, and today more acutely than ever, because most people, including women, have entered modernity.

The love or service that St. Paul talks about is not exactly the traditional solidarity of family, homeland, and church. Christendom brought things to the point where Christian love was almost identified with traditional social solidarity. The Christian message was not like that in the beginning. With the passing of christendom, distinctions should have been made during the centuries of modernity, but in fact they were not made. For a time, traditional solidarity may have been an adequate expression of Christian love, but it is really of another nature. Hence, we must examine the meaning of love and of service in the New Testament, especially in Paul.

In the New Testament there is no contradiction between love and freedom. Love and freedom converge and belong to the same projection of personality. However, in order to attain this same convergence today we must get beyond both modern individualism and traditional communitarianism.

The gospels show that the love of Jesus was not in any way conventional—it had nothing in common with solidarities of the collective unconscious. It was not limited by the family nor did it privilege the family (Mt 10:34-39). It was not oriented toward tribal solidarity: Jesus was also concerned with non-Jews, broke traditional barriers, and was open to the Samaritans who were regarded as heretics and to the Romans who were the oppressors. Jesus did not stand in solidarity with the religious system and he sought out sinners, that is, those excommunicated from the religious system, more than the official representatives of the religion of Israel. The love of Jesus had nothing to do with that kind of solidarity.

Jesus' way of acting highlights the essential. Loving does not mean supporting the collective body to which we belong. To love means first to recognize the other, the one who is different.[18] Traditional love is not personalizing. The love of Jesus is personalizing; it first of all situates before us the other as he or she is. The other is regarded as the person who is not from one's own family, tribe, language, race, or culture. The other is especially the person who is not of one's own religion. For the early Christians, the Jew's other was the pagan; the Greek's other was the barbarian; the man's other was the woman; the master's other was the slave. Today there are many more contrasting poles, more differences, but the challenge is the same.

The other can also be recognized within the family, the tribe, and the church. Nevertheless, in these areas it is easier to love because of similarity rather than difference. Outside the traditional frameworks the challenge of love is more obvious.

To recognize the other is to accept his or her existence, to accept his or her right to live, act, take initiatives, occupy space, and move ahead. Recognizing the other means being willing to be inconvenienced by him or her, precisely because of the difference. To love is not simply to acknowledge but also to help, or as Paul says, "to serve." Serving does not mean abasing oneself, being made dependent, falling into servility, becoming a slave, but actually being of help in the other's liberation. Loving is always sharing, and hence giving, letting go of privileges, or of exclusivism—not merely acknowledging the other's right to be different, but helping him or her to be different, that is, to grow in his or her own personality.

Finally, to love is to receive from the other's difference, to open oneself to difference and to receive from it. There is no love without dialogue, because there is no acceptance of the other if one is unwilling to receive anything from him or her. Love leads to the reciprocal gift in which each gives of what is one's own and receives from the other. The two terms are not merged together but complete one another. If such is love, it is understandable that it fits perfectly well with freedom. Far from limiting freedom, serving in this manner promotes it.

The freedom seeking movements during modernity highlight all kinds of emancipation. They have been devoted to "freedom from" and have not emphasized "*freedom for.*" Struggles against all kinds of domination have been taking place for centuries. Such movements have shaped modern individualism which today attains its supreme expression in the new ruling class of the Western world, with its most advanced point in the United States. There comes a moment when the question must be raised: why this freedom? Why so many emancipation struggles? To fashion an isolated individual struggling against all, in the defense of his or her individual rights? What real freedom can there be in such a situation?

In the encyclical *Veritatis Splendor* (VS), Pope John Paul II highlights the positive aspects of freedom. Freedom is the capacity to achieve one's own being, the capacity of the human being to become human by oneself, the ability of human beings to make themselves human. Human beings are born unfinished, with the calling to fashion themselves, thereby responding to and entering into open dialogue with the Creator. Freedom carries out this calling in achieving sovereignty and control over the world, but especially in building up one's own personality.

> Taking up the words of Sirach, the Second Vatican Council explains the meaning of that "genuine freedom" which is "an outstanding manifestation of the divine image" in man: "God willed to leave man in the power of his own counsel, so that he would seek his Creator of his own accord and would freely arrive at full and blessed perfection by cleaving to God." These words indicate the wonderful depth of the *sharing in God's dominion* to which man has been called: they indicate that man's dominion extends in a certain sense over man himself (VS 38).
>
> Not only the world, however, but also *man himself* has been *entrusted to his own care and responsibility*. God left man "in the power of his own counsel" (Sir 15:14), that he might seek his Creator and freely attain perfection. Attaining such perfection means *personally building up that perfection in himself* (VS 39).

The encyclical explains that human beings realize this calling to fashion themselves "by practicing morally good acts" (VS 39), which is not really any explanation.[19]

The human being is not fulfilled in isolation. A human being left abandoned, without any life shared with others, would inevitably lose his or her
humanity. One needs a certain rhythm of coming and going: withdrawing
and returning to others. The human being is fulfilled with others, in the midst
of others, and in exchange with others.

Freedom that makes a person independent of everyone else is insufficient.
Freedom lies in the ability to open a dialogue among equals with others. A
human being who is unable to relate and establish ties with others is not free.

The freedom of Jesus offers an exemplary case. Jesus goes out to the other,
to the one who is different. He breaks down the barriers that limit common
life to relating with one's family, tribe, and religion. His freedom consists of
overcoming barriers, and so he converses with the Samaritan woman,
approaches the prostitute and the adulterous woman by treating them in a
human way, and approaches the leper and the pagan. Jesus does this very
openly so that it will be clear that he is violating norms and destroying the
limits of the established society. Jesus chooses those excluded from his society. His freedom lies not only in independence toward established norms,
but especially in the ability to create a new way of relating: no one knew
how to communicate with a leper, and in official society, how to deal with
a prostitute. By choosing the other—the new, the excluded, the poor—Jesus
invents a new kind of life in common. He is original: he does not copy conventional behaviors, but invents something new. In the conversation with
the Samaritan woman he shows who he is, and is not restricted to repeating
routine patterns.

Freedom consists in opening dialogue with "other" persons, even those
who are not included in common social life. In this new relation of love there
is something particular and unique. The human being is not acting as a captive of social and cultural structures, and not simply because it is convenient
to act in such a manner. He or she creates something new.

In beginning a shared life with "others," a man or woman becomes creator of freedom. God shows that God is free in calling the human being to
freedom. Likewise, the human being becomes free in calling others to freedom. By breaking down barriers, by going out to meet the outcast, the "poor"
who are outcast precisely because they are poor, the human being is awakening to freedom. He or she opens prospects for the other, opens for him or
her the chance to be free. One who is treated as free awakens to freedom.

The service that love practices tends to create freedom. Human beings
become free by creating freedom within the limits of their possibilities, by
helping to awaken and constitute the freedom of others. To serve one another
mutually is to help one another be free. Love does not make others slaves
but tends to free them or help them win freedom.

Why does freedom demand service? Why not be content with pure dialogue, with the exchange of signs, words, or gestures manifesting acknowledgment and love? Because human beings are bodily and are full of material
needs. There is no point in telling someone who is hungry that you acknowledge him or her as a person, if you don't provide bread to eat. Of course

material food alone is not a solution. The most important thing is the relationship of kinship that removes the barrier of exclusion and takes the poor out of their humiliation. Nevertheless, without the bread, everything else is make-believe. Hence, freedom includes mutual service and not just being together or conversing. For without service there is no true love.

We can thus conclude that far from excluding each other, love and freedom are mutually inclusive. For freedom is only won in the formation of bonds with "others," and true love is the effect of a personal option and not of conscious or unconscious social pressure.

Truth and Freedom

Veritatis Splendor deals precisely with the relationship between truth and freedom. This encyclical marks an important advance over the 1984 and 1986 instructions of the Congregation for the Doctrine of the Faith. It invokes as its foundation the well-known paragraph 17 of *Gaudium et Spes*. It has many references to biblical and patristic texts. It is no doubt the result of a long and broad research. It strives to go out to meet the aspirations of humankind to freedom. For many traditional Catholics and for many non-Catholics as well, the encyclical had to have been a surprise because of the openness of its horizons and its aspiration to be in tune with the concerns of our age. Even so, it does not settle all doubts and some questions remain pending. We would like to present them here by way of suggestion.

As is common in texts of the magisterium, there are many biblical references, but the text is prepared with no consideration to the meaning of the biblical texts invoked, and the teaching is based on principles taken from other sources—in this instance from scholastic theology. For example, to speak of an "assumed conflict between freedom and the law" (35, 46) is to give little consideration to the Pauline teaching on the law and freedom. There is no point in piling up citations for the Pauline epistles if you are ignoring what is the heart of Paul's message.

The encyclical itself presents as its core, as a basic text containing the summation of all its teaching, John 8:32. The encyclical claims to draw from this passage in John the principle that it proposes as the center of the encyclical and of Catholic teaching: "the dependence of freedom on truth" (34). The encyclical speaks of "the fundamental dependence of freedom upon truth, a dependence which has found its clearest and most authoritative expression in the words of Christ: 'You will know the truth, and the truth will set you free' (Jn 8:32)" (VS 34).[20]

The problem is that there is a great distance between the meaning of the words "truth" and "freedom" in the fourth gospel and in the encyclical. It seems that the encyclical's teaching did not start with John, but rather with other sources, and the text from John is cited as an illustration, without paying much attention to just what it means. Indeed, in the encyclical the idea of truth continually has to do with universal and unchanging moral principles of the divine law, both natural and positive, with particular insistence on the natural law. The attributes of truth are "universality and immutability" (VS 51).

Now, in the Gospel according to John, the truth is Jesus himself. "I am . . . the truth" (Jn 14:6). Jesus is the truth because in him and through him is made manifest the true God and God's truth. However, the truth of God that Jesus manifests is that God is love. The truth is that God is love and this truth becomes manifest in Jesus. Being the truth, Jesus is also the way, because only he can lead to the love of God. According to John, the truth does not have to do with any law, and it is not about moral principles, much less unchanging principles. If God is love, the immutability so emphasized by Greek philosophy and scholastic theology becomes meaningless.

Jesus says that freedom comes from this truth. He thereby means that the root of freedom is the love of God. In Jesus God's love becomes immediately perceptible, infinitely close. Jesus is creative of freedom. He himself, in his humanity, becomes the free image of the Father's freedom. The love of God that is made manifest in him is the source of human freedom. Love creates freedom.

The context of the well-known statement of Jesus in chapter 8 sheds even more light on the scope of the text. Jesus is truth as opposed to others who are falsehood and live in falsehood. In chapter 8, lying is with those known as "Jews." They have the devil for their father (Jn 8:44), and the devil "is a liar and the father of lies" (Jn 8:44). They abide in falsehood. They oppose "their" law, supposedly God's law, to Jesus (Jn 8:17). According to John, truth, far from being identified with a law, stands against it. That is why it is really inappropriate to refer to this text in order to affirm the primacy of immutable and universal moral principles.

Freedom proceeds from the truth that is Jesus. That is the very thing we are saying in this chapter. Just as the encyclical replaces John's concept of truth with one taken from scholastic theology, so it does with the concept of freedom.

The document refers to *Gaudium et Spes*, and several times invokes an idea of freedom in tune with the Council's teaching (VS 38-39). However, when it seeks to pull the argumentation together and move toward practical conclusions, the encyclical puts aside the Bible and the Council, and uses another definition of freedom.

The basic idea underlying the encyclical is that freedom consists of "the free obedience of the human being to God's law" (VS 41). With this definition it can be concluded that there is no conflict between law and freedom inasmuch as freedom is totally subordinated to law. This is the exact opposite of Paul's gospel. According to Paul, freedom overcomes the law; according to the encyclical, freedom is a matter of obeying the law. We thus return—at least if the words are taken in their plain meaning—to the doctrine of the Judeo-Christians against whom Paul directs his fury.

The encyclical invokes the authority of St. Thomas Aquinas (cf. VS 45), attempting to draw from a passage from Aquinas writing on the "law of the

Spirit" in Romans 8:2 an exaltation of the law in Paul. That would be in contradiction to the teaching of the epistle to the Galatians. However, St. Thomas explains intelligently—like someone who has a good grasp of the scope of the Pauline message—that, for Paul, the law of the Spirit is the Holy Spirit himself who illuminates the mind or the resulting faith. St. Thomas does not accentuate the "law" as such. Nevertheless, the encyclical cites the Angelic Doctor as though the passage cited would support its case, whereas it actually runs counter to it.

All indications are that this notion of freedom as obedience, which is the standard used by the encyclical, comes from ordinary scholastic theology. However, as already noted, it has failed to understand, much less accept, biblical freedom. It has remained a captive of Greek philosophy, for which freedom is an imperfection that has to be reduced as much as possible.[21]

For scholasticism, the goal of the human person is the attainment of a universal and unchangeable nature. The road is made up of immutable and universal principles. The human being is an "order," occupying its own place in the "order" of the universe. The value of human beings lies in the collaboration that they offer to the order of the whole. Respecting order is the highest duty and calling of each individual. To some extent, the ideal would be that all human beings should achieve "order" and thereby leave a universe without stain or flaw. Unfortunately, freedom creates a danger and risk: human beings may fail to occupy their place in the order and may create disorder in the universe. Hence, it is emphasized that the raison d'être of freedom is to observe order, to voluntarily obey God's law, since it has not been possible to make such obedience necessary, even though that would assure greater perfection.

Scholasticism has never valued freedom. If freedom consists of freely obeying God's law, it is reduced to a limited choice: obeying or not obeying, doing or not doing what the law commands. The whole pattern for life is already completed. God's laws have already established the order of the universe. Only one thing remains for a human being: saying yes or no. Such a freedom cannot arouse enthusiasm. That is why modernity has rejected scholastic theology and sought other ideas. For many people, however, this scholastic theology has concealed the message of the Bible, and Thomas's own commentaries on the epistles of Paul have been forgotten or distorted.

Actually, if freedom consisted simply of the obligation to obey God's law, it would have been much better for humanity not to have been free. From this standpoint, freedom is actually a cruel ploy on God's part, forcing human beings to decide for themselves what has already been decided by someone else. It would have been better to have to obey spontaneously without the obligation to ratify by one's free consent, which creates the temptation to not obey, and hence the danger of being punished.

Freedom is something other than this, and we regret that the church's magisterium is afraid to deal with the question. The Council laid some foundations, but it did not carry out the construction. Some day, however, we will have to return to the gospel as it was in early Christianity.

We are not very likely to be able to evangelize the world today on the basis of this freedom which consists of obeying God's universal and immutable law. Indeed, that would not be a new evangelization but rather the renewal of the old gospel proclaimed during christendom when there was no need to be persuasive because the support of the secular arm was there at hand.

Of course, St. Paul knows that freedom can be abused, "But do not use this freedom as an opportunity for the flesh" (Gal 5:13). He presents a list of "desires of the flesh" (Gal 5:19-21). Freedom builds the human being. If it destroys, it is not freedom, but slavery, submission, and death wishes. In the human being, both individually and collectively, there are desires that destroy, and to submit oneself to such desires is not freedom but slavery. However, the route from such desires of the flesh to the "universal and immutable principles" of scholastic theology remains an open problem that the encyclical does not clarify. It takes scholasticism as its absolute and obvious starting point. It states that these principles derive from God's revelation, but it does not establish that. Hence it does not resolve doubts.

Such is biblical freedom. God has left human beings unfinished, and has left them the task of inventing themselves and building themselves. The destiny of the human being is not to remain alone. To build humankind means building a network of relationships, and having the human being be connected to others through countless bonds. Freedom consists in creating a life in common, open to ever more distant others. Freedom is not choosing between yes and no. It is doing something new, bringing into existence something human that never existed before. Freedom means struggling against the established structures that offer security, overcoming the fear of what is new, overcoming the barriers between human beings, overcoming prudence and timidity, and experiencing the not yet known.

The sixteenth century Portuguese ships were the image of freedom: they ventured out into the unknown ocean to discover the unknown without any point of support. If that venture included the conquest of other peoples, that was not determined beforehand. Those setting forth did not know that they were going to be meeting other peoples, whether weaker or stronger. When faced with previously undiscovered peoples, they did not have the courage to agree to live together and to establish a new life in common; they gave in to the desires of the flesh.

What they failed to do in the sixteenth century continues to be a challenge to be taken on. The freedom that ventured out onto the open seas can venture to make room for a shared human life beyond the borders of what used to be christendom. It is still possible to open to the other; it is still possible for humankind to take a new step. The call for this new step would be new evangelization. The evangelization that was not achieved in the sixteenth century could be taken on today. That is what a historically contextualized new evangelization is all about. After all, this evangelization, like all evangelization, can only have as its object the gospel of freedom. From Jesus, the apostles held the conviction that the gospel to be announced was this one, radically different from the teaching that they had learned and from the philosophies that they encountered in the world of their time.

3

FREEDOM AND LIBERATION

Liberation theology has gone along its way paying practically no attention to the theology of freedom—at least until recently with the works of Juan Luis Segundo. He inevitably had to come to a theology of freedom, however, because years ago he had argued that a "liberation of theology" was a condition for a theology of liberation.

Liberation theology needs the theology of freedom in order to take its proper place within the whole body of theology and to be received as theology in the full sense—and not simply as an appendix to a section in the treatise in justice, as Cardinal Daniélou once said in Buenos Aires. Moreover, the theology of freedom offers a broader perspective, thereby preventing liberation theology from being regarded as a circumstantial theology lasting only for a generation or as long as a particular set of social issues lasts.

Only on the basis of a theology of freedom can the dualism over the gospel that can also be found in liberation theology be overcome. We will first see how liberation theology remains a captive of dualism, despite efforts to avoid it. Then we will see how to situate liberation in the context of freedom.

Liberation and Twofold Gospel

Earlier we saw how, until Leo XIII, christendom always presented a single uniform gospel, and how since Leo XIII, the church's message has been divided into two parts: the religious doctrine of christendom, drawing inspiration from scholasticism, and the church's social doctrine, likewise drawing inspiration from scholasticism but also from the experience of contemporary social life. The religious doctrine is said to be fixed and immutable, while the social doctrine is enriched as new social situations come along and create new challenges and new responses.

We have seen how evangelization has been affected by this duality. While some have been attracted by the social doctrine, they have not been able to assimilate the legacy of scholasticism. Conversely, traditional Catholics have clung to the scholasticism of christendom and have rejected the social teaching. There have been a number of efforts in both theology and practice to overcome dualism, but they have not been successfully integrated into the church. Not even Vatican II overcame the dualism between social and religious doctrine. The fact that one treatise, *Lumen Gentium*, is separated from another, *Gaudium et Spes*, and that they have two different methodologies, is the most obvious sign of a split over the gospel.

What is the relationship between liberation theology and the church's social teaching?[1] This is always a troubling question. For their part, the liberation theologians refuse to be assimilated. If their work were merely a commentary related to the church's social doctrine, it would not deserve to be called theology. It would be an appendix, it would be the second aspect of the gospel, but considerably below the first one which is the object of traditional theology. It would not be broadly encompassing knowledge, but merely a chapter.

However, people from outside who were attempting to situate this new development concluded that liberation theology was a Latin American version—quite original—but a *version* of the church's social doctrine, namely the social doctrine applied to Latin America. Indeed, the social doctrine and liberation theology were talking about the same issues: social sin, justice, development, human dignity, and liberation.

The theologians drew on a number of arguments, including the fact that its root is the praxis of liberation and its theology is the expression of individual theologians and not a church document. However, such arguments were not always convincing because the church's social teaching is also based on a praxis of Catholics and it is prepared by theologians before being integrated into the teaching of the magisterium.

The Puebla document easily makes such an assimilation. "The contribution of the Church to liberation and human promotion has gradually been taking shape in a series of doctrinal guidelines and criteria for action that we are now accustomed to call 'the social teaching of the Church'" (Puebla 472). "But the aim of this doctrine of the Church . . . is always the promotion and integral liberation of human beings in terms of both their earthly and their transcendent dimensions. It is a contribution to the construction of the ultimate and definitive Kingdom, although it does not equate earthly progress with Christ's Kingdom" (Puebla 475).

Since its earliest works, liberation theology has defined itself in relationship to the doctrine of salvation. Gustavo Gutiérrez connects his first sketch to the theological issue of whether there is one salvation or two, a topic much discussed in the 1950s and 1960s by the theologians who prepared the Council and wanted to get away from dualism.[2] How to connect eternal salvation to temporal liberation, and salvation in heaven to liberation on earth?

When liberation theology emerged, the documents of the magisterium situated it in the dualist perspective, as had been common since Leo XIII. *Evangelii Nuntiandi* had the effect of enshrining dualism. Never had it been stated so clearly that the church's social doctrine was a necessary part of evangelization. According to *Evangelii Nuntiandi* evangelization is dual in nature and the gospel has two objects. The first, which is always placed first and is cited as obvious and traditional, is what is called "salvation in Jesus Christ" (EN 27, 35). The second is called "human liberation" and also "human promotion."

But is not this human liberation part of salvation in Jesus Christ? The theologians who prepared the document clearly did not have a well-defined vocabulary. Nevertheless, by bringing human liberation into evangelization, Paul VI had the impression that he had taken a step forward.

Actually, ever since *Rerum Novarum* it was clear that there was something new in the church's teaching, something that stood out from the traditional deposit: while the religious aspect was retained from christendom, the social aspect was replaced by something new. From this point on, then, there were two objects in the church's teaching. However, the status of the social teaching had not been defined. Now human liberation enters explicitly into evangelization. The pope changed the vocabulary a little, taking a cue from Gustavo Gutiérrez. Instead of stating the social teaching, he was adopting the salvation-liberation framework. The aim of *Evangelii Nuntiandi* was precisely to justify the introduction of liberation into the gospel alongside salvation.

There remained, however, the problem of how to define the relationship of the two objects, a problem which was taken up by Gutiérrez's theology of liberation. For Pope Paul VI, there is a profound link between salvation and liberation. "Between evangelization and human advancement—development and liberation—there are in fact profound links" (EN 31). "The church links human liberation and salvation in Jesus Christ, but it never identifies them . . ." (EN 35).

What might be the nature of this link between salvation and liberation? It is not explained, but the link seems to be an extrinsic one. Liberation does not seem to be part of salvation in Jesus Christ, nor does liberation seem to be the result of salvation. It is striking that there is no allusion to Paul's teaching on freedom. Nor does the papal document present an elaboration of the content of the gospel. It lists a disjointed series of propositions as forming part of the gospel, but there is no clear notion of just what the gospel is. There still seems to be an attachment to the legacy of christendom, when the gospel was identified with scholastic teaching and the documents of the magisterium.

The link seems extrinsic because salvation contains no reference to a message of freedom. Moreover, liberation always seems to refer to specific political activities and has no broader extension. Hence there is nothing that could fashion this connection except a decree of the will. The decision is made to link the two objects, even though it is not clear why. A decision is made to announce one gospel in two parts.

This continues to be how the relationship between salvation and liberation is seen in subsequent documents. It is present in the instruction, *Libertatis Conscientia*, which was intended to approach liberation theology in a positive way: "Evangelization is the proclamation of salvation, which is a gift of God" (LC 63). The document goes on to say, "But the love which impels the church to communicate to all persons a sharing in the grace of divine life also causes it . . . to promote an integral liberation from everything that hinders the development of individuals" (LC 63). Salvation and liberation are thus united by the common love of the church which is concerned for both objects. Such union is purely extrinsic.

Interestingly, the instruction speaks a great deal about the Christian teaching on freedom, citing the relevant texts from Paul and going so far as to title chapter 2, "The Human Vocation to Freedom and the Tragedy of Sin." Unfortunately, the body of the chapter shows that it is not about Paul's message, and absolutely nothing is said about the vocation to freedom. This chapter devoted to freedom speaks only of freedom in a negative sense in order to point out dangers, necessary constraints, and dire consequences. Far from providing a unifying principle, freedom is treated only in negative terms.

The mindset of the writer is revealed when he says, "It is because of its awareness of this deadly ambiguity that through its magisterium the church has raised its voice over the centuries to warn against aberrations that could easily bring enthusiasm for liberation to bitter disillusionment. The church has often been misunderstood in so doing. With the passage of time, however, it is possible to do greater justice to the church's point of view" (LC 20). Praise for the Syllabus of Errors! We see here the document's underlying thinking about freedom. Such considerations nullify all references to the Bible, as well as statements of good intentions.

The pope's letter to the Brazilian bishops conference about the church's mission and liberation theology (September 4, 1986) is the magisterial document that has striven most to unite the two objects of evangelization. The pope speaks about:

- the "mystery of liberation in the cross and resurrection of Christ";
- the "two constitutive dimensions of liberation in its Christian conception" and the "gospel of radical and integral liberation"; and
- the "correct and necessary theology of liberation."

He says that "the theology of liberation is not only timely but useful and necessary," and he adds that the church in Brazil can play "an important and at the same time delicate role" as it promotes this correct theology of liberation.

There is no reason to think that the pope has changed his mind or that liberation theology has ceased being useful and necessary. However, the world has changed since then. Liberation theology needs to examine the changes that have occurred.

At the 1992 assembly in Santo Domingo the word "liberation" was eliminated from the vocabulary. Instead, the word "advancement" [*promoción*] was used. Human advancement was likewise separated from evangelization—or at least the connection between the two was very much relativized. The final document says, "The church's concern for the social . . . is part of its evangelizing mission" (SD 158). The message of freedom was either forgotten or intentionally dropped. There remains merely a "concern for the social."

However, the Santo Domingo assembly does not necessarily represent the real thinking of the bishops and the Latin American churches. In any case, there is no doubt that the Santo Domingo document was not of any help in clarifying the relationship between the two classic objects of evangelization.

Summing up the contributions of the documents of the magisterium, we can say that on the whole they remain on the same level of generality as the Council: "Earthly progress must be carefully distinguished from the growth of Christ's kingdom. Nevertheless, to the extent that the former can contribute to the better ordering of human society, it is of vital concern to the kingdom of God" (GS 39).

Not even liberation theologians have always been concerned to seek the unity between Christ's salvation and temporal liberation. That has been Gutiérrez's concern from the beginning. He has based his pursuit on the position that there is but one salvation history and that there is a unity between creation and redemption, issues commonly discussed around the time of the Council.

Some accept and openly argue for a clear distinction. Such is the case of Clodovis Boff, who has made a distinction between two theologies—a "theology 1" and a "theology 2"—corresponding to two very distinct objects. "The first is directly concerned with specifically 'religious' matters." That is where the classic treatises are to be found: God, creation and sin, Christ, grace, eschatology, sacraments, ecclesiology, and so forth. The second deals with "secular" matters: culture, sexuality, history, politics. Politics and history are acknowledged to have no intrinsic tie to God, Christ, or the sacraments.[3]

The distinction—indeed the separation or quasi-separation—between "theology 1" and "theology 2" has actually been practiced, particularly by a significant number of pastoral activists. Some people have reserved their time, concerns, energies, and activities for a practice supposedly about liberation, which in fact had to do with "secular" matters without making any reference to "religious" matters. They dealt with the objects of theology 2. They said that they were evangelizing because evangelization was a matter of working for "secular" liberation. But their evangelical practice and their traditional pastoral work had nothing to do with each other. These people could devote a portion of their time to the established religious activities, but such activities had little or no relation to the "secular" activities. Thus there was, or still is, a de facto separation between the two evangelizations. Social activity and religious activity were separated.[4]

This whole phenomenon was certainly affected by the fact that it coincided with the historic moment of secularization affecting christendom after World War II, whose high point was 1955 to 1970, the very years when liberation theology was elaborated and the public that was going to receive it was prepared. The liberation theology movement went through the very same crisis of secularization that virtually wiped out Catholic Action movements.

Once they entered into "secular" activity, large numbers of priests, religious, sisters, and lay people moved away from religious activities. They discovered that there was nothing in common between the two areas except the intention of being Christians, which seemed quite extrinsic.

The wave of popular religion came along in the 1970s. Under the banner of popular religion, many pastoral agents returned to the "religious." They discovered, or thought they were discovering, that popular religion could have "political" and "temporal" effects. Nevertheless, popular religion has not provided the solution to the challenge of the unity of salvation and of evangelization. Indeed, the pastoral agents who returned to encouraging popular religion did not believe in it for themselves. They merely pretended to believe, and this lack of faith had an impact on the people. They were practicing this religion not because of its intrinsic religious value, but for the political effects attributed to it, whether correctly or—more likely—incorrectly.

Moreover, by this time popular religion was declining and its decline continues inexorably. It is still practiced by older people, but has no luck in converting new followers. In comparison to the effective proselytizing of the pentecostal churches or the Catholic charismatic renewal, popular religion is powerless. Year by year fewer people are involved.

In practice the separation between salvation and liberation, and between the two evangelizations, has been very harmful to the sectors of the church that have taken up tasks of liberation or temporal advancement. On one hand, the religious dimension has been seized by the new movements that take advantage of the renewal of religion in our contemporary world. The vast majority of Catholic or Protestant "religious" people have joined pietist movements that are all emotion or charitable aid. On the other hand, the "liberationists" have not renewed their ranks; they have not converted a second generation. They are getting old and are not growing, and are even declining. It seems to us that the de facto separation between liberation and religion in the traditional sense has been decisive in this decline.

There is no more urgent task than that of again uniting what has been separated for so long, the "political" and the "religious," the "social" and the "mystical." This is more a practical than a theoretical task, although theory would have to make a contribution to anchor and guide an effective practice.

Today, the crisis of secularization has vanished. The "religious" is once more valued. A more comprehensive theology can be fashioned. However, the triumph of pietistic movements has very much diminished interest in theology or in any kind of intellectual reflection. The new movements are more concerned with experience than with intellectual reflection, and they mistrust any critical reflection that can stifle experience. For them, our age does not need theology.[5]

Even so the problems remain intact and some day there will be renewed interest in them. At the moment, theological reflection is intended more for a future generation than for the current one. Even if theology does not seem necessary today, it will become necessary some day.

Toward a Theology of Freedom

Emerging from Isolation

For a generation, the particularity of the new Latin American theology has been emphasized a great deal. Any likening of it to something earlier or to other areas was treated as an assault on the authenticity of Latin American theology. Liberation theology sought to be utterly new and original, with no antecedents and nothing similar to it. A great deal of intellectual work consisted in studying the differences between this new theology and all others.[6]

This created the impression that the theologians wanted to be more original and further removed from their colleagues in the European tradition than they actually managed to be. There were unquestionably differences and new elements. However, it was dangerous to create the impression of wanting to move away from the entire Western tradition, because most Latin American Christians do not want to move away from the European tradition. Indeed, most identify with that tradition. Hence, instead of attracting people, the claim of originality led to a reaction of defensiveness and rejection. Rome could not have produced the two instructions of the Congregation for the Doctrine of the Faith unless it had felt supported by broad sectors of Latin American Catholics.[7] Similar reactions have occurred in the Protestant churches.

A theology that stresses its Latin American originality ends up being rejected by most Latin American Christians; the majority does not see itself there and reacts with fear and mistrust. In order to understand this situation, we have to situate it within the broad movement of Latin American culture. What is happening with Christian theology is also happening in other cultural domains.

In colonial times there was an ongoing rivalry between Europeans and "creoles," that is, the descendants of Spaniards and Portuguese born in the Americas. Even so, the creoles did not want a different culture; they wanted to imitate and reproduce the culture of Portugal and Spain. Thus, no space was left for the indigenous cultures, which survived only out of sight, and did not become publicly visible. Nor did they want to create a mestizo culture, because they were unwilling to accept their own condition as mestizos. The Guarani language was supplanted by Portuguese, just as Spanish was imposed over the Nahuatl and Quechua languages. Along with the language came the imposition of the entire culture which is transmitted through language.

Independence changed nothing; it opened the door for English or French culture, but it did not create a specifically Latin American culture. Everything "native" was "barbarian," as Sarmiento said so convincingly, and as all the elites thought well into our own century. Only in the twentieth century did the proclamation of a mestizo culture begin. Mestizos began to multiply. The mestizo character of a good portion of the population began to be accepted, and mestizos began to accept that that is what they are. In the twentieth century, the mestizo character begins to be affirmed in the arts: painting, sculpture, cinema, and to some degree in literature. In Brazil it was only with Gilberto Freyre that the mestizo character received citizenship rights.

Even so, mestizos are only a small segment. The totality continues to be defined by European white culture. To this day all public and private school curricula, from pre-school to the university, are curricula in Western culture. Now, as the twentieth century draws to a close, the Westernization of culture can be said to be increasing while the mestizo characteristics are on the wane. The triumph of computers is only increasing Western penetration. To this day the ambition of many artists is to be a success in the United States. For writers the Nobel prize is the supreme anointing. On the whole, the culture remains fascinated by the West. Only some mestizo elites strive to move away from this source. They are not likely to succeed, however, and even when they do, they are not recognized.

It is clear that deep in the bowels of Latin America lie indigenous culture, black culture, and one or multiple mestizo cultures. However, with a few exceptions, they do not have access to public life: they are not admitted in teaching, in culture-producing companies (press, television, etc.), and they do not have financing. Hence the dominant culture is still a copy of Western culture, and that is what the vast majority wants: the vast majority accepts television along Western, and typically American, lines. The time for characteristically mestizo cultures has still not arrived. North American culture is even beginning to dominate areas as private as food, drink, sexuality, and medicine.

How could we expect religion or theology to be any different? With regard to religion, even though today there is a great deal of talk about "inculturation," what is really happening is a "de-inculturation" that is unstoppable. Almost all the new spiritual movements come from North America (Charismatic Renewal) or Europe (Focolari, Schönstatt, Communione e Liberazione, Opus Dei, etc.). We are witnessing a shocking "de-inculturation." The more traditional devotions are giving way to new Western forms of piety.

If a liberation theology were grounded in a strong autonomous culture, such as a mestizo culture or an indigenous culture which had achieved a dynamic strength for integrating other cultures, there could be an autonomous theology, recognized and accepted as such. Given the current state of Latin American culture, such a situation is still a dream.

Hence the widespread rejection: where is Latin American liberation taught today? Who reads it? Who is familiar with its texts? In Latin America, a tiny minority of the educated religious public. Rejection has produced an isolation, the upshot of which is that liberation theology is better known and more read in Europe and the United States than in Latin America itself.

It is legitimate to assert those aspects in which Latin American theology is original. At the same time, it must be situated within a movement of the whole of Christian theology since its origins. Unless that continuity can be shown, it will not be accepted.[8] It would be difficult to show continuity with scholastic theology alone, even though there are very serviceable elements in scholasticism and even in the neo-scholasticism elaborated by the Spanish Dominicans and then by the Spanish Jesuits in the sixteenth century. Scholastic theology does not encompass the entire Christian theological tradition, however.[9]

It is not enough to go directly to the Bible without going through the history of exegesis. Ignoring the history of the biblical tradition leads to the risk of falling into theological "concordisms" which are no better than fundamentalist "concordisms."[10]

In order to draw liberation theology out of its isolation, it will be well to place it in a current of a theology of freedom which in some manner has always sought to find a way in the history of Christianity.

Emerging from the Particular

The worst thing that could happen to liberation theology would be for it to be regarded as a circumstantial theology—a discourse that was valid at a particular moment in history, but has ceased to be relevant once that moment has passed.

Liberation theology certainly arose in a very specific context and it bears the marks of that period. It emerged in the 1960s, when a vast endeavor of Latin American liberation was in the air, one that would be a political, economic, social, and cultural revolution all at once. In the air was the idea of a specific kind of development that would include true independence. In the air was the project of a total transformation comparable to the great revolutions that gave rise to the nations of Europe and North America. There were a number of specific projects, but they were connected by a certain family resemblance. The Medellín conference was one reflection of the mental excitement of that period. Many thought that great things could happen; for many, the 1959 Cuban revolution augured major developments for the whole continent.

What has actually happened, of course, is quite different. Instead of being transformed, traditional society has been stabilized by civilian or military national security regimes. These regimes have taken a route directly contrary to that imagined in the 1960s: rather than independence, they have sought to be more integrated into the Western world, first in order to defend themselves from communism, and then in the name of modernization and in order to enter the age of the new technologies.

The younger generation has no memory of all the excitement of the 1960s; it cannot imagine the hopes of that time, and cannot comprehend the cultural expressions of that period: protest music and songs, films, celebrations, ways of greeting one another. Few remember Che Guevara; no one remembers Camilo Torres. And Salvador Allende? Forgotten. The heroes of the struggles against the military regime in Brazil? Integrated into the system— even in Congress and government ministries. They gave up on the ideals of their youth some time ago. In Brazil the supreme irony is that the crown prince of the sociologists of liberation, the one who provided the theology of that period with its "scientific" mediations, has reached the presidency of the country, elected by all the country's conservative forces, and he now heads a government in which the traditional "colonels" [rural strongmen] place all their hopes. Times really have changed.[11]

If liberation theology had been simply the theory of the practice of the 1960s, history would indeed have cast it off by now. It would be the theory of a failed practice. It would have failed as theory as well. However, it was more than a theory linked to a practice, even if that is how some understood it and defended it. The situation provided the opportunity. Within that situation, this Latin American theology was the rediscovery of perennial Christian themes, which have been present since their biblical origins but have often been hidden by the ideologies of christendom. The themes that were disinterred and highlighted go much further than the situation of the 1960s.

Some voices within liberation theology itself have occasionally furnished arguments for considering this theology as something purely circumstantial. Indeed, if one thinks that Latin American liberation theology has to do only with "theology 2" and leaves "theology 1" intact, it can easily be concluded that once the circumstance that brought about "theology 2" has passed, "theology 1" severs all ties with it and continues blithely along the same path as ever, quite unaffected.

Actually what is of value in liberation theology is that it questions theology as a whole, and demands, as Juan Luis Segundo used to say, a "liberation of theology"—of *all* theology, and not just "theology 2." Precisely because liberation theology entails an overall change, it goes beyond the circumstance in which it arose. It joins other factors to direct Christian thinking beyond traditional scholastic theology and the church's traditional social teaching inspired by that theology.

Since the 1970s, in view of the failures of the revolutionary frameworks conceived during the previous decade, some have sought substitutes, as though other movements might provide the "revolutionary class," that is, the social force capable of changing society. Thus, people began to place their trust and draw up projects on the basis of the indigenous movement, the black movement, or the feminist movement. In them would lie the continuation or replacement of the previous social movements that had not attained the hoped-for results. Indeed, these movements have developed since the 1970s.[12]

Nevertheless, some observations should be made in this regard. Blacks, Indians, and women have specific projects, and they are not the same as the previous revolutionary project. Indigenous people want an indigenous society alongside, or instead of, the current national society. They are not pursuing a transformation of this white society with which they are not deeply familiar. Black people want to go on living and be respected, but they run up against racism. In no country are they a majority and in no country are they in a position to take power, as in South Africa. Finally, what women want is not achieved by taking power, or by transforming social structures or legislation alone. They want a total transformation of the culture, and that requires processes of another kind. Indigenous, black, and feminist movements open new areas for the pursuit of freedom, but they are something else. They do not replace the struggles of the previous decade to transform society.

Hence the object of liberation theology cannot be exclusive. This theology is part of a much broader movement. Each specific project is an expression of the human calling to freedom. All flow into one another in an overall theology of freedom.

Latin American liberation theology is not something in isolation. It is the expression of a vast many-sided and differentiated movement that involves the whole of humankind and is expressed in a variety of ways in accordance with the diversity of situations. Had it been a temporary expression it would already be consigned to history. The particular situation has passed, but thinking can continue and begin anew.

Can a form of theology disappear? It most certainly can. For example, there was a liberal theology during the first half of the nineteenth century in various regions in Latin America, particularly in Brazil. It was the theology that drove first the independence movements, and the republican movements that failed.[13] Conservative regimes prevailed and liberal theology died: the ultramontane theology accompanying the new Romanization in the second half of the nineteenth century won out.

Theology of Freedom

Greek philosophy is unaware of the comprehensive meaning of freedom in the Bible. Roman law is even more radically unfamiliar with it. To the extent that Christianity integrated Greek philosophy and Roman law, it withdrew ever more from the biblical sources. It created and lived the model of a fixed society, ever the same, living by rules and stable structures. Value was always placed on stability, invariability, and submission. Under such conditions, freedom could only be a source of disorder, a weakness, a flaw in the order of society which supposedly corresponded to an imagined order of the universe.

Scholastic theology adopted many elements from Greek philosophy and Roman law. It also exalted "order" as the highest value. It held that action must be subjected to a universal order. The human being contributed to the order of the universe by his or her action. Nevertheless, in the Christian tradition there have always been some people, especially in the mystical tradition, who did not submit to scholasticism. Even though the official ideology of christendom was predominant, they held onto the originality of the Bible's message. That was where a theology of freedom has been passed on.

Hence a theology of freedom does not emerge from modernity, but has its roots in the Christian tradition as a whole and ultimately in the Bible—whose message has always remained consciously alive at least in some sectors of the church, despite the ideological interpretations of christendom.

Insofar as the Reformation was a movement of return to the Bible—and bypassing scholasticism and christendom—we can say that a theology of freedom stands in the line of the Reformation—it takes up again, continues, and reassumes the Reformation project. What is being sought today is a continuation of the Reformation in its deep inspiration but without its schismatic results. The breaking away of the reformed churches from the main trunk of the medieval church was a disaster. It prompted a reactionary hardening on the part of Roman Catholicism. Indeed, several reformed churches very quickly fell into the same defect: the struggle between the churches had the effect of placing them all in a state of war, as they became hardened in their distinctive features which they regarded as sacred. What separated them became more important than what united them. The theology of freedom was persecuted for centuries. Even the churches that raised it as a banner reduced it to purely theoretical claims that were belied by their practice. The Reformation sought the freedom described by Paul and John, but the wars of religion sidelined that concern.

Vatican II assumed a portion of the Reformation's concern for freedom, but it halted part way, not daring to go the full distance. It began a journey that is still unfinished. The task of a theology of freedom would be to reassume Vatican II's intuitions and go further than the Council went.

The roots of the theology of freedom are very plainly in the Bible. By linking up to a theology of freedom, a theology of liberation makes evident its roots in the Bible and tradition. By refusing to approach a theology of freedom, liberation theology has weakened itself and allowed for a certain ambiguity that its adversaries have exploited: it has allowed the value of what were called the "mediations" of the human sciences to be exaggerated. The topic of freedom seemed to draw much of its inspiration from modern ideologies: many pressed the point by denouncing the influence of Marxist ideas.[14]

Latin American theologians have been afraid to be categorized as mere repeaters of well-worn topics. They wanted to highlight their connection to what was happening in the present. At the time that may have seemed more useful, but over the long run it has been the cause of many misunderstandings. It can be argued that in any case the decisions have already been made and the die is cast, and nothing can prevent the widespread rejection that has occurred after the Roman instructions. Perhaps, but even so, it is always better not to wager on defeat, but rather to try to save the situation by any means possible. In any case, in looking toward the future, the way to save the situation is to establish a strict connection to a biblical theology of freedom, following the lead of Paul and John, and extended over a centuries-long tradition, albeit one that was usually that of a minority given the context of christendom.

Liberation and Modernity

The theology of freedom and the theology of liberation are not the product of modernity or of modern ideologies. Yet, freedom is a summation of the language of modernity; it is the air that modernity breathes and its ever present underlying common foundation. There is a wide variety of expressions and concepts of freedom, but freedom is modernity's climate, its atmosphere, its ongoing concern. In this regard, postmodernity is even more insistent. The ideas of freedom in circulation may be contradictory, but freedom is the common language, the lingua franca that allows for communication.

Anyone who is outside this atmosphere of freedom cuts communication with the modern world. In this sense, it was unfortunate that Vatican II did not have the courage to take its stand boldly within the language of freedom in order to enable the Christian conception of freedom to appear from within that language. The present papacy has gone no further, and gives the impression that it has remained behind the conciliar discourse. At least that is the impression that emerges from the 1984 and 1986 instructions, which are intended to be a Christian doctrine on freedom and yet manage to present nothing more than a Christian doctrine against freedom, where freedom is seen more as a danger than as God's gift and human calling. Freedom is apparently more a concession made by God than a benefit. Despite the best of intentions, the encyclical *Veritatis Splendor* fails to be a teaching on Christian freedom.

Liberation theology sought to distance itself from modern liberalism, and to some extent came to the point of sometimes coinciding with conservative theology. It is true that in Latin America, liberals, or so-called "liberals," have always been a small elite of intellectuals identified with the culture, and often enough with the interests of so-called "liberal" and "democratic" countries. Latin American political liberalism has never gone so far as to struggle for the freedoms of the poor. Just like the revolutionaries of the 1960s, the liberation theologians have despised liberals and liberalism.

Sometimes one heard from them something of an echo of the Marxist condemnation of the so-called "formal" freedoms of Western-type democracies. However, when the national security dictatorships began to persecute their foes, they began to appreciate the "formal freedoms" of democracies. Today many thousands have done penance, been converted, and are firm defenders of the formal freedoms of the liberals, that is, of Western-style formal democracy.

Today, it makes no sense to reject the freedoms of the democratic system. They offer many more possibilities for the struggle of the poor than the alternatives that Latin America has witnessed. The notion that "the worse things get, so much the better" does not work. The worst has come and it did not bring about the better. The so-called "democratic freedoms" are a starting point or a foothold. There is no point in standing outside the contemporary world, by rejecting the whole language of freedom. It is within this modern language that we must situate the Christian message of the call to freedom. Moreover, political liberalism is not the totality of modern freedoms. The climate of freedom goes much further than the political system, and of course beyond economic liberalism.

In order to keep going and to save itself from sharing the fate of passing phenomena, Latin American liberation theology must merge with the great current that derives from the New Testament's message of freedom and which runs through all of christendom, even though it is often at the margins, affirms its power in the Reformation, confronts modernity, of which it is one of the sources, and is in dialogue with this modernity up to our own times.

Latin America still does not have its own autonomous mestizo culture, one that could create its own language. The churches of Africa and Asia have not yet reached the level of development that would enable them to express themselves in the categories of traditional Chinese, Japanese, Indian, or African thought. To this day there is no theology that does not use the categories and forms of logic of the West—which does not mean that that may not be the case some generations from now. Thus far there is no Latin American theology that can have its own means of expression. Indeed, that is why books of liberation theology are read and discussed more in the First World than in Latin America.

4

SOCIAL LIBERATION

The gospel is the proclamation of God's love, love poured into our hearts, love by which God gives up being all-powerful and creates the freedom of God's human creatures. By entering into the human condition, however, love becomes multiple and varied, producing extremely diverse expressions, which we cannot condemn as corruptions or deviations by their very nature. Love is diversified and has largely helped produce diversity in history. It is not only the variety of sin, but also the variety of love that makes history a movement that cannot be predicted and that makes developments unforeseeable.

In Latin America for a generation—the generation that turned twenty in the 1960s—the image of love that for many years seduced, attracted, convinced or else prompted repudiation, indignation, and uneasiness, was Camilo Torres. Camilo died thirty years ago, on February 15, 1966. Only thirty years and yet it seems that centuries have passed.

How the world has changed since then! How Latin America has changed! How the church has changed! Only thirty years and everything has become so different! Love remains the predominant concern, the essential motivation. Yet how greatly the way love is understood has changed! Holding a press conference on the letter that he had just delivered to the Cardinal archbishop of Bogotá requesting to be reduced to the lay state, Camilo Torres said:

> I feel that the revolutionary struggle is a Christian and priestly struggle. Only through this, given the specific situation of our country, can we fulfill the love that human beings should have for their neighbors . . .
>
> I think my commitment to my fellow human beings to effectively fulfill the precept of love for neighbor imposes this sacrifice on me. The ultimate criterion of human decisions must be charity, it must be supernatural love. I am going to expose myself to all the risks that this criterion requires of me.[1]

In a message to Christians, published on the day that he went underground, he wrote:

I think that I have given myself over to the Revolution out of love for neighbor. I have given up celebrating Mass in order to achieve this love for neighbor in the temporal, economic, and social realm. When my neighbor no longer has anything against me, when the Revolution has been achieved, I will again celebrate Mass, if God grants it to me.[2]

Naturally, few followed Camilo Torres in his option. But his message prodded and guided a generation. It lasted into the early 1990s in Central America, although it had disappeared in South America many years earlier.

At that time, in a church so peacefully integrated into the established system, the voice of Camilo Torres resounded like a thunderclap. A call so strong has not resounded in vain. For a generation, many believed that it was obvious that love for neighbor demanded a determined struggle to transform society. That is what the documents of the bishops conferences have been understood to mean. Even the papal encyclicals have included the struggle for social transformation among the duties of charity. This teaching has not been given the same degree of emphasis in all circles. By and large, however, we can say that this reflects the overall mind of the Latin American church. Of course it did not reach the masses of the people, who still think that religion has nothing to do with "politics," that is, with situations in society which belong to the nature of things: if that is how things are, it must be because God wants them to be that way.

In Latin America today, and especially in Brazil, the prevailing idea of love is quite different. The extreme and radical form of the new expression of love is found in esoteric religions, sects, or philosophies. They present themselves as sciences, although they essentially critique the "modern" sciences. They claim to be the real science of total (holistic) reality of which the sciences are unaware. There is a wide variety of schools and systems. Already in our large cities there are large contingents of them. What they have in common is the notion that the human being becomes one element in a vast living organism enveloping the universe. Human beings feel that they are in communication with all beings in the universe, and hence are able to know the whole. Their activity is part of the unfolding of an overall energy. Love is sympathy, a communication linking all beings. Loving means feeling united to everything and to all, breathing together with the whole, and letting the energies of the universe—which are love—flow through oneself. Love is, as it were, an experience of universal communion.[3]

In today's Catholic movements we find these same themes in a Christian garb that is perfectly orthodox and in harmony with the dogmas of the church. The overall meaning is nevertheless the same, and love is primarily an "experience," a feeling of union with others. The religious "experience" of the charismatic renewal is also an experience of love: universal, not personalized, love; a feeling of being in sympathetic communion with others and with the entire universe. The hierarchy is rather hesitant in the face of this avalanche of religious feeling, but all indications are that it will end up being infected, because the movement is quite strong.

We have here a conception of love diametrically opposed to the idea of the 1960s. Can we conclude that Christians have given up struggles for social change and have surrounded themselves in the waves of Universal Energy, in a vast cosmic Love that encompasses everything and mixes it all together? Perhaps not, but the enthusiasm with which young people are entering this movement can only be compared to the enthusiasm with which they allowed themselves to be won over by social struggle in the sixties.

Esoteric or "spiritualistic" movements are not so indifferent to specific acts of love. They may carry out works of charity. Spiritual movements sometimes engage in major works of charity: they provide help to drug users, alcoholics, people with AIDS, the mentally ill, poor women, and so forth. However, they have little or no sensitivity to social action, that is, to activity to change social structures. Indeed, they instinctively shy away from anything that could create conflict, as if they were allergic to any conflict. For them love means absence of conflict, absence of struggle or any expression of aggression. When communicated to the poor, this rejection of all conflict means passive acceptance of the situation, resignation, denial of reality, and salvation by fleeing into unreal dreams.

All indications are that for some years to come the prevailing idea of love will be spiritualistic and "holistic," in its more radical forms outside the church, or in its more moderate forms inside the church. This does not mean that activity aiming at social liberation has to disappear. It is continuing, although with fewer people and with less public awareness. Actually, there are intermediate positions between the two extremes, seeking to reconcile internal liberation with social liberation. Young people are often more radical and prefer the extreme positions, but as they gain experience positions in between gradually gain ground.

Even so, social liberation today is seen quite differently. We are in a new phase of social history in Latin America. What seemed obvious thirty years ago has become incomprehensible today, and what was rejected then is now esteemed. At that time you could not speak of reform; you had to be pursuing a revolution. Today no one speaks of revolution anymore, not even the guerrillas of the Zapatista army in Mexico; everyone is seeking reform. Thirty years ago "reformism" was a bad word; today it is the word in vogue among the most progressive.[4] In this chapter we are going to examine what social liberation means to those Christians who seek to be fully faithful to the gospel of love.

Social Apartheid in Latin America

From Inequality to Apartheid

In church pronouncements, the situation in Latin America has been primarily described in terms of inequality. The documents state that inequality is growing: the rich are becoming richer and the poor are becoming poorer.

The situation of inequality is blamed on an "institutionalized violence."

Lately the topic of "apartheid" is emerging as predominant.[5] The new wealthy of today seem to be trying to separate themselves from the masses of their people. They do not want to live near the poor, but by themselves. They set up for themselves cities completely separated from the rest of the population, true Edens: ecological islands of well-being and abundance, tranquility and peace, far away from danger and dirt, from the various and growing pollutions of the cities. The model of "Apartheid Brazilian Style" is Alphaville, near São Paulo. More and more "Alphavilles" are springing up and will continue to spring up near the large Brazilian state capitals. Similar phenomena exist in other countries.

These Alphavilles are bringing about a separation into two peoples, two countries, two cultures, two civilizations, and indeed, two races. From now on, the new Edens of the rich are going to move along on their own, entirely without any contact with anyone else. They are going to be integrated into a worldwide network of privileged Edens protected from being contaminated by second-class humanity which will be left to its own devices without a future. Most people will live off the refuse from the Edens.

And so the large cities can be calmly handed over to violence: let poor people kill each other. They can be handed over to pollution, to the weariness of long trips on public transportation, to the tightly limited spaces for housing and leisure, to dangers along the road. None of that matters. The privileged don't have to venture into these infernal cities. They live far away, are even unaware of what is happening in the cities. They have their Edens. All the resources of governments and all the resources of their own classes are devoted to putting them at ease. Meanwhile, the cities will never again be able to collect enough money to resolve their problems.

The model for this apartheid is in the United States. There the new elites have gotten out of New York, Chicago, Los Angeles, or Washington some time ago. What happens there no longer concerns them. Nothing goes on in their Edens, except for continual enjoyment.

The elites have their "Alphavilles" protected by private police forces that are better organized than the government police. They have their shopping centers also protected by private security forces. They have their beaches, their clubs, their recreation areas, their schools and universities far from the violence of the cities.

The world of the elites is continually moving ahead. The sub-world of the urban masses, on the contrary, is condemned to a gradual deterioration: deterioration in the environment, in social relations, in education, in health care, in culture. The two peoples do not know one another and never meet. An ever-growing police force, especially private security forces, assures a minimum of the absolutely necessary communication between the two worlds. The system is not fully organized but that is the way things are going. One need only look at advertisements in daily papers: they are all about the creation of such Edens far from the cities, which are being left on their own with few resources.[6]

The Past and the Future

Obviously, many things in Latin America's past have paved the way for apartheid. In colonial times, whites, Indians, blacks, and mestizos lived by different legal codes. Indians, slaves, whites, and mestizos each had their own laws. Their activities were separated even in religion. Their way of life was different, including the way they dressed. The four groups, in fact, lived under separate classifications.

In principle, independence, the abolition of slavery, and the establishment of the republic suppressed all forms of discrimination and separation, but in practice the changes were not so deep. Very few individuals from the lower categories had access to the upper classes. Governments actually engaged in a "whitening" policy by encouraging immigration of whites. Today many descendants of these white immigrants are integrated into the ruling classes. The Indians have not risen, while most blacks have not risen and still make up the largest contingents of illiterates and people in extreme poverty. Mestizos have had little access to the ruling classes—or else they are mestizos who consider themselves white and are regarded as such by society.

Even though discrimination is outlawed, in practice everyone knows which people can and cannot enter the Alphaville, the mall, hotel, restaurant, private club, a particular beach, and so forth. As long as the lower classes submit to the established criteria, there is no conflict. That is why inequality of resources, culture, way of life, and so forth are regarded as normal and accepted with resignation, as though they were part of the normal order of things. Hence, there is no reaction to what is happening today. The poor do not see what is taking place as anything new.

It is lower middle-class whites who are shocked; they cannot afford to buy a house in an Alphaville. With the formation of the new ruling class and their secession into their exclusive Edens, the lower middle class is going to be stuck in the cities by force, sharing the evils that afflict the poor and knowing that they—the lower middle class—are being left out of the new system.

The new apartheid emerging in Brazil and Latin America imitates the system that is already firmly established in the United States: it is the work of the new ruling class, the new elite, something they demand. In Latin America many members of the old elite have been able to enter the new elite. They have been able to give their children the education that has opened for them the doors into the new elite. A portion of the middle class has also been able to enter, especially the children of immigrants, that is, the children of those families that have invested most in their children's education. An advanced degree from the United States, or at least from Europe, is absolutely required for getting into the new class. Only with a great deal of money can one compensate for the lack of the precious diploma.

The New Elite

The new elite is both agent and product of the third industrial revolution, which began in the 1970s and into which some Latin American countries are entering now or began to enter in the 1980s. This most recent industrial revolution is the consequence of the new technologies, especially communications technologies. It used to be that the major economic issue was production. Industry sought to respond to demand for the most necessary products. Today industry produces primarily superfluous or useless goods. The economic problem is to create buyers, to create markets. There is no point in producing if you cannot sell. The important person is the one who knows how to open or conquer a market and launch into the marketplace something that can be sold. Techniques and technologies exist at the service of this new economy.

Thus there appears a new class, one oriented more toward consumption than toward production. The person who produces is worth less and earns less; the new moneymaker is the person who succeeds in selling. The company managers regarded as winners are those who know how to persuade the public to buy a product that they have launched on the market a few weeks ahead of their competitors. Hence we have a new bourgeoisie for whom the supreme value is no longer work, but astuteness, agility, knowing the market.

The new class is that of executives. The executive class is acquiring more and more social prestige, and their resources are increasing all the time. From now on, the class that decides is the executive class. It will not be those who own the companies, or those who own capital, but those who own knowledge (knowing how to win in the marketplace).[7]

Wages of production workers are continually declining as a share of company expenses, reward to capital is small, the proportion for raw materials is continually going down, and tax cuts and various kinds of fiscal privileges are being obtained. So where is the money going? One thing is always going up, and rises more each year: executive pay.[8]

It is estimated that in the United States in 1950, the manager of a company received, after taxes, twelve times the pay of an entry-level worker. In 1990 the executive received, after taxes, seventy times the wages of an entry-level worker.[9]

In Brazil the gap, which has always been great, is widening even more, and so the entire economic, social, political, and cultural life of the nation is concentrated more and more around the class of executives. All advertising revolves around them. Ultimately, production itself takes place around them. They are the ones who buy. They order the nation's production, and they buy it. The economy lives around the executive class.

What are the attributes of this new class? According to Robert Reich, former U.S. Secretary of Labor, their functions can be defined as follows.

They have titles like engineer, director, designer, coordinator, consultant, manager, advisor, planner, and so forth.

Of what?

Of planning, administration, processing, development, strategy, policy, utilization, research, and so forth. Regarding: finances, communications, systems, projects, business, resources, products, and so forth.

Hence we have titles of project engineers, systems engineers, civil engineers, biotechnicians, sound engineers, public relations executives, investment bankers, lawyers. They are financing, management, tax, and energy consultants, information specialists, systems analysts, advertising specialists, talent hunters for companies, marketing strategists, art directors, filmmakers, and the like.[10]

In the United States this new class represents 20% of the population. In Brazil it is certainly less—might it reach as high as 5% or 10%? In any case, the new class is acquiring all the privileges. It is a cosmopolitan class and works either in multinational complexes or in connection with them. They move from one country to another, and have no homeland. Their homeland speaks English, but it is spread all over the world, wherever the multinationals are set up.

In the United States, the Reagan and Bush policies over twelve years gave this class a spectacular boost. The Republican administrations favored the concentration of wealth in the hands of this class with the idea that wealth thus accumulated would lead to new investments. They were wrong; the new class got all kinds of breaks—e.g., lower taxes—but did not invest at all. In fact, instead of investing, executives engage in luxury overconsumption.[11]

This new bourgeoisie is quite different from the industrial bourgeoisie of earlier generations who presided over the great industrialization of the United States from 1880 to 1970. The older capitalists wanted to earn money to invest more. They wanted to provide more work. They also wanted the workers to be well paid so they could buy what they were producing. They accepted the welfare state. In that, they felt a part of the whole nation and were moved by feelings of patriotism. Their supreme values were work and nation. The older bourgeoisie worked for the future.

But the new bourgeoisie does not respect work. They live in unending competition with their rivals to dominate the market. They have no country; mentally they live in the entire world, and have their eyes on stock exchanges spread around the world, and following the markets. For this bourgeoisie, the nation and the state are not the answer but the problem, as Ronald Reagan used to say.

The new class feels no solidarity with other classes, especially with the poor. Its members believe they deserve what they receive. The new elite do not think about the future, but live only in the present. Their only rule is consumption, the sole value in the world.[12] They orient production toward ever more sophisticated products, which distance them ever farther from everyone else. They conceive of the economy in terms of their own consumption and completely ignore what is happening with the majority of the population, since they live a long way from them and never meet them in their daily life.

The members of this new class live in the closed world of their Edens.[13] They practice what Christopher Lasch calls the "culture of narcissism."[14] They look only at themselves and are incapable of paying attention to others. They need to consume in order to prove to themselves that they exist. They need to play the role of a celebrity, always on stage. They live surrounded by people who are like themselves but who are at the same time their rivals, ever awaiting a moment of weakness to then get the jump on them. This class does not have long-range collective aspirations; they live in the present moment and cultivate primarily a feeling that all is well. Thus there is a host of specialists in feeling good physically or psychologically. Members of the new class are continually undergoing several kinds of treatment simultaneously in order to improve their overall feeling.[15]

This is becoming the general characterization of the new bourgeoisie in the United States, which is the absolute and unquestioned standard for the new bourgeoisie in Latin America, and particularly in Brazil. It is still in the early stages, but we can anticipate what the situation of these elites will be ten or twenty years from how. They will form a ruling class utterly insensitive to any social problem, and completely incapable of solidarity. They will defend their privileges with no reservations whatsoever. And they will have no idea whatsoever of how the rest of the country lives; nor will they want to know.

The former ruling classes, such as rural landholders known as "colonels," were paternalistic. Clientelism makes possible personal, almost physical, contact between rich and poor; the rich can at least smell the poor. The new executives, living in their air-conditioned Edens, have not the slightest idea of what that might be like.

What a challenge to the nation! What a challenge to the church!

Everyone Else

What is happening with the subordinated social classes? What changes are underway for them? Now that Latin American nations—and Brazil in particular—have entered into a process of assimilation into the United States, it is well to look at what is going on there. Of course, underdevelopment creates unequal conditions, but first-world trends are driving the changes in the Third World, even though these latter may be at least somewhat different.

Peasants

Traditional peasants are destined to disappear in Brazil; young peasants are convinced of that. Saving the peasantry would require such a reversal of all national policies that it can be regarded as historically impossible. That is why young people are emigrating to the cities; they are ashamed to admit that they are peasants and they are not interested in land struggles. The result is an even greater shift to the cities[16]—starting in agricultural schools themselves where young people develop their personality, thereby facilitating the move to the city. With the awakening of their personality, young people see that they have no future in the countryside.

Instead, the future is with agribusiness companies. They take advantage of all the kinds of help provided by governments. They are modernizing and are using less and less labor. In the United States the primary sector (agriculture and mining) occupies 5% of the active labor force, and that is enough to produce the largest harvest in the world. In Brazil the evolution will be slower, but it will follow the same direction. Ten or twenty years from now, only 5% or 10% of the population will make its living in agriculture.

The working class

In classic socialist doctrine, the revolutionary class par excellence is the working class. At the end of the last century and early in this century, it was thought that industrial workers and employees would occupy the largest portion of labor. That has not happened. Today in the more industrialized world, the number of workers employed by industry is declining, even as production rises. New technologies and outsourcing are sharply cutting the number of workers, especially in heavy industry.

In the United States, the most industrialized country in the world, the industrial working class—laborers and salaried employees—still comprises 25% of the work force. Each year the number is declining further, and it is estimated that it will soon reach 10%. For example, in 1980, U.S. Steel, the largest steelmaker in the United States, employed 120,000 workers. In 1990, it employed 20,000 while maintaining the same level of production. It is calculated that the same amount of production could be maintained with five times fewer workers.[17]

In Brazil modernization is not so far along, but things are going to move in the same direction. Industry will grow a great deal, but the number of workers in the economically active population will decline. Many workers are technicians and enjoy a relatively favored situation, but they do not take responsibility for advancing other less favored classes, let alone the unemployed and the outcast. Labor unions will keep losing strength, and will simply defend the immediate interests of their membership.

Government workers (including those working in education and health)

In the United States this group makes up 20% of the labor force. In Brazil, the figure is lower, although the number will have to grow as a result of the growing need for public services, despite all the preaching about cutting the number of government employees. In the industrialized nations, the situation of public employees is declining little by little. In Latin America, their condition is still precarious except in some privileged sectors of little quantitative significance. All indications are that their condition will remain precarious in the future, given the shortage of federal, state, and municipal resources.[18]

Personal services

These are the humbler services that have expanded throughout the twentieth century. In the United States workers in personal services represent 30% of the labor force. They are salespeople, cashiers, doormen, janitors, domestic workers, workers in hotels, restaurants, cafes, drivers, night watchmen. The fastest growing category in the United States is that of private security guards (2.6% of the labor force in the country, equal to the entire category of farm workers). Wages in this kind of work are the lowest. The work demands little in the way of qualifications, and productivity is weak. Hence, all indications are that their condition will not improve.

In Brazil and Latin America, this category is still more significant. Alongside the jobs mentioned, the mass of the unemployed has invented a vast number of pseudo-employments, which are little more than odd jobs: load carriers, parking space guards, street vendors, children who run errands, and so forth. Private security services are expanding every day. It is said that in some cities like Lima, the population involved in this area of alternative survival services is as much as 70% of the labor force. However, it is hard to trust statistics in this area: how can all the services that do not appear on any official documentation be registered? In the short or medium run, most people in the cities will make their living from personal services, whether officially registered or not. Those registered earn the minimum wage or a little more; those not registered usually do not even earn the minimum wage.

Retirees

In Brazil and Latin America, given the vast extent of disguised or undeclared unemployment, many families live off the grandparents' pension. Such families make up the largest portion of those in extreme poverty; sometimes their living conditions are even lower than those of beggars themselves.

If the foregoing is, in brief, the picture of the new society now taking shape, what does social liberation mean? Where can such a liberation come from?

Thirty years ago most would have said that social liberation could come from the joint action of the working class and poor peasants. But today poor peasants are giving up work in the countryside and going to the city, while workers are declining in number and power—they are in a way a privileged class and are defending primarily their own status, which is a little above that of the vast mass of those underemployed in the parallel or informal economy. It is hard to imagine how the population devoted to services, including day laborers, watchmen, custodians, and self-appointed "guards," can constitute a liberation movement.

Hence the driving force of any social liberation in Brazil and Latin America will continue to be, as it always has been (despite illusions projected by ideologies), intellectuals as a class.[19] At the moment, most intellectuals are working for the dominant class—in keeping with the prevailing climate in universities and cultural work. They are fascinated by the executive class and their way of life. For the new class has established a new aristocracy that has introduced the new look of the "American way of life" into Brazil. They are also suffering from the fascination of neoliberalism that a systematic propaganda has very skillfully cultivated. This double fascination is not likely to last forever.

Since the eighteenth century, intellectuals have been the driving force of change throughout Latin America. Intellectuals have always been the revolutionary class and will be so for a long time to come. The intellectuals of today and tomorrow will inevitably rediscover their historic calling. They have been taken aback by the fall of the communist world, but their historic task has never been closely tied to Marxist communism. Their roots are linked to the history of the continent itself.[20] As always, future revolutionary intellectual leaders are likely to come from the midst of the ruling class itself. The great mass will come from children of the lower middle classes.

The clergy has always played an active and important part in the revolutionary action of the intellectual class. In the past, priests made up the largest contingent within the intellectual class. Today they are numerically less significant but they continue to make up part of the intellectual class. Certainly the most recent measures of the Holy See on the life and training of priests is tending to distance priests from active political life. It will not work, however; history is stronger than legislation. Priests will inevitably rediscover the same task that their predecessors assumed in the past. Given their training in seminaries, priests have the mindset of intellectuals and they react within their class.[21]

What would constitute a liberating transformation of the new society? Here it is well not to lose sight of the fact that the fundamental social issue in Latin America is the separation that has never been overcome and that today is deeper as a result of the recent trends of the two peoples, two nations, or rather a people and a non-people, a nation and a non-nation. It is the problem of elevating the outcast, the rejected races, the manual laborers who have always been treated as semi-slaves. How can this be brought about? In the following sections we will offer some guidelines on the basis of history. The chapters on economic liberation and political liberation will shed some light on the economic and political mediations for transforming society.

The Irruption of the Poor

The topic of the "irruption of the poor" has been present in liberation theology and in the ideology of the base communities.[22] The Puebla document echoed this theme when it referred to "the evangelizing power of the poor," and when it said, "The poor, too, have been encouraged by the Church. They have begun to organize themselves to live their faith in an integral way, and hence to reclaim their rights."[23]

It is a good idea not to give the word "irruption" too absolute a meaning, as though the organizations of the poor today were beginning from scratch. The poor have never remained passive. Nevertheless, something new is underway, particularly since the world depression of the 1930s and World War II, something that has begun to be perceived in the church as the "irruption of the poor" since the 1960s and in the context of Vatican II.

What has been recognized since the 1960s as the "irruption of the poor" used to be regarded as the "communist threat," "danger from the barbarians," "social anarchy," "religious fanaticism," and so forth. The new terminology of "irruption of the poor" signals primarily a change of perception on the part of the clergy and of those Catholics who are faithful to the clergy. Since the 1960s, a more positive explanation has been given to popular revolts and broad proposals for social change. The "irruption of the poor" has actually always existed, but now it is beginning to be seen in a positive light.

The "Irruption of the Poor" in the Past

Ever since the conquest and the slave trade there have been revolts of indigenous people and black slaves, but they were not regarded as movements of the poor, since they were triggered not by poverty but by the struggle of the indigenous against the invaders, or by the slaves' desire for freedom.

In the nineteenth century, some movements could be interpreted as mass movements of the poor, of marginalized mestizos claiming a share in society. That is the case of the Reform led by Benito Juarez in Mexico and the war against the French invasion and Emperor Maximilian, or the Rosas government in Argentina, which took the form of a government of the gauchos against the white bourgeoisie in Buenos Aires.

Only in the twentieth century, however, did "populisms" appear and attack the real problem. They attempted to unseat the "oligarchies," as they were called in Argentina, from their privileged positions, and to establish a government of the "people." The people versus the oligarchy or the aristocracy—mestizos versus whites—that is the real clash in Latin American society.

Meanwhile, the first socialist political parties arose in the twentieth century. They introduced a new interpretation, seeking to define social issues in the categories of socialist ideologies. Anarchism was short-lived; Marxism became the dominant ideology of the new movements and parties after World War I, resulting, of course, from the victorious revolution in Russia.[24]

For Marxism, "people" is not a scientific concept. What we have are proletarians in the countryside and the city, in agriculture or industry. Instead of the people we have the alliance of the proletariat, that is, of workers in the countryside and the city. Changes in strategy later brought the "national bourgeoisie" into this alliance, because during the cold war the struggle against "imperialism" became the number one priority of the social revolution. The "organic intellectuals" of the revolution were also introduced, thanks to Gramsci.[25]

The Marxist interpretation was adopted by activists in Marxist parties naturally, but it did not achieve widespread spontaneous acceptance, because it was too foreign to the real situation. At a time when the greatest ambition of farmers is to no longer be farmers, and when incipient industry employs only a small portion of the labor force, society is not likely to see itself reflected in Marxist ideology. Moreover, the vast majority of Latin Americans make their living from services, whether in the parallel economy or in a not very robust formal economy. Marxist theory does not grant them any existence,

besides identifying them as "lumpen." Likewise, the idea of a "national bourgeoisie" does not hold up: the owners of national industries are tied either
to the traditional aristocracy or to foreign multinationals; they are not the
bearers of projects for transforming society.

Inspired by Marxist or socialist movements, some efforts at land reform have
been made, but they have either failed or been coopted by the state, or the previous situation has been reimposed, as in Mexico and Bolivia. A vast movement
of the countryside against the city as envisioned in Mao's theory has never taken
place; when peasants are seeking to migrate to the city, they are not likely to go
to war against it. Agrarian reform movements have been very spotty, and
quickly coopted, and they have never been a great "popular" cause. (Indigenous
movements in which land is claimed not for economic reasons but rather for
reasons of survival as a nation or a tribe are another matter.)

Struggles of industrial workers reached their high point in Salvador
Allende's Chile. When the industrial proletariat failed to prevent the Allende
government from being overthrown, it became clear that the Latin American
industrial proletariat would never be strong, nor would they have enough of
a political will to be able to change society. A good portion of the "people"
had remained foreign to the cause.

Movements of urban revolt began to appear in the 1980s in the form of
looting supermarkets, burning government buildings, and indiscriminate
killing. These are outbreaks of violence set off by minor incidents that manifest a state of imbalance or even social anomie. Such movements do not
have continuity, however. They have no positive proposals and are not based
on political movements capable of offering an alternative to the established
system.

Who Are the Poor?

"Poor" is not a sociological category. It is very hard to define a poor person
in sociological categories, because it is hard to give concrete and observable
attributes to poverty. Where are the boundaries of poverty? Even so, everyone in Latin America is very aware of what a poor person is, and the poor
use the term to define themselves. This notion does not come to them from
social science but from Christian culture, that is, from the theology underlying that culture.

The category of "poor" is used especially by the church and in everyday
language. That is why Christians have often been accused of lacking in scientific rigor. We must see the reason and intention behind the use of the category of the poor.

"Poor" is a biblical category, a term correlative to "rich." There would
be no poor if there were no rich—and vice versa. The existence of poor and
rich is an injustice. Division into rich and poor is the expression of social sin;
that is what the Bible teaches. Jesus proclaims that the terms are being turned
upside down. There will be compensation: the rich will be made poor and
the poor rich.

Thus, the "dignity of the poor" is part of Christian doctrine. No Christian can be against the poor or remain indifferent to the poor. In Christian tradition, the church is the refuge, the defense, the hope of the poor. During christendom, the church officially accepted responsibility for the poor. Society entrusted it to care for its poor in the name of the entire society. And the society provided the church with the resources needed to care for the poor.

Under christendom Catholics generally believed that the poor were cared for. The church maintained a network of institutions to attend to all their needs. The poor had no reasons to complain because the church offered help. One needed only to knock on the right door and the poor person would be cared for. The problem of the poor was solved; the poor were known, registered, and properly attended. Even today, in more conservative circles that is the view. But in such a context, raising the issue of the poor is seen as demagoguery, because the solution has been provided for centuries.

The expression "irruption of the poor" meant first of all that christendom was being questioned. If the poor "irrupt," it is a sign that something is wrong in the way they are being treated; the system for dealing with the poor is not working satisfactorily. The poor are a problem.

The problem of the poor and the church was raised in Brazil by Father Júlio Maria at the time of the founding of the Republic in the late nineteenth century, when church and state were separated. It was raised later in Chile by Father Fernando Vives and then by his follower, Father Alberto Hurtado—recently beatified—in his book, ¿Es Chile un País Católico? [Is Chile a Catholic Country?].

However, the issue of poverty and of the poor as a challenge to the church was deepened behind the scenes at Vatican II, and was clearly posed by the Latin American church after the Council. That led to Medellín, where the issue of poverty as a challenge to the church was central. The poor were seen as a new challenge—one to which the church has still not responded and that demands profound changes both in the presence of the church in the world and in its internal structure. Medellín recognized an "irruption of the poor": the poor had upset the tranquility in which previous generations had lived. The poor have "irrupted" in the sense that they have been conceded to be a challenge previously not acknowledged.

Secondly, the "irruption of the poor" has been a matter of identifying the poor with categories previously not associated with them as such. Among the poor were placed the Indians, who used to be known as "our Indians," but not as poor. The Indians were in their place, occupying the space that history had granted them. They maintained their ways; they were obedient and did not disturb things much. If they are now recognized as poor, a whole new responsibility for the church suddenly opens up.

In the case of blacks, the understanding used to be that society had done its duty when the abolition of slavery was proclaimed. After that blacks had no reason to complain. If blacks are now regarded as among the poor, they also question the responsibility of church and society.

Then come landless peasants, the elderly, the sick with no one to care for them, and recently, the unemployed and underemployed in the city. The number of the poor is increasing. From now on, it will no longer be possible to say that the church has resolved the problem with its charitable works. Announcing the "irruption of the poor" meant making a list of the poor as was done in the Puebla document and later rounded out by the Santo Domingo document.

Third, the "irruption of the poor" indicates that the poor are entering into a terrain from which they used to be excluded. What is this terrain? It is society itself. They were outcast, excluded from society, and so they could be forgotten. They were hidden. Social problems were a problem for the police, as a politician from that time said. "Irrupting" means that they are becoming visible; they appear, they make noise, they penetrate into the terrain of organized society to protest and make claims.

Actually, various categories of the poor have been making noise and demonstrating for some time now, but in the church that was not interpreted as the "irruption of the poor." A strike was not understood as the "irruption of the poor," a street demonstration was not regarded as an "irruption of the poor," but as a disturbance of order by "hooligans"; actions taken by the Indians were revolts in the jungle against civilization, not the "irruption of the poor," and so forth.

Under the notion of the "irruption of the poor," the church has learned to look more positively and to welcome the movements of the poor and oppressed. This was the only way to change the behavior of Christians.

Fourth, the word "irruption" meant that the poor were taking the initiative. They began to make demands. In context, the word was always given a positive meaning, and hence the demand was seen to be legitimate. The "irruption of the poor" says that the poor are asking for their rights. Since *Rerum Novarum*, Catholics have recognized that the claims of the poor could be legitimate because their misery was "undeserved," as Leo XIII said.

The power of the word "irruption" hinted that the movement of the poor making their demands was strong, imperative, able to bring about changes in society, and that it could not be ignored.

Specifically, who were the poor?

They were not simply beggars who came asking for help or the needy who by custom were cared for through charitable works. They were not the proletariat in the Marxist sense. They included broad categories. In a way, there was a convergence between the "people" [Portuguese *povo*, Spanish *pueblo*] as understood in the various examples of populism and in everyday language and the "poor" in the language of the church. The poor were the vast majority. They were not a small portion whose existence would not have justified a noun as emphatic as "irruption." Hence "people" and "poor" have been virtually synonymous, especially in the Argentine version of liberation theology.

The concept of the poor has been used in order to describe Latin American society as structurally unjust, divided into two poles, the rich and the poor, in which the trend is for the distance between the two poles to increase.

In the distinction between people and aristocracy or oligarchy, as in populist ideology, the people in some sense constitute the entire nation, and the oligarchies are the foreigners who have taken possession of the country. The oligarchical class is anti-national, the presence of a foreign element in the body of the nation; the oligarchy are interlopers. The term opposite to *poor* is not *foreigners*, but rather the *rich*, who are also oppressors.

Has There Been an "Irruption"?

An "irruption of the poor" has occurred in the sense that the church has become aware of the poor. Whether there has been an "irruption" in the sense of achieving power is far more open to question.

Certainly in the sixties there was a rumbling about the power of the poor. Conservatives were really quite fearful that the poor threatened their privileges. Left movements have also had the illusion of a people's power able to carry out a revolution. Those on the left inflated the discourse, perhaps unconsciously because they were aware of the weakness of the popular movements and of the organizations of all categories of poor people, and felt the need to convince themselves that they were strong, strong enough to overthrow age-old structures.[26]

This strength never existed, and since the military coup in Chile, it has been obvious that it did not exist. Most of all, there was no united force of the poor. The Indians had their objectives: winning back their lost past, primarily their lands. Blacks are just starting to awaken and do not have an overall proposal for society. Women likewise are barely beginning to awaken, and what they are seeking is not obtained through a social revolution. Peasants have different interests among themselves—they have taken action only in an isolated way in certain areas. The masses who are involved in the parallel economy do not feel that they are understood, and are looking for a protector: they would like a new clientelism. Workers seek better working conditions and pay, and they are happy if they manage to salvage something that they have already won. Nothing is holding all of this together; unity comes from either a populist movement or intellectuals.

However, populism did not succeed in establishing a new society: neither Peronism in Argentina, nor APRA in Peru, nor their stand-ins elsewhere. Populisms have been defeated or assimilated by the system. The melancholy spectacle of Peronism is a sad illustration of this story. The strongest popular political parties have been those of the Popular Unity in Chile under Salvador Allende. If they were unsuccessful, who could bring about a victorious "irruption" through political parties?

In recent years, a number of pastoral agents have become discouraged over what they call a lack of drive, a lack of commitment or lack of combative spirit among the popular masses. Once they exaggerated the power of the poor, and now they complain of its weakness. The poor have nothing to do with this. The fact is that when the vanguards were counting on the support of the people, the people were somewhere else. The vanguards wanted to head up a strong social movement in order to transform society. The people were somewhere else. They were migrating from the countryside to the city, and struggling to survive in the city. They were busy with immediate problems that seemed more pressing to them.

The Great Migration

The sixties mark the high point of the intellectual movement that began early in the century and grew gradually, and then rapidly after World War II. Little by little the intellectual class identified what was specific in the identity of Latin America and of each nation and its culture. It began to reject servile imitation of foreign ways. An initial awareness of being mestizo peoples with their own culture came into being. Intellectuals sought not only to defend but to promote the specific culture of their people and to contribute to their identity. This movement can be called nationalism provided it be kept in mind that "nation" refers to what is specific and proper in a new culture born in Latin America out of the merging of the indigenous, the African, and the European.[27]

In the 1960s, the nationalist drive produced a strong movement for political independence and economic autonomy. Cuba seemed to be the beacon indicating the destination to move toward. Some day they would all carry out their Cuban revolution, although each was going to do so in its own fashion. That was the conviction of the left. It was obvious that Latin America would take its own route and would move away from the path taken by the Western nations.[28]

That is what intellectuals wanted. They wanted the whole people, especially this mestizo people, the bearer of the new culture, to understand this and to become involved. But the people did not understand and did not become involved. In some instances, the two came together to some degree. It was thought that the people were there, that they were united to their vanguards. That was an illusion—the people were there but for other reasons. They were present in the same demonstration but their motives were different. They followed the party, but only up to a certain point. If the vanguard sought to manipulate the people, the people for their part sought to manipulate the party.

The people were involved in the most momentous social development of the century, the migration from the countryside to the city. The vast majority of families are involved in this process of emigrating to the city. This is not simply a change of location, but a move from one civilization to another, from one period of history to another. For in the city, everything is different; in the city everything remains to be done.

When the poor migrate to the city, they do so under miserable conditions. Society does not help; recent arrivals have to do everything. They come to an area of land with nothing, and they have to do everything: win a plot of ground, put up a shack first, then wander all over the city in order to find a job, become initiated in how the city works, and discover where to find everything they need. Becoming integrated into the city requires longer than a generation. It takes decades of unending work, because everything has to be done by oneself with the help of one's neighbors, all equally left to their own devices. To become established in the city is a struggle over many years. Surviving in the city is another ongoing and never-ending struggle.

The poor are not inert, passive, resigned, or alienated; they are active and working all the time. After working to earn money to survive on, they need to work to build their house, urbanize their surroundings, and obtain those things that make life bearable. They are very active, but their activity is absorbed by immediate needs. Changing society will have to wait: it is a very abstract objective in comparison with the pressing demands of immediate need.

Besides that, the poor who are building their life in the city do not feel oppressed; their basic experience is of freedom. For them life in the countryside was the image of slavery. In the countryside it was impossible to get ahead. In the countryside what held sway was traditions, customs, the strict patriarchal tradition, and submission to the powerful, to authoritarian, abusive, arrogant, and exploiting owners. In the countryside they had no prospects and no future. How many young people pondering their parents' lives, became alarmed.

"Me, spend my life like my father? Never. God help us!"

"My father exhausted himself all life long. And what did he get? He has nothing, stuck with a miserable pension payment."

Life is harsh in the city and the shantytown, but you have the impression you are getting ahead, that you can have a future. Everyone is much more independent; everyone lives the way he or she wants, and does not worry about what the neighbors might say.

They are experiencing a great endeavor, they are building history. They are proud of their city, despite suffering so much. They feel that their neighborhood is improving and the shantytown also. The city dwellers struggle, but their psychological state is not that of the defeated. They believe in the future; they think that they will be able to achieve some of what they intend. Their benchmark is their previous life in the countryside. They do not compare their life with that of the elites with which they are not familiar. They compare their life in the city to the life they or their parents had in the countryside and they feel more fulfilled.

Later, when no one recalls the sufferings in the countryside anymore, these impressions may possibly change along with their aspirations. At present, however, the people are struggling to build their "nest" in the city, and they are learning to live according to the rules of the city. That task is enough to occupy a whole lifetime.

The Vanguards

In any social movement there is always a minority that is more committed to it, more conscious of its objectives, and more firmly decided on achieving them. In this sense there is always a vanguard—in any soccer club or samba school, as well as in political movements. The vanguard took on a very special meaning in Latin American revolutionary movements in the 1960s.

There was a huge difference between the awareness, aspirations, and simply the culture of the popular classes, and the awareness and the proposals of movements seeking the liberation of the people. The problem was this: according to the ideology of socialist movements the social revolution ought to be the endeavor of the working class, whether connected to the peasant class or not. However, the vast majority of workers and peasants were far from assuming or even understanding what was being explained to them as their historic mission. The revolutionary parties and movements, which were the only really revolutionary class, did not want to stand alone; to do so they would contradict their ideology. So what was their role? They could not be the revolutionary class; they would be simply the vanguard.

This vanguard, however, had the task of doing almost everything. First, the vanguard had to change the consciousness of the popular masses. What was presented as consciousness-raising should in theory be an awakening of the popular consciousness. In actuality, it was a work of injecting ideology into the mind of the popular classes: a task of instilling doctrine so that the people would learn to feel what the theory said that they ought to feel and to want what the theory said that they ought to want.

Consciousness-raising meant transferring an activist's conscience into the naive consciousness of a peasant who belonged to another age of humankind. The latter were taught how to repeat slogans, but slogans alone do not lead to action. The vanguard is a vanguard only when it achieves communication with the majority. If the vanguard does not succeed in transmitting its aspirations and its objectives to the masses, it is not a vanguard, and it remains enclosed within itself.

The problem is not the existence of vanguards, because vanguards are always necessary. The problem occurs when a vanguard does not succeed in its leadership role. That was largely what happened. Naturally, partial acceptance sometimes took place, but there was no overall movement. Even in Chile, where the political parties of the left always went further in their task as vanguards, there was not enough communication. The more clearsighted leaders of the Communist Party knew that the people would not go to the point of civil war and would not defend the Allende government—although there were some who did nourish that illusion.[29]

A vanguard cannot become too distant from its people, or it will cease to be a vanguard. In Latin America vanguard and mass are separated by a difference in culture. The vanguard speaks a language that the masses do not understand—and the masses react in a way that the vanguard does not understand. There is no dialogue because different cultures are juxtaposed.

Many do not understand that today to a great extent the people are not seeking a vanguard but a "godfather." The people are very aware of their weakness. They are much more aware of the true relationships of forces; they know what they can say or do and what they cannot; they know that the poor, even united, are still weak and in need of protection.

Clientelism is still the basis of social relations. A poor person knows that in a case of need it is well to have someone you know you can go to. It may be a mayor, a council person, a local political boss; it may be a charitable organization, a priest, a parish, someone who has good connections, someone who knows how to get into the hospital, or the prison, or other closed institutions. Even with the independence attained in the city, emancipation is not complete; one must know how to make use of powerful institutions.

That is why the "irruption of the poor" still has very strict limits. There have been changes in the twentieth century, especially with migration from the countryside to the city and the spread of urban culture. However, the "irruption of the poor" cannot yet bring about a radical change in society.

This does not mean that the intellectual classes have to withdraw. They cannot cherish the illusion that they are a vanguard that is going to channel a non-existent power of the poor. Indeed, they must assume the power that is theirs: they are the only class that can question and challenge the power of the ruling classes.

Significance of the "Irruption of the Poor"

The meaning of the "irruption of the poor" is essentially theological rather than sociological. It describes not a social phenomenon but rather the gospel. Thus, the "irruption of the poor" takes place within the context of Christianity. For proof, one need only read the gospels or the entire Bible, for that is where the poor "irrupt."

For our contemporaries, the poor are nowhere to be seen. The gospels do not describe a society; they point to a path. The "irruption of the poor" prompts the option for the poor. Its meaning is precisely to prompt that option. It was with the gospel that the poor began to be seen in the world. The church recovers its gospel vocation. The poor make their way into human awareness thanks to the gospel of Jesus Christ.

What makes the poor a class is only their poverty. The poor are the polar opposite to the rich. For Christians that is enough to dictate the path to follow: between the rich and the poor, one must choose the poor and stand alongside them. This option does not require any analysis. To identify the rich and the poor one needs no analysis. The difference between rich and poor is obvious and immediate. You need only open your eyes and in a moment and at a glance it is clear who is rich and who is poor.

An "irruption of the poor" takes place whenever the gospel is made manifest, whenever the church is renewed, whenever the church returns to its origins. That was what happened around Vatican II, and in Latin America especially around Medellín. There is no question that this "irruption" is not so strong today, because the gospel-mindedness of the church has declined.

It has always been the case that some portions of the church have remained indifferent to the option for the poor and have continued working to serve the privileged—as in the ages of christendom. Today these sectors are very strong. A great portion of Catholic institutions (universities, high schools, primary schools, parishes) favors or provides services primarily to the very wealthy.

But on the level of society as a whole, certain features of poverty have been more visible in recent decades. With migration to the cities, poverty has become more visible: there is greater poverty in the countryside, but it is more spread out and less visible because it is hard to reach, and journalists do not often venture into the countryside. Migration has led to disorderly growth of cities: dire poverty cannot be completely hidden. Shantytowns have sprung up in very visible places, such as Rio de Janeiro. With demographic growth, dire poverty has spread a great deal and that has made it more visible. One shantytown in a city attracts no attention, but a hundred or a thousand shantytowns do.

Visibility does not mean strength or power. There is no proof that the poor have acquired greater power. The poor are often mentioned in speeches, and also in the newspapers, the academic world, and the media. Of course, since the extension of the right to vote to the masses, poverty has been mentioned much more in political discourse. However, the extension of the right to vote was much more a conquest of intellectuals who wanted to imitate First World countries and introduce the political customs of the Western democracies than a conquest of the poor themselves. For that reason discourse on poverty has little effect after elections. More words devoted to the poor do not mean that the poor have greater social power.

It has been demonstrated that the redemocratization of the 1980s has not brought the poor greater political power. On the contrary, inequality has increased since the new wave of democratization (Brazil, Chile, Argentina, and so forth). Democratic institutions have not been able to threaten the dual structure of society. As the twentieth century draws to a close, it cannot be said that there is less inequality than there was when it began. There have been changes in the makeup of the privileged class, but the structure of society remains the same.

Society has not changed because the poor do not constitute a cohesive social and political force; they do not constitute a united front. There is no organization uniting the indigenous, blacks, the masses of landless peasants, shantytown dwellers, the unemployed, day laborers, rural casual workers, custodians, bodyguards, and the totality of poorly paid lines of work. Today this huge contingent of persons has still not come together so as to constitute a force capable of shaking the structure of society. Taken altogether they make up 80% of the population and in some areas 90%, but this 80% or 90% does not have any power comparable to the organized power of the other 10% or 20%.

The 1960s were a time of illusions. Many intellectuals went so far as to claim that Latin American society was in an explosive situation, that the only resolution was a social revolution and the establishment of socialism. As always happens in history, many wanted to be on the side of the winner; many found that they had a calling as social revolutionaries because they believed in the hasty proclamations and believed that the poor were going to change society. In the church as well there were those who let themselves be deceived by the prevailing discourses of that age. Many thought that a social revolution was imminent. Many thought that the only alternatives were revolution in freedom or revolution in violence. They thought that, in any case, a social revolution was inevitable.

Actually many of these ideas and especially the fervor surrounding them were imported. They were the reflection of Marxist discourse or of the student revolts in the First World (Berkeley, Paris). Objectively, there was not much justification within the Latin American peoples for anticipating a social revolution.

For Christians, however, it does not matter that such hopes have proven illusory. Christians do not make an option for the poor because they are the winners, but precisely because they are the losers. The fact that the poor have not won the political and social battles since the 1960s does not change the Christian vocation at all. On the contrary, the successive defeats of the poor since the 1960s ought to be a stimulus reinforcing commitment to their cause even more. Because inequality has grown and the poor are more numerous and weaker than before, the reasons for renewing the option for the poor are all the stronger.

There is no doubt, however, that Christians—and even pastoral agents— feel discouraged. That may be a sign that they previously confused the evangelical option for the poor with the option for victory.

There was a time in the twentieth century when the situation of the poor improved. It was after the great depression of the 1930s with the advent of populist and nationalist regimes. The populists extended the right to vote, created the first social legislation, set up labor unions even though they were controlled, allowed a certain amount of organization of popular forces, even though the intention was to use them to garner support for the regime. To some extent, the various populisms were stimulated by European fascisms, and for that very reason their social reforms were distorted. However, it was under populism that the poor fared best. Since 1960, the standard of living of the poor has been declining (in Chile since 1973, but the Frei and Allende governments were more populist than revolutionary or socialist). For some years, various kinds of nationalism managed to achieve a kind of patriotic front in which the privileged accepted some concessions to the poor.

The poor are the vast majority, but they have no strength when they are not united. What is it that could bring about a degree of unity, a degree of organization within these masses of poor people? The history of the nineteenth and twentieth centuries shows it to us.

The only force that can hold the majorities together always has been that of nationalist and populist movements, and such will continue to be the case for a long time. Democratic forms constitute obstacles: they are stabilizing structures that do not allow changes. Western-style democracy paralyzes society. It only works if it is jolted by sudden disruptions in which new balances of power are defined. Organizing the poor will be the work of charismatic leaders heading up populist movements; the power of populism, in turn, lies in nationalism, for nationalism is the only force that can bring the privileged classes to accept sacrifices. (We take up the issue of politics in chapter 6.)

In any case it is useless to try to elude history. A Latin American history that has already established historic structures exists. History has given Latin American nations a certain configuration, a certain relationship between social forces. Importing foreign ideologies like Marxism or free-trade liberalism will not be able to change the thrust of history. Reality is stronger than ideologies.

Community Utopia

Besides the option for the poor, the issue most highlighted by the Catholic church since the 1960s has been that of community, especially in the form of the Christian base communities or CEBs (*comunidades eclesias de base*, "ecclesial base communities"). This issue of community has given expression to two things: on the one hand, a proposal for the reform of church structures, often regarded as the decentralization of the parish, and on the other hand, a proposal for reforming society which draws inspiration from the utopia of community.

The base community idea came from priests and sisters—not from the people themselves. It arose partly out of pastoral concerns in view of the lack of clergy or the unworkability of the parish structure. To a lesser extent perhaps, a notion of a community utopia was also at work. This utopia was rooted in specifically Christian and Catholic sources, and sources common to all of Western society at that time. No significant influence of indigenous or black culture can be discerned in the roots of CEBs.

The utopia of community certainly drew inspiration from the ecclesiology of Vatican II.[30] This ecclesiology had shortcomings and has not produced the same effects in Europe or North America, but it has had a significant impact in Latin America and also in Africa.

A theology can become a utopia if the effort is made to draw from it a life project immediately, without human mediations. The life-project drawn from it will continue to hover over reality, seeking to penetrate into it, but the results will be limited. For a theological concept never expresses a concrete reality. No concrete model of association can be drawn out of the ideas of communion and community that can be found in the Bible. Many had the impression, however, that the CEB was the immediate and necessary translation of the new ecclesiology. Some went so far as to think that from now on the CEB would be the new way of being church, and that the entire church would take on the form of the CEB.[31]

Conciliar theology provided inspiration for a communitarian utopia precisely because it was seen to be more biblical than the previous ecclesiology. The Bible also provided the material for a utopia. Especially invoked were the summaries that Luke placed in the description of the early Jerusalem community. Luke is the biblical author most inclined to utopia. All his descriptions have something utopian about them. That is particularly true of the description of the Jerusalem community. Luke had little information available. He generalized on the basis of this scant information and provided short summaries which have been the source of so many initiatives and so many projects in the history of the church, especially in the history of monasticism and religious life.

In this instance, the summaries taken from the book of the Acts of the Apostles have been applied not only to religious, but also to the entire Christian people. People imagined that the whole Christian people could draw inspiration from these descriptions of the early community. The Bible was also given a concordist reading. A model of community was drawn from Acts, when it was actually coming from the cultural sources proper to a particular age.

Sources of the Social Utopia

The first such source is a nostalgia for the rural world. People living in the rural world do not idealize their condition. They emigrate to the cities precisely because they feel all the limitations of life in the countryside and all the dominations of rural society, constrained as it is by its customs and by the fact that people are continually under one another's gaze. At the same time, the church, which does not live in the countryside, idealizes it. In this idealized view, rural society seems to be a place of vital interpersonal relationships, a place of reciprocal giving and community, where families supposedly help each other, a place of kinship where everything is discussed and decided together. In the eyes of the utopians, rural society—the small local community, the hamlet or village and so forth—is regarded as a place that is on a human scale, an informal society that is not bureaucratized, a society where everything is spontaneous, and where solidarity makes laws and regulations unnecessary. Moreover, it is a community where everything is linked together: religion, culture, the economy—it is all a single reality and religion is present in life.

Accordingly, the CEBs would constitute a rebuilding of the former rural community. Indeed, in many instances, CEBs have been simply identified with already existing rural communities. When a pastor is asked how many CEBs there are in his parish, before answering, he stops to count the chapels located within the parish boundaries.

For priests or religious, the CEBs also reconstitute the foundation of traditional patriarchy (or matriarchy) which is so hard to relinquish because the entire priestly tradition is patriarchal, and this tradition is what is passed on more than anything else. It should be noted that priests or sisters are never themselves members of the community: they do not place their goods in common with the families of the community. They are above the community like patriarchs or matriarchs. Indeed, they can be removed by a superior at any time, and the community cannot demand a commitment from them.

The second source is the return to the countryside, the return to tradition, which is a manifestation of a reaction against modernity. As modernity expands, it also arouses anti-modern reactions. One of these reactions is the return to the countryside and the formation of small communities by people born in the city: communities of young people, alternative enterprises, community enterprises, or craft enterprises. In this sense, there was a booming anti-modern youth movement in Latin America in the 1960s. While a revolutionary movement was indeed drawing inspiration from modernity (including Marxist modernity) there was also a movement of return to older, premodern values; hence, the mushrooming small communities that generally lasted a few months or a few years.

It was a reaction against the individualism of urban society, against "one-dimensionality," as Marcuse put it, against life reduced to the economic, against the mechanization of life reduced to automatic actions in which the values of life disappeared, a reaction against the bureaucratization of society. Small communities were going to rediscover the values of personal relationships and spontaneity. As of the 1970s this return to the premodern has fed into a broader, ecological movement, with all the varieties of "Greens" which have now reached the point of building political parties, without, however, changing the fundamental political constellation of nations.

Protests against modern society have also had parallel reactions in the church: protests against organization, bureaucratization, formalism, and other phenomena hastily identified with the presence of modernity in the church. There was some connection between the base community and protests against "structures."

The unfolding of the ecology movement notwithstanding, community tendencies began to decline starting in the 1980s. Doubts and uncertainties about CEBs arose during the same period. It is not only a church problem but one that affects Western society. Modernization is moving forward despite resistance, the rural world is disappearing, and communitarianism finds ever less of the human resources that can serve as its basis of support.

Community Utopia and Reality

Experience has shown that Christian base communities have developed essentially in rural areas, far from the parish headquarters, and in neighborhoods on the city outskirts inhabited by people recently arrived from the countryside. They have not developed among the middle classes—in either large or small cities—among traditional people in urban or rural parishes, within the more advanced working class, nor among the very poor in the countryside or the city.

We can conclude that the CEBs suit poor people (but not those in extreme poverty) who are still very much imbued with the traditional rural way of living. Moreover, even in the countryside, everyone acknowledges that the introduction of television has struck the most serious blow against community life. With TV comes modernity, the mindset of the city—beginning with the expression of individualism that consists in sitting down in front of the TV set oblivious to anything else. This means that the portion of the population open to participating in a truly community life, according to the manner expected of CEBs, will inevitably decline.

Indeed, even in the more united communities, real sharing of goods, willingness to place gifts in common, real sharing of all, have always fallen far short of the desires of pastoral agents. Aspirations that were not really those of the community members, and projects that did not fit their real capacities or their true cultural situation have often been projected onto communities. In reality, the history of mestizos in Brazil was no preparation for community life. To expect from them something like the community life of the indigenous could only lead to disappointment. Thus, a number of pastoral agents have been disappointed because they have projected their own dreams onto a people whose aspirations were quite different. It is really quite difficult to infuse a community spirit into a people who are in a historic phase of discovering individualism.

The problems and conflicts notwithstanding, some things have been accomplished: a community flour mill, community plot, community path, creation of cooperatives—all with less sharing than hoped for and always with the threat of being "privatized" by the more powerful members of the community.

In the city, much was expected of cooperatives for building homes, creating neighborhood associations, associations of mothers or of parents of schoolchildren, and so forth. Such groups work while they are involved in the issue that concerns them, but they do not generate permanent communities, and they do not lead their members to comprehensive commitments. They are modern, urban, so-called "secondary" types of associations, and they cannot resurrect the mindset of the associations of the primary type in the rural world, precisely because people have been emancipated from those very associations.

In modern society, from which fewer and fewer groups escape, community sharing takes place in another manner: largely through politics, through social legislation, or through the action of non-governmental organizations involving large numbers of citizens. These organizations are never sufficient for resolving all problems, and there will always be a need for local aid, and for spontaneous services to respond to immediate needs. But families or persons cannot be expected to share their possessions in common. Today not even members of religious orders place everything in common. Each has his or her library, computer, sound system, often even a car.

Community practice has become complicated, and inevitably bureaucratized. That is the price of urban life and of large concentrations of people.

Discouragement and Hope

The utopia of community is losing ground in the church, as was bound to happen after thirty years of running up against reality. It is losing ground first of all among pastoral agents. The practical difficulties have become clear. A good part of the communitarian utopia has been nourished by the experiences of small religious communities. However, such experiences have been the very place where the disappointment has first appeared.

It seems that it is sometimes more difficult to practice the virtue of patience toward companions in a small community, where personality clashes take place continually, than in a large community, where distances are greater and the larger space makes contact less frequent. This means that possibilities for communication between persons are limited, no matter how holy such persons may be. Even among saints, shared life has its problems. Moreover, when there are no superiors, all team members are obliged to resolve the problems of their shared life themselves. The superior used to be someone in-between who limited clashes and took responsibility for most communication.

As a result of what happened, many small communities ended up declining to the point of comprising groups of only two members. In some instances the two eventually separated and constituted two candidates for religious life living alone waiting for whoever wanted to form community. Many wanted to form small communities, but they could not find anyone with whom to form them.

The fact is that in modern life—with growing intellectual and critical development, with the trend toward the development of one's personality, in a competitive culture where each individual must pursue his or her possibilities to the utmost—community must be completely reconceived. What is in common? What can be shared? What can be lived in common? As religious take on tasks in the contemporary world, they see that the former rules of shared life are inapplicable. They also see that contemporary life makes difficult any communication except that which is functional. It is plainly not enough to bring together four people of good will and expect a "community" to spring forth from them.

Lay groups encounter similar problems. There is an immense desire for communication and communion, but when it comes time to change something in their life for the sake of such community, no one agrees. No one wants a community that forces people to give up something that is theirs. Thus, there is no way to create a community based on a common culture, in a shared way of life or in a passive acceptance of others.

And yet, community is a permanent aim of the church. In today's new urban culture the challenges are great and almost everything must still be invented to place people in contact with one another, so that they can relearn a community work style. Community does not arise spontaneously in the urban setting; everything must be built. A new spontaneity will be the result of a long apprenticeship.

Marxists regard the communitarian movement as a vestige of utopianism. Although some Christians might have hoped that base communities could provide a model of society for a Latin American socialism, Marxists regarded that as sheer utopian socialism. They recalled that in the early days of socialism there were Protestant pastors and Catholic priests who wanted it to be based on Christian community; such people were rejected, and were branded utopian socialists. It is true that utopian socialism provided valid points of inspiration, and still does. But those points will have to be rethought in the specific circumstances of the new urban society now under construction.[32]

The CEBs have supplied the Workers Party (PT) with many activists. One side effect is that the issue of whether membership in a community and membership in a political movement are compatible has been raised. In theory there is no problem, but in practice, activists complain that they do not receive the community's support. For their part, the communities complain that activists lose interest in them. CEBs also provide points of support: they help out in strikes, land occupations, election campaigns, and legal defenses.

With regard to making them the driving force of social transformations or the foundation of a new society, such objectives plainly are beyond their capacities. A social transformation cannot come from groups that largely represent the old society and old forms of solidarity; something new will have to be invented, and what is new will be invented by young people and by those who are confronting the new situations.

The Ecclesial Problem

Instead of saying "ecclesial problem" it would be more accurate to say "intra-ecclesial problem." Some have thought that the CEBs would resolve two problems at the same time: the transformation of society and the transformation of the church. That is a manifestation of the overall pattern that typifies pre-modern thinking. In the last thirty years, as we have seen, most of the population has entered the modern world. They have come in through the back door, but they have entered. People no longer live like rural communities used to live, and what still remains of community life cannot be the basis for reconstituting a social fabric in today's cities. The poor masses, the very poor, do not join CEBs; they are not in a position to do so.

CEBs are too rationalized to be accessible to the very poorest, and on the other hand, not rationalized enough to respond to the needs of those who are fully engaged in city life. The segment in between, whose aspirations they represent, is declining, as it is squeezed by the advance of the less developed and the more developed.

Then, there is the problem of the church. The urban parish is reaching a tiny portion of those baptized at the very time when there is arising in the masses a need for greater religious personalization. The so-called "sects," which are primarily pentecostal churches, are spreading and constitute an extensive network of communities. The parish is inert, stable, paralyzed by the ecclesiastical bureaucracy which imposes on it a complicated set of programs; it has no missionary capability. The patriarchal figure of the parish priest takes up all the room and leaves lay people immobilized. All this has been known since the end of the last century and has been demonstrated by sociologists of religion for a hundred years.

Experience has shown that it is almost impossible to live the Christian life without being connected to a group or community. Christians used to belong to a group and to a parish that encompassed from three hundred to five hundred inhabitants and hence people could be in direct contact with one another. Since the creation of modern large cities in the nineteenth century, many Catholics have been unconnected to any group or community. New, very heavily populated parishes have been created, but they do not solve the problem. Indeed, the parish structure is not suited for city people. It is heterogeneous and bureaucratic, has no horizontal communication, and is shot through with patriarchalism.

CEBs seemed to offer solutions to these problems.[33] But they succeeded only very partially because they were, or were intended to be, both cells of a new society (core groups for social and political activity) and ecclesial community. But the vast majority of those baptized are not willing to enter social and political vanguard groups. And others see in the CEB a miniature parish and find it as boring as the parish.

It is going to be necessary to define just what is wanted. If CEBs do not emerge from their present ambiguous situation and do not define their role in the framework of contemporary society, they are going to disappear, reabsorbed by parishes, and they will suffer the fate of parishes.

CEBs—or base groups—must be free and independent to carry out their own activities, and not be subordinated to parish or diocesan programming. They must be culturally homogeneous, and not seek to bring together people who have nothing to say to one another because they lead completely different lives. And they must be flexible in their form and strongly inspired in their faith and Christian formation. Some communities may develop into bases of operations for social or political movements, but that depends on each particular community; there can be no uniform model.

Naturally, in the urban context, the scope of community life will have to be redefined in each category: what can groups of twenty, fifty, or two hundred persons have in common? What does community life mean? There will be no single definition of a community program. Indeed, the community spirit extends far beyond the limits of the small base community. There are many levels of community, from the level of the block to that of the entire universe.

The Christian communitarian utopia is also reflected in the new movements. Further new phenomena will undoubtedly make their appearance, for the terrain is vast and many new kinds of community need to be created. The Christian utopia is in ferment. The CEBs of the 1960s and 1970s were one manifestation; they need to be redefined in the framework of urban society.

Building the City

It is not our intention to suggest a program for social transformation; that is the role of political parties and their intellectuals. What we are seeking is to uncover the directions for the activity of the Christian church in the world in which we find ourselves on the basis of the "signs of the times."

Despite the current retreat of the "social" and the advance of the "religious" in Latin America (and in Brazil in particular), social liberation is still,

in fact more than ever, a priority. And it must not only be proclaimed in statements but be put into practice every day, even though today many have lost
sight of that. To some extent, we have to row upstream, and that may be the
case for some years to come.

However, what is meant by "the social" changes as time goes on. Today
the social has to do primarily with building the city. We are at the climax of
the great migration from countryside to city. The last millions of peasants
are getting ready to move to the cities. For most people, the immediate and
urgent problem is to become established in the city. The primary issue to be
resolved is what to do to build freedom in the city. The new content of liberation consists of learning to be a citizen, a member of the city.[34]

Vast contingents of people have come from the countryside to the city
under the pull of freedom. They have emerged from the oppression of the
rural world and have discovered freedom in the city: they knew that it was
better to live in a shantytown in the city than on a plantation in the interior.
Despite everything, they have more freedom; in the city they begin to share
in freedom.

One need only look at young women or young men after a few years spent
in the city: their appearance changes, they become persons, they live in very
harsh conditions, they struggle to survive, but that struggle is not in vain like
the struggle in the country. Some fail, but most succeed.

The search for freedom still has a long way to go, however. The city presents many obstacles to the poor. The paths of liberation are very difficult.
But young men and women choose this: they are engaged in this daily battle for freedom. There is no point in proposing other more remote or more
abstract objectives. Liberation must be won on the terrain chosen by the people and not by intellectuals on the basis of comprehensive projects that may
be theoretically more on target but are absent from the popular mind.

Thirty years ago the great alternative was reform or revolution. For
purists, reform was synonymous with being soft; it meant taking the easy
way, or giving in to the system, a failure of nerve. Even then, however, the
people were migrating. Over the course of thirty years, dozens and dozens
of millions of people have built cities, hundreds of square miles of cities. They
have built them whether the authorities provided help or not. They have set
up cities that are often disorderly and improvised, but they have built them.
That has been the liberation they have chosen.

Latin American cities are the material expression of the structure of society. They are divided cities, or juxtapositions of two cities. In former times
the separation was not so great. The rich still lived close to the poor; they
were still within reach of beggars. But over the course of this century, the
elites have retreated to outlying neighborhoods, where they have built themselves truly urbanized areas. They have reserved the best resources of municipalities for their own privileged neighborhoods. Until a few years ago, they
were still within the city limits; now they are beginning to build artificial
Edens far from the cities.

As we noted at the beginning of this chapter, in Brazil the prototype of such paradises is Alphaville (a place near São Paulo). "Alphavilles" are going to spread. The existence of such places means that the rich want to avoid any contact with poor people as a group. They want to stay far away and have erected such high walls, defended by private police forces so well armed that they are really protected from any contamination from poor cities. Social apartheid is inscribed in the fabric of the cities. The elites are fleeing, striving to live far away from their real country, and they no longer want to be familiar with it. The rich think that they are free in their Alphavilles, but actually they are the prisoners of their security; they are condemning themselves to live behind their grates, even if they are golden grates in a golden prison.

The cities, especially large cities, capital cities, are increasingly surrendered to the poor. The middle classes are striving to defend themselves there because they cannot afford to live in an Eden. They feel very uncomfortable because they have to put up with the presence of the mass of the poor. For the poor struggling in a city, with few resources, abandoned by those who monopolize resources, it is a terrible challenge. That is where the great struggle for liberation is taking place.

The poor have made their "irruption" into the city; now they have to build it. When the poor made their "irruption," the rich fled and went to build their Edens out of the reach of the poor. The poor are thus faced with the challenge of building for themselves, upon the leftovers from the rich.

Models of City

Earlier cities of a few thousand inhabitants are very different from contemporary cities containing millions. Even so, the basic models are still largely the same.

The model of the city of power

This model has been present since the origins of cities. Many cities have been established, built, and extended to introduce a power, display it, and consolidate it. That is how the cities were founded in the Americas by the monarchs of Spain and Portugal. They were set up to assert the power of monarchs, and to provide them with a material basis from which they could impose their rule over all the inhabitants of the region.

Cities of power arose around royal palaces to house the court servants, public officials, and the monarch's armies. Or they arose around temples to house the servants, priests, pilgrims, and all their auxiliaries. The colonial cities of the Americas were made up initially of public buildings and churches (with their huge religious houses), and their population was composed of those who served the government and the churches, along with the necessary artisans and merchants. Palaces, churches, and religious houses occupied most of the surface of the cities and almost their entire core. Starting in the nineteenth century, religious power began to decline and economic power increased. Cities switched to being organized around economic power. Banks came to occupy the foremost position, which had formerly been occupied by churches. Palaces were replaced by the headquarters of large companies. The whole rhythm of the city was organized around industry and trade. Only recently did those holding power begin to see that the cities were dangerous, uncomfortable, and stressful. Those wielding power have moved further away.

Today, the orientation coming from the United States points toward abandoning cities that are dehumanized by the poor masses: the elites are emigrating to set up ideal cities. In the television era there is not so much need for display. Great monuments used to serve a consciousness-raising function: they were intended to be a reminder of the presence of the civil power and religious power. With television such propaganda penetrates into the homes of the citizenry. Little by little, industries are going to leave the cities, as will the shopping centers. The cities will be only the place for collecting garbage: that is where the poor will be.

We have not yet reached that point. For the poor the city remains what it has been for thousands of years: the site of liberation. However, the day will come—as has already happened in the United States—when liberation will consist of fleeing from the city. That will happen unless work is done to transform existing cities.

The so-called "radial" city of Le Corbusier
Nineteenth-century cities, cities of coal and steel, were ugly and dirty. In reaction, twentieth-century urbanism has sought to create "radial" cities. Several principles were intended to make cities beautiful, beginning with separating the various sectors. That is why space was set aside for factories in industrial districts outside the city. There would be sites for housing and schools, sites for games and sports, sites for government agencies, sites for work and a rapid transportation system between these areas.

This model has been most fully achieved in Brasilia. To allow for ample green spaces, construction took a vertical form. Blocks of buildings are separated by broad green spaces. There is an area for schools, an administrative area, and so forth. There is light, green area, clean air, space—all of this should make people happy.[35] Even so, everything is far away. Everyone has to travel long distances for everything; you have to have a car.

The "radial" city is flawed, however. First, it is forced to have many transportation services available. Second, it destroys life in relationship, by eliminating streets and public squares. It eliminates local business, places where people come together. To meet one another, people have to visit each other at home, and that is quite constraining. The "radial" city has proven more individualistic than all its predecessors. It enables individuals to carry out their activities in a more pleasant setting, but it isolates them.

It has other disadvantages which become apparent particularly in the underdeveloped world, and very obviously in Brasilia. Brasilia is a city for rich people; the poor do not fit in there. The fact is that the poor were not even considered when Brasilia was being planned, but they arrived and have remained. There was no place for them in the initial plan. Since then, what are called satellite cities have been set up. Actually Brasilia consists of Brasilia plus the satellite cities—Brasilia's gains are the satellite cities' losses. The "radial" city is an island of prosperity, the price of which is the satellite cities: images of exclusion, the satellite cities are the antithesis of the "radial" city. Everything that was avoided in Brasilia is there, and everything gained in Brasilia is absent there. Le Corbusier's "radial" city leads to urban apartheid: two separate cities, the city of privilege exploiting the other one without assuming its problems. No wonder that the model of the "radial" city has inspired so many "Alphavilles" around the world. It has everything necessary; nothing is missing.

What if everyone could live in Alphavilles? That is an utterly unattainable utopia. A model based on the monopoly of resources in the hands of a minority can never be a universal model. The fact is that the aspirations of the privileged grow faster than the resources available, and the pressure that the rich put on the poor grows as well.

The city of relationships or the people's city

Many cities were originally founded in a spirit of liberation from oppressive rural structures. That was the origin of numerous medieval cities that became "communes" and were able to defend their freedoms against the spirit of domination of the local lords. In Brazil as well, many cities have arisen out of the initiative of peasants who fled the slavery of the countryside. The most famous example, and the one most dear to the heart of the people of the northeast, is that of Juazeiro do Norte. Father Cícero Romão Batista stands at the origin of the city because he welcomed thousands of wandering poor farmers. He encouraged them to stop working on other people's lands. In the city he encouraged them to learn a trade. Cities composed of citizens arise out of the association of workers from many trades and professions who pool their resources to create or improve public services.

Over time certain cities may lose some of their freedoms, and lose the yearning for equality. They can fall into the hands of greater powers, as happened in Europe at the time of the absolute monarchs in the seventeenth and eighteenth centuries. However, cities that have been born free always retain an air of freedom much more than cities that have been born at the service of the powers that be.

The goal of all cities is that their inhabitants really regain control over them. Many third-world cities have fallen into the hands of elites who have drained them to increase their own wealth even more, for example, through speculation in land or real estate. The valorization of city spaces, which is produced by everyone's labor, has always been seized by private owners to the detriment of the whole city. The rich are like pirates taking the fortunes away from cities and then abandoning them without resources.

By contrast, cities fashioned by citizens emphasize their human relationships. Many initiatives and many activities are carried out in community. Many private associations promote the interests of everyone—or at least of a number of groups. The poor live in greater dependence on others. It is more difficult for the poor to build an island of happiness for themselves, where they can have everything on hand, without depending on anyone. Hence the poor always live more out in the street or in public squares than the non-poor. Lacking private spaces of their own, the poor create public spaces in which all participate.

Cities as They Are

Cities in Brazil vary widely. Here we will be speaking primarily of the large cities, the state capitals and others of a similar size. Cities in the south are very different from those in the north of the country. Even so, with some exceptions, there are common features with variations in accent.

The first and most striking thing is that the people do a lot of building. They work on days off, they work after their regular jobs, they work with neighbors or relatives. They have built millions of houses, with almost no government involvement. These ordinary people build, improve what they have built, and urbanize their surroundings. They struggle to attain a few basic services: water, electricity, sewers, a small clinic, and schools. In ten or twenty years and with a vast output of energy they obtain what the wealthy neighborhoods obtain in a few months. When the rich go into a new house, everything is ready to go.

A great deal of literature exists showing all the flaws of third-world cities and of Brazil in particular; the information is widely available. We must emphasize, however, the positive work carried out by the people. With years of work they succeed in urbanizing or improving shantytowns, poor barrios, and downtown tenements.[36]

The starting point is one of desolation. The poor build where there is nothing. Or they recover deteriorating buildings in the neighborhoods that used to be good housing, and turn them into tenements. Even though they have so little to work with, they manage to put up cities that are more or less liveable.

These people have created a huge network of social relationships. At the lowest level there are informal associations: neighbors who help one another, often relatives or people who have come from the same remote location in the interior. They form cells at the bottom of society, linking two, three or more families. They unite to meet their daily needs: food, clothing, services in the home, child care, and so forth.[37]

At a higher level, there are countless informal associations for games or sports; young people or older people come together often, even daily, to share their lives, talk about events, share their plans or their disappointments. Associations of men and women are set up.

At a third and higher level are formal associations: neighborhood associations, clubs, mothers groups, samba schools, centers for candomblé, macumba, and umbanda, festival or cultural organizations, and religious communities. There is a social life, although it is very little known or studied from the other

side of the barrier. The poor are not completely isolated.[38] Above the neighborhoods there are labor unions and a variety of popular movements,[39]
including popular political parties linking thousands of members.

Even so, two observations are always made. The first is that this network
of social relations and associations is still not enough. Many people are
involved only on the lowest level. The second observation is that taken as a
whole, popular associations still do not have access to public life. Only excep-
tionally do they reach public life. Popular associations do not become effective on a city level; that is, they do not have an impact on the entire society
unless intellectuals become involved in them. Popular culture is still very
weak, even weaker in Brazil than in other Latin American nations. People in
popular culture do not have the ability to administer or lead organizations
that go beyond the neighborhood.

With leadership from intellectuals, however, popular organizations
together can assert themselves in society on the city level. The proof is that
they have won municipal elections in several of the largest cities in Brazil,
and there is no doubt that these leaders have the political skill to run the large
municipalities in that country. The problem does not lie in an inability to
reach governing positions over the cities, but in the lack of resources for dealing with so many needs because of the flight of the wealthy. The money is
going to leave the poor cities—indeed, it is already leaving. Once the privileged are no longer able to control city governments, they are going to start
moving out, or they will do as they have done in Santiago, Chile: they divided
the city into dozens of municipalities, so that municipalities of wealthy res-
idential areas now have vast resources, while those of poor neighborhoods
are deprived of means to improve their situation.

Decentralization of Politics

Decentralizing politics is about returning to citizens the set of responsibilities that they can assume. They have been accustomed to expecting everything from the authorities. They are disillusioned but they console themselves
by nourishing new illusions. Grassroots initiatives cannot provide an answer
to all problems, but they can channel many solutions and can respond to
many needs—through groups, local councils, associations, leagues, and so
forth. Only a mobilization of the people in cities will be able to humanize
the cities themselves. Humane cities are not going to arise some day out of
the minds of city planners or from superintelligent computers. Only a mobilization of citizens will be able to modify the current direction of cities and
the deep trends toward deterioration found in many of them, especially the
largest cities.

The freedom of citizens is built by promoting security, housing, education, and so forth. Without such reforms, freedom remains repressed.
Liberation is a matter of people building by themselves the conditions for
their own achievement.

Of course, as in all sectors, here also the people will need help from those who are more highly qualified, who are more able to take advantage of available techniques, or more highly trained for organizing community action in a modern context. However, intellectuals and professional people will not be able to change the situation appreciably unless the people themselves are mobilized and take the initiative.

The help of government agencies is also absolutely necessary. Here again, however, they will not be able to do much if they think they can impose planning from a desk, and if they are not willing to support the initiatives that come from below.[40]

Such a perspective may seem utopian. However, it is a utopia that is not beyond the realm of reality: it can become a reality and in fact something like this is already being done in all the areas discussed here.

Conclusion

Today social liberation is taking place in the city; that is where all the great social problems are concentrated. It is in the city that one can conceive of a civic activity at a time when political activity is becoming ever more impossible. The true community is the city with all its levels of participation and all the complexity of its structures.

Cities are threatened by the prospect of the withdrawal of the rich; the departure of the rich amounts to the consummation of the dual society and social apartheid. If "Alphavilles" are allowed to keep spreading, ten or twenty years from now, apartheid will be a fait accompli and cities will be unlivable. Exclusion will be written right into material structure itself.

How avoid the flight of the elites to artificial Edens if the gap between rich and poor is not reduced? In the United States and in the industrialized world in general, the first challenge, the first task, is to reduce the distance between rich and poor, between the extremes that are tending to increase, while the classes in between are tending to diminish. This challenge cannot be answered without touching the privileges of the 20% who are privileged, and this cannot be done without a radical imposition.[41]

In the Third World, the distance between rich and poor is even greater. And in Brazil this difference is among the most extreme in the world. Here also the distance cannot be reduced without affecting the privileges of the wealthiest. Whom? How? When?

5

ECONOMIC LIBERATION

Thirty years ago everything seemed very simple. Economists, sociologists, and political scientists in Latin America were tending toward a consensus; they had the impression that they knew what was happening and what ought to be done. Both ECLA (United Nations Economic Commission on Latin America), led by Raul Prebisch, and dependency theory were pointing in the same direction.[1]

They believed that the problem of Latin America was dependency, and that dependent capitalism would never be able to achieve development for Latin America. They even thought—the more radical among them—that this dependent capitalism was no longer viable and that its crisis, which was inevitable and imminent, would ignite political and social revolutions.

The solution was to create a national economy freed from the ties of dependency, that is, to shut out the world market and shape an economy that would produce for the internal market. The state had to be the driving force of such an economy. The economy had to be planned and led by the state, supported by a nationwide agreement between the "national" bourgeoisie and the working class. The more radical held that only a socialist economy would be able to develop Latin America. They pointed to Cuba as an example: Cuba's achievements, especially in the areas of health and education, provided visible evidence to validate the theoretical argumentation.

In fact, almost all nations experimented with going down this road—some less, some more. Even the military regimes in Peru and Ecuador adopted it. In Peru, the government of General Velasco did not shy away from the word "socialism." At that time, the Peruvian bishops conference issued a document that came closer to socialism than any other in the history of the church in Latin America.

Even so, after the fall of Salvador Allende in 1973, the bells tolled. Everyone began to shift directions. The model of the national market and import substitution began to decline. The oil crisis occurred at that time, suddenly freeing up huge amounts of capital. The Arab sheiks placed their huge and unforeseen fortunes in Western banks and cheap capital was available.

Latin American governments heard the seductive call of the sirens and fell into the trap of the foreign debt.

Oil was only one episode, however. It should be noted that in the 1970s the economy of the Western world entered a period of profound change. Little by little, Latin America began to suffer the consequences of these changes. At the same time, neoliberalism achieved high visibility in Western culture. It hit Latin America like a hurricane in the late 1980s, and served to legitimize a new economic transformation whose first effects we are now beginning to feel.

Until late 1994, economists seemed to be tending toward a new consensus, this time one that was neoliberal. Then in 1995 came the sudden thunderbolt of the monetary crisis in Mexico. Since then the enthusiasm of the neoliberals has waned a great deal. All indications are that we are entering into a time of doubt and uncertainty. No one has the answer anymore.

The Western economy has influenced the whole world economy, but the people of the West have no theory for understanding what is happening—and much less do third-world economists. Under these conditions, there is no longer any clear and conscious alternative. Governments are groping; owners of capital are also groping. So what can economic liberation be about? That is what we are seeking to examine in this chapter.

Changes in the Economy

Observers tend to agree in acknowledging a basic fact: since the 1970s we are entering into a third industrial revolution. It began in the Western world, but it is gradually spreading throughout the world.

In the former Soviet Union and its satellites socialism fell because of this major economic fact. Socialism was economically viable, but it could not compete with the West in the third revolution. In the minds of the socialist elites, the objective was not only to compete with the Western capitalism but to outdo it. Once the elites were convinced that they could not be competitive, they became discouraged and let down their guard; they acknowledged that they had been beaten. The revolution in the Soviet Union, then, came not from the people but from the elites who lost faith in the socialism that they had created, because the third worldwide revolution was changing the social conditions and relationships between the state and civil society.

Socialism predicted the end of capitalism. But what has actually happened has been the beginning of a new phase. Today, no one can proclaim that capitalism is coming to an end, because it is once more expanding full speed. The human problems that it causes remain and are increasing. But no system disappears simply because it is evil. History does not respect ethics. History is cruel and has evolved slowly—if indeed it has evolved at all, in any deep sense.

The Three Economic Revolutions in the Industrial World

a) *The first industrial revolution* lasted from 1770 (its birth in England) to 1880 (in countries that entered into the phase of industrialization).[2]

In a number of countries that entered into industrialization later, as in the Third World, several features of the first revolution took place later.

The characteristics of the first revolution were as follows:

- huge machines were invented, and requiring a great deal of capital, large factories, a great deal of energy expenditure (coal). Factories with thousands of workers were built. That is the origin of workers' cities that look like concentration camps;
- machines were rough and at a low level of technology. There was no need for engineers in factories because the technology was very simple. By the same token, machines required a great deal of manual labor. Much of the work consisted of moving heavy objects from one place to another. Manual labor was not very productive, and it made the human being the slave of the machine;
- pay was very low and yields to capital were very high. Capital was often concentrated in a few families.

Such an industry produced a clearly polarized society: a small class of bosses who were also the capitalists, those who owned everything, and a huge mass of very poor workers who performed exhausting work and who continually nourished the idea that they were slaves of a few capitalists. Workers had the impression that the boss had not contributed anything and that they themselves, without a boss, could make the factory run better. The boss was a "sheer exploiter" who abused his control over capital. If capital were in the hands of the workers everything would function better and the living conditions of workers would be much different—hence, the aim of collectivizing industry as a practical embodiment of the idea of socialism. Indeed, socialist parties went on to concentrate their whole program around the collectivization of industry.

Collectivization was applied in the former Soviet Union and in the nations that entered into its sphere of influence. It was partially carried out by social democracy and partly imitated by populisms in Latin America. The polarization of industrial capitalist society did not issue in further socialist revolutions because industrialization was not instantaneous and a great portion of the population continued to live in preindustrial and precapitalist structures until the second half of the twentieth century. It was only after 1950 that the most economically advanced nations became completely industrialized. Socialism was prevented from achieving greater success by the advent of the second industrial revolution.

b) *The second industrial revolution* began around 1880 in the United States and gradually spread to the rest of the world up to 1960. It entered the former colonies, although unevenly. To some extent, it continues to exert its influence even today, although now the third revolution is what is decisive. The second revolution was that of productivity. New inventions, the industrial application of science, and the replacement of coal by petroleum and electricity reduced manual labor more and more; machines accomplished what muscle used to do. Workers were no longer so subordinated to machines. The trend was toward mechanical automation. Work tended to consist of maintaining and controlling machines.[3]

Since 1880 labor productivity has been rising by 3.5% to 4% a year.

In the past century, labor productivity in industry has been multiplied by fifty—a worker today produces fifty times as much as his counterpart a hundred years ago. Not only have machines become more productive, but Taylorism has studied work scientifically to make it more productive.

Work is not only less tiring, but working time has been reduced. In 1910, an industry laborer worked 3,000 hours a year. A Japanese worker in 1990 worked 2,000 hours; an American, 1,800 hours; a German, 1,600 hours. At the same time, wages have risen a great deal. The set of social reforms known as the welfare state which began with Bismarck's policy after 1880, has spread. Programs of universal education, public health, unemployment insurance, retirement insurance, and the like have emerged to offer workers protection. The welfare state is established in the Western industrialized countries, and to some extent in Latin America.

As the welfare state has become established, labor unions have ceased being revolutionary. They have gone over to defending the interests of industry in order to save workers' jobs. Industrial workers have become rather diversified categories so that the interests of all no longer coincide. It has become more difficult to organize an overall challenge to society.

By approximately 1970, industrial workers had achieved a middle-class status: they had a car, vacations, their own house, appliances, phone, and television set. Since then, as a result of the third revolution, their situation has become more precarious. Still, it continues to be better than that of other categories of people. In Latin America, social structures basically hinder such a development. Industrialization has not taken place everywhere at the same pace. Even so, within the population as a whole, in comparison to the agriculture sector or the informal sector, workers in industry are relatively privileged—so much so that there are ten applicants for every factory job that opens.

Capital has expanded enormously and is more widely shared. It no longer belongs to great families—even though some very rich families remain, more in the United States, less in Japan and Europe. The share held by great families in Latin America is a sign of how great the resistance of the traditional social structure remains. Nevertheless, in the industrialized world, since 1970 most industrial capital is widely distributed. It has been pulverized into a multiplicity of small shareholders. In the United States, the largest amounts of capital are held by pension funds and insurance companies. It is becoming more difficult to situate capitalists because the workers themselves are capitalists. Those who are able to manipulate capital, such as financial companies, are more influential than the owners of capital.

The purpose of industrial production is to produce on a large scale relatively simple goods whose designs do not change too quickly. The accent is on the amount produced. Companies seek to conquer the market so as to produce as much as possible. Industries tend to grow; they practice competition—which is increasing especially between countries.

A typical product of the second revolution is the Volkswagen "Bug." The second industrial revolution is still marching along in many sectors of the economy, but it is no longer what is driving the economy forward. New forces have arisen, and because they have come together at the same time, they constitute a third industrial revolution.

c) *The third industrial revolution.* It would be absurd to imagine that this is a logically coherent system. In history, systems of forces are not necessarily connected. A number of phenomena come together by chance, combine, and react upon one another and in the end shape systems that are more or less coherent. Likewise, each region has its own constellation of phenomena. There is no rigid structure that could be called the third revolution, that could then be applied to the letter in each country. Indeed, each author has his or her own interpretation of the facts and personal overall vision. Even so, some thematic lines are so clear that everyone identifies them as important for anyone wishing to understand what is happening today.[4]

First, since the 1970s, we are witnessing such an acceleration of scientific discovery, and of the application of science to technology and of technological innovation that the realm of production is completely changed. Competition between companies is a matter of launching new products onto the market before one's competitor does so—hence the avalanche of new products. Instead of producing many similar products, production is now trying to diversify and be overhauled continually. Products are ever more sophisticated, lasting only a few years before being replaced. Machines are made to last five years, or often just three. In some branches of industry, by the time an item reaches the market it is out of date: the factory is already being tooled for another product that is more "modern." The acceleration of invention especially affects electronics, computers, and biotechnology.

Second, what is most profitable is no longer selling a large amount of similar products, but producing and selling a few items that are expensive. Hence, the pursuit of new materials, new ingredients, new gadgets, new commodities. Capital is less interested in traditional branches of industry and is seeking new things.[5]

Third, goods today are made up of many basic products, many separable components. An airplane, for instance, is made of hundreds of thousands of different parts which can be produced in different locations, thereby making it possible to decentralize. Factories that produce everything make it difficult to manage production. It is more practical, and much more economical, to decentralize production.[6] By outsourcing, a company entrusts other companies with everything that is of lesser importance in production: e.g., maintenance, cleaning, security, transportation, and so forth. Production itself is broken down into several pieces or several stages. The ability of companies to move around allows them to produce each part in a different location, or different country, by using the human resources that offer the best conditions. Today, the components of a complicated machine like an airplane are produced in ten or twenty different countries, in hundreds of different factories. The weight of raw materials has declined, as has their volume. Computerization makes it possible to have immediate communication between hundreds of production units; being together physically is no longer necessary. Factories can be located thousands of miles away from each other and yet everything can be synchronized. Hence, the formation of large multinational conglomerates that overspill the borders of nations. Today almost half of world trade consists of exchanges between the various affiliates or companies associated with those multinationals. Hence the so-called "globalization of production." Each country produces a portion of the final product. Under such conditions, what does "national industry" mean?[7]

In the economy the accent is shifting from production to distribution. New products are not a response to a need; people are not waiting for them. Products, then, do not have a natural market—a market has to be created. The less a product serves a useful purpose, the more advertising it needs in order to sell. As a result, conquering and creating the market is increasingly becoming the center of a company's concerns, and the people who work at these functions are the most important. The importance of the workers who produce them has declined. What is important is to know how to guide fashions and public taste: to create a need and be the first to serve it.[8]

With regard to production, it now makes sense that workers be involved in the process. Production increasingly needs to be able to count on the intelligence and collaboration of workers. Hence the "Toyotization" of work, so named because it was created by Toyota in Japan. Instead of having the production line go to the end, and then perform quality control on products, workers can halt the line at any moment and from any location in order to correct a defect, thereby avoiding waste. But workers have to be trusted. Factories integrate workers in the context of their whole lives: they offer recreation, housing, transportation, courses, retraining; they make the company a "family." That is why labor conflicts and tensions have been reduced so much in Japan and then in the countries that have imitated it. Once the quality of production is uppermost, the workers' intelligence and their good will become a basic factor.[9]

The communications age (computers, telecommunications, and so forth) makes it possible not only to decentralize production, but also to shift capital around the entire world. Hence, the incredible continual movement from one stock exchange to another, from one country to another. Billions and hundreds of billions of dollars are continually going around the world through simple computer maneuvers. This has increased speculation enormously and made nations unable to control their currency. Speculative movements can destabilize a currency, and along with it a government or the economy of a whole nation.[10]

This third revolution produces effects in all areas of life. In the previous chapter, we saw that it gives rise to the new ruling class and a whole restructuring of industrial societies, and thereby of other societies as well. In this chapter, we are going to consider the various aspects of changes in the economy.

Neoliberal Ideology

The Aim of Neoliberal Ideology

Neoliberal ideology would never have been so successful had it not been taken up by the American political right just when the third industrial revolution was taking place. Neoliberal ideology has served multinationals as a weapon when they needed to become established in other countries, conquer or dominate world markets, and have money and goods circulate throughout the world without nationalistic restrictions. The right used this weapon against the Great Society project of the Democrats.

The ideas in neoliberal ideology were nothing new[11]—they were a repetition of the old ideas of earlier ultraliberals like Hayek. At the University of Chicago, Milton Friedman set up a school of economics that achieved utterly undeserved fame as the result of favorable circumstances. Once the Chicago school had had some impact in the United States, it spread throughout the rest of the world. In Latin America, it was the source of the famous "Chicago boys" who in Chile were able to carry out the most famous radical experiment in liberalism with the help of Pinochet's iron fist.

Neoliberalism preaches that the free market is the solution to all problems: it advocates the destruction of barriers and borders that hinder the free circulation of goods or capital. If the free market causes problems, the remedy is always the same: more market.[12]

The fact is that in so-called "free trade" nations 90% of international trade is regulated in myriad ways, officially or unofficially. Thus, neoliberals state their principles against all the evidence, and no one would pay any attention unless their own interests were involved.[13]

Neoliberals regard government as the enemy. As Ronald Reagan once said, "Government is not the answer; government is the problem." The state must decline by giving up all involvement in economic life. It is claimed—gratuitously and against all evidence—that state companies work poorly, run deficits, and harm the economy. Government assistance programs are condemned as unworkable, with no proof whatsoever, but rather on the a priori grounds that government can never do anything good.

They claim that the free market has brought about the development of the more prosperous nations and has produced greater equality between social classes, without taking into account that it was with strict control over the market that Japan and the Asian "tigers" were able to get ahead, and that the great difference between Europe and the United States lies in the fact that Europe displays greater social equality because of firm state involvement in the overall economy in order to redistribute the fruits of greater productivity, while that has not been done in the United States.

Market freedom is said to be the foundation for all freedoms. But that is just what history refutes. If the market were completely unfettered, all indications are that alongside a few privileged, there would be a much larger mass of people left out.

Finally, the claims of neoliberalism are nothing but a series of gratuitous statements refuted by the history of this century. It has been successful only because it responded to particular interests that have turned it into very well presented propaganda. The way that advertising for the neoliberal system has been organized demonstrates the power of propaganda in contemporary society.[14]

Behind the Ideology

Behind neoliberal ideology lies a rising new class, the class of managers, experts, and consultants, the class directing the new economy. This class ignores social commitments. It has come along after the welfare state and rejects it. It regards everything that the government spends on social services as useless, wasteful spending. Those who belong to this class or feel in tune with it demand less government, that is, less taxes. They say that their taxes are being wasted on social policies that create idle people who live off government programs.

Multinational companies want to get into all markets without limits. They want to downsize the state, but they also want their government to work against the protectionist policies of other governments. They want the U.S. government to force Japan to allow their products to enter; they want to limit the entry of Japanese products; they want to dismantle European agricultural policy; they want protectionism against foreign rivals and free entry into those same foreign countries.

Multinationals have spread and multiplied. There are now tens of thousands of them, and they constitute the largest portion of the productive apparatus of the industrial world. They wanted to suppress borders and unify the world in a single market in order to operate freely. They have no regard for the fate of nations and peoples. Having expanded so enormously, they take advantage of their new power to impose their own conditions. Unfortunately, what is good for a corporation is not necessarily good for the rest of the world. Free expansion of multinationals is not necessarily the best path for the world to take.[15]

U.S. Administrations

During the 1980s, the United States assumed the leadership of the industrialized world more decisively and pursued its policies aggressively. For twelve years, the Reagan and Bush administrations carried out a policy that systemically favored the concentration of the wealth and privileges of the new class. Inequality between rich and poor increased. The working class lost ground and millions of low qualification service positions were created. By all measurements, poverty increased. In foreign policy, the United States put pressure on Japan and Europe. It succeeded in having Japan and Germany pay for the war against Iraq.

The U.S. government has been able to manipulate the International Monetary Fund and the World Bank so as to impose neoliberal principles—free access to capital and to North American companies—on the Third World.

Bush was defeated by the excesses of the policy of downsizing government. He cut taxes, but he had to maintain a defense policy that was larger than could be afforded. On the other hand, he was unable to dismantle the policy of redistribution to the poor.

The poor were still there; they can't be put in prison—it would be impossible to pay for so many prisons. The United States already has more than a million prisoners. Even if the far right would like to quadruple the number of prisoners, the government would not have enough funding to do so. Ultimately, the growing federal budget deficit brought his policy into disfavor.

Despite the dismantling of the Democratic Party, Bill Clinton succeeded in winning the election in 1992. He found himself facing insoluble problems. Here we have come to the matter of politics, which will be taken up in more depth in the next chapter. In anticipation, however, we note that, for the United States, Clinton signifies the decline of neoliberal ideology, although it is being upheld in dependent countries. Even if it is no longer useful in the United States, it can still be advantageous in the world. Their ultraliberal rhetoric notwithstanding, it is not very likely that the Republicans can return to Reagan's style which thrust millions of destitute citizens into the streets of America.

In Europe, citizens are increasingly desperate as they face the prospects of the creation of the European Union. They see it as something inevitable that will only bring calamity down upon the people—even though it will make the multinationals happy, especially the American and Japanese. The creation of the European Union, which is intended to benefit the large corporations, may lead to the ruin of the social legislation that has been in place for a hundred years. There is a great fear that the European Union will let itself be guided by neoliberal principles. The European authorities do not permit any oversight by the people. The so-called "European parliament" has no power whatsoever. What exists is a technocratic dictatorship that is subject to the pressures from campaigns mounted by economic conglomerates.

The Problem of Social Programs

One of the neoliberals' major arguments is that government social programs are ineffective: such programs do not overcome poverty; on the contrary, by encouraging laziness they have expanded poverty. Moreover, social programs have served primarily to give good jobs to inefficient officials who devote their time to publicizing the poverty that justifies their jobs. Ultimately, the misery of the poor is believed to be an invention of such officials to legitimize thousands of make-believe jobs.

In the neoliberal view, the government in the name of social justice increases its own power, hinders the economy, and harms those who are productive for the benefit of those who produce nothing. The state is regarded as a power machine whose purpose is to divert resources needed for production into unproductive spending that sustains a host of lazy people.

What are we to think of such ideas? First, they do not add anything to what the rich have always said of the poor: the poor are poor because they are lazy, and aiding them only encourages vice. To give alms is to encourage vice, gang activity, and laziness. That is nothing new. Second, social programs do not attack the root of the problem. They help some, they save some from dire poverty, but the system inevitably generates new people in want.

Capitalism is economically efficient, but it creates poverty, because it excludes whatever does not serve it. Aid programs do not address the source of problems. They deal with symptoms, but not the disease, not because government officials do not want to do so, but because they cannot. Social programs change nothing in the way society is organized to serve capitalism.

To think that doing away with assistance programs would solve the problem would be naive—if not simply cruel and bad faith. It is plain to see that simply doing away with assistance programs would increase dire poverty. Cutting back such programs in the 1980s in the United States, for example, brought about a notable rise in poverty.

That does not mean that such programs could not be more efficient. There may indeed be an excessive administrative structure and an overabundance of employees who do not work where problems are, but are content to talk about them in meetings, congresses, demonstrations, planning sessions, research, and so forth. Such defects also arise in church programs and in nongovernment organizations that aid development. Even so, it is better not to generalize.

Decentralizing government services more and entrusting services to private bodies through contracts would probably make services more efficient. The state is a slow administrative machine that is not every flexible and is expensive. Private organizations can be more efficient, provided they do not place public resources at the service of their private interests.

The Changes in Latin America

The Crisis of the Import Substitution Model

Latin America entered the age of industrialization late because of the resistance of its aristocratic elites. The elites kept alive the dream of the conquistadors—the dream of El Dorado: there is gold in the Americas; wealth is a matter of discovering a gold mine. When gold disappears, another kind of natural wealth is sought to replace it, a wealth that one need only gather, and that therefore requires little or no work. The solution was found to be cattle in Argentina, Uruguay, and southern Brazil; elsewhere it was sugar, coffee, copper or nitrate, wood, and fish.

This myth of the aristocracy—extract natural wealth and get a lot of money right now!—which later passed into the population as a whole, is the opposite of the bourgeois and capitalist mindset for which the source of wealth is labor, and capital is the fruit of labor.

The aristocracy foiled the efforts of some pioneers, including the Baron of Mauá and Delmiro Gouveia, who wanted to begin to industrialize. It was the European immigrants who introduced the industrial spirit. Even so, they had an uphill struggle. An incipient industry got underway, but when it had to compete with the production of other countries, the government did not take any interest in promoting national industry. The myth that the country had a calling to agriculture or mining remained an indestructible one. For industrial products one had foreign countries: products imported from Europe or the United States would always be better.

The elites wanted to imitate the European way of life. For a long time, they thought that they could do so by importing European or North American products. Then came the great crash of 1929 and its aftermath. The price of raw materials fell and the elites could no longer import. For a decade things were unclear; the beginnings of industrialization did not have the backing of a firm decisive policy. Then came World War II, which made raw materials valuable once more, but at the same time limited possibilities of importing. It was after 1950 that Latin America entered decisively into the age of industrialization: first in Brazil and Mexico, then Chile and Argentina, less so in the Andean countries, and not at all in Central America and the Caribbean.

That was when the decision was made to industrialize in order to replace imports. That decision was taken practically without discussion; it seemed plain and obvious. Right and left agreed; the only ones who resisted were blind conservatives who still thought it was possible to go back to a colonial economy.

The decision to replace imports affected the whole future. Why was it made? Latin American elites and the new tiny middle classes were blinded by Europe and North America. What they wanted was the way of life and consumption level of the First World. Since that way of life was no longer possible through imports, the country had to produce their equivalent.[16] This decision entailed a cultural option (we will return to the issue in the chapter on culture). It was an option for Western culture—even if it was only for a small elite.

Import substitution has been carried out since that time. Brazil managed to set up an industry that is practically complete, capable of replacing almost all imports. In the early 1990s, Brazil had a quasi-closed and self-sufficient economy. But something was wrong; something had not been done right. The error lay in this: the substitute production succeeded in providing a European living standard for 20% of the population, but it left everyone else in a miserable state—Brazil has the second greatest inequality in the world. Europe was imitated even in the welfare state: everything limited to an elite.

The first mistake was in the reason for industrializing. Latin Americans looked to Europe and the United States, but they did so without considering the history of those economies. They did not look toward Japan, Korea, or the other Asian tigers, just as today they are not looking at the second generation tigers (Thailand, Malaysia, Indonesia). The Asians have chosen industrialization for export—in order to compete on world markets, and conquer markets—even at the cost of a great deal of suffering and of many sacrifices, by putting off until later the enjoyment of consumption.

The second mistake was the choice of a strategy for import substitutions. A "big push" strategy was chosen. First came an intensive injection of capital by the state, which set up or attracted companies by granting them excessive privileges. Then, the state attracted foreign companies, particularly multinationals, which brought in a fully functioning system. Industrialization was carried out from the top. Industry was simply imported, without any work, any conquest, any apprenticeship on the part of the Brazilian people. Hence, a small portion of the people entered into this system and received a privileged position without having done anything to deserve it, while the great masses remained completely outside the changes. A new breach in the country was created; a minority learned to work in the industrial system, while the majority went on to live off odd jobs or completely unproductive kinds of work and the country had no access to production goods. It became impossible to allow everyone to enter into the world of industry. Alongside the new industrial sector there was created a vast sector of those excluded, and for whom the development strategy has no provision.[17]

The upshot is a social crisis caused by the import substitution model. Nevertheless, that is not the crisis that causes most discomfort to economies and ruling elites. The crisis is one whose consequences are more immediate. The crisis that most immediately concerns the elites is called the "exhaustion of the import substitution model." Why exhaustion? Industries are operating and producing, but their products are not competitive—they cannot compete on the world market. While a few products manufactured here in Latin America do compete successfully, most do not—hence the crisis.[18]

The elites are discovering that their industries do not produce the equivalent of first-world industries, which under the pressure of ongoing competition are continually modernizing. They are forced to overhaul themselves or they die. In Latin America, industries are overprotected. They get privileges and subsidies, they are often exempted from taxes, and they have entered the clientelist society. They do not allow themselves to be overhauled. They know that in order to make more money it is more important to get a tax reduction or other privileges than to modernize production. After ten or twenty years the elites now see what they interpret as the failure of the model.

In actuality, they brought in foreign factories, but they did not bring in the industrial spirit, the effort at renewal. Introducing machines alone does not change culture. They have bought technologies, but have not formed local technicians.

Nevertheless, the elites are not firm in critiquing the economic model as a whole, let alone the cultural model in which they live. Here is the problem: which model can give us what import substitution has not been able to give us? Is it the North American way of life? The problem for the elites is how to change the economy without changing European-American culture or the traditional dual society.

Adoption of the Neoliberal Model

No region in the world has welcomed neoliberal ideology more enthusiastically—and more blindly—than Latin America. In just a decade, Latin America has managed to make it the official doctrine now presented as dogma. In propaganda, neoliberalism is regarded as the only "scientific" theory, like economics, which has finally become a science; no one can question it.[19] Always it is imposed as if it were the truth coming from Europe and the United States, even though in those places it is still very much questioned, and refuted by the facts. But it has permeated Latin America with dazzling success. Hence Hernán Büchi in Chile, Carlos Salinas de Gortari in Mexico, and Domingo Cavallo in Argentina seem to be the new wizards who have been able to repair their nations and who have brought them to the sanctuary of the First World, ever the supreme goal of the elites.

The fact is that ideology enshrines recipes proposed by the International Monetary Fund and the World Bank—in other words, United States interests. For the United States, freedom of the market means opening international markets to American products with no assurance of reciprocity. In any case, the de facto alliance between the "sages" of the economy and the IMF has been a major force. They are joined by the "modernizers" who think that the neoliberal recipes are the best and the shortest route for reaching the First World.

Neoliberalism was charged with resolving the problem that arose as a result of the crisis of the import substitution model. The new model began in Chile under Pinochet. Subsequent governments have maintained it, although with some corrections to redistribute a portion of the new wealth produced. Later it was Mexico's turn with the Salinas government (1989; he began in the previous government when he was minister of the Treasury). Argentina entered flashily with Cavallo, Carlos Menem's minister of the economy. Other countries are entering partially; they were never very industrialized and have much less to change. Brazil is still hesitant; it enters part way but then withdraws and hesitates. Indeed Brazil has a great deal to lose. In changing models it is risking much more than the rest.

What does the neoliberal model entail?

It has been termed a "readjustment," but that does not express the full importance of the changes involved.

a) *Opening of borders to free competition.* From now on, national industries will have to change. According to this theory, the consequence of opening the market will be that industries will modernize. In practice that does not happen. Industrialists have another option that is much more comfortable: become import companies.

b) *Emphasis on exports.* "Produce in order to export," goes the slogan. Industries are supposed to produce for export, but that is not really what happens. As in the past, it is natural resources extracted with no industrial process that are being exported. Thus, products with little added value are exported, and that is always unfavorable in world competition. Thus, Chile is exporting copper, lumber, fish, and fruit—but few industrial products. Over the long run, that is very risky. Presently, Argentina is going back to exporting agricultural and livestock products and is sacrificing its industry.

c) *Privatization of government companies.* The theory claims that government companies are not economically profitable. But that does not take the real conditions into account. It is normal for companies providing public services to the very poor to be subsidized; that is one way of redistributing national production. Moreover, some companies run a deficit because the government does not provide them the funding they need, or forces them to offer services that are not paid for, etc. In some cases, privatization is justified, but each case must be examined on its own merits; there is no basis for the general principles. Privatizations by and large have been grants made by the state to privileged groups.

d) *Assumption that these measures will allow Latin America to participate in the world market more intensively.* Thus far, there is no convincing proof that that is what is taking place.

The social consequences of the new model can already be seen, especially in Mexico and Argentina: widening unemployment and severe poverty, greater concentration of wealth and greater inequality between social classes, higher indices of poverty. No social problem has been resolved: on the contrary, the situation has gotten worse.[20]

The Crisis of the Neoliberal Model

One foretaste of the crisis of the neoliberal model was the public emergence of the Zapatista army in Mexico, on January 1, 1994. For a whole year, events took place under the Zapatista cloud, especially during the election campaign. Finally, a month after the inauguration of the new president, in the midst of ongoing tragedies, the system exploded. The January 1995 monetary crisis in Mexico ruined the credibility of the neoliberal model. Argentina has been shaken by small tremors that are presaging an earthquake. Brazil is frightened. The most recent elections in Latin America (Venezuela, Colombia, Uruguay) show the left gaining.

The crisis of the model presents Latin Americans with the same old problem: how to reach the First World without changing the social structure, that is, without sacrificing the privileges the elites have always enjoyed? Could there be an alternative? Certainly the experts are studying the situation.

Can one foresee a questioning of the social structure itself and the creation of an economic model that leads to a social transformation? At the moment there are no foreseeable signs of such a prospect, at least in the near future. History is nonetheless full of unforeseen events. Structures that seemed solid suddenly collapse when struck by unforeseen blows. In any case, the current worldwide context is not favorable to large changes.

Openings Today

Endless discussion can be devoted to trying to discover whether the fall of the Soviet Union was or was not inevitable, and whether the socialism practiced in the world under Soviet influence is still viable or not. In any case, that kind of socialism is simply no longer a possibility in today's world. All socialist countries ultimately open up to the capitalist world, introducing some aspects of a market economy into their system in a gradual evolution that seems irreversible (e.g., China, Cuba, Vietnam, even North Korea).[21]

For the immediate future, there is no socialist alternative in sight. Socialism certainly remains, and will remain, in the form of utopia, dream, and aspiration. There will be further attempts to embody it in history, but not very soon. It is very likely that future attempts will be different from the form known in the twentieth century.[22]

Socialism's greatest problem is the difficulty of saying just what it is. In the twentieth century, socialism has meant collectivizing the means of production, essentially land and industries, and capital as well. Socialism was national: each nation made up a self-enclosed independent economic unit. However, the conditions of the economy have changed. At present internationalization seems unavoidable for a number of reasons that need not be reiterated here.

Collectivizing the means of production is a myth when the main factor of economic life is market control, and when distribution is more important than production. What is important is not producing but knowing how to sell. But how is selling to be socialized? Does it serve workers to be owners of the factory if that factory is unable to sell?

Hence, today the market economy is unavoidable. Some glorify it and regard it as proclaiming a prosperous future. Others make the capitalist road a road to liberation. Most people accept it simply for want of alternatives.

Among the popular masses in Latin America, there is no deep wave of resistance or opposition; there is no mass rejection of the new capitalist model. Most people believe that the present situation offers prospects for advancement in the future. Otherwise, how explain the overall acceptance of the neoliberal model in Chile? How explain the support given to the readjustment (and the reelection of Carlos Menem) in Argentina, despite its very brutal aspects and the fact that some sectors of the population have been pushed back? How explain such wide acceptance of the Real Plan (measures to halt inflation in 1994) in Brazil? How explain the Peruvian people's loyalty to Fujimori? How explain the lack of popular reaction and the PRI electoral victory in 1994, despite so many revelations of corruption and rottenness within the government party? In Mexico it has been the Indians who have reacted. However, the indigenous people are opposing not so much the market economic model as the invasion of their lands by the Spaniards and their descendants. The resistance of the indigenous people has been used against the current government, but it is actually responding to five centuries of invasion. The Latin American population as a whole is not systematically opposed to the neoliberal economic model.

Actually, there is nothing new about the lack of popular resistance—it is a constant through history. The peoples of Latin America become stirred up when there arises a class of nationalistic and populist leaders who have the skill to lead them. At certain times, left intellectuals have served as revolutionary leaders to this elite. Hence, what is making the market economy inevitable is not so much the passivity of the popular masses—which is nothing new—but the lack of a left intelligentsia willing to lead a popular insurrection. Even the Zapatista army in Chiapas is not seeking to take power in order to establish a socialist society.[23] In the absence of a class of left intellectuals set on promoting it, no socialist model is feasible at this moment in history.

The Latin American left is full of self-blame. Leftists blame themselves for their failures over the past thirty years. They feel guilty over the fall of the Soviet Union, and even more over the retreat of socialism in Western Europe: for an intellectual class with its gaze ever on Europe, the decline of socialism in European public opinion is traumatizing. Left intellectuals cannot get beyond the crisis of 1989. The generation that made history from 1960 to 1990 is unlikely to present a socialist option. We will have to wait for another generation to come along that does not feel that it is to blame for everything that happened during those thirty years.

The lack of a socialist alternative does not mean that Latin America is condemned to the neoliberal model that the United States might want to establish or consolidate throughout the continent (by means of NAFTA , for example).[24] The neoliberal model is already stirring up a great deal of opposition, even among the ruling classes who are beginning to realize how radical it is. The neoliberal model is exacerbating rather than relieving the continent's longstanding social problems, and runs the risk of provoking social explosions. The example of what happened in Mexico on January 1, 1994, opened many people's eyes.[25] The elites will probably seek less radical approaches to a market economy. Indeed, that is what is happening in Brazil.

What stance should Christians take toward this situation?

An initial response is that Christians should be prophetic. As a prophet, the church denounces the evil in the world, injustice, the destruction of the human being and of all creation; it denounces the capitalist model of the economy that causes injustice and oppression.

Neoliberal ideology entails a sacralization of money and wealth, an idolatry of money that is the very opposite of the Christian message.[26] Neoliberalism allows the complete emancipation of the economy from any ethics. *Gaudium et Spes* sets limits to the autonomy of the temporal and earthly values, including the economy.

Hence it is imperative that there be a response of prophetic witness in condemnation. In Santo Domingo, the bishops conference denounced the neoliberal model but perhaps not forcefully enough to arouse the consciousness of the local churches and of Catholics in general.[27] There are various kinds of prophetic witness. Pentecostal churches condemn the world and all worldly activities; they condemn economics, politics, and culture because everything is contaminated with sin, and everything is idolatry. They accordingly proclaim that this world is ending and the reign of God is coming soon. They assume no responsibility for this world that has abandoned God and that God has abandoned. Their message is, "Let us save ourselves from this world. Let us flee far away from here!"

But the prevailing theme in Catholic tradition is not the witness of radical rejection of this world. Not all is lost in this world, and a beginning of the reign of God is possible here. Hence, Catholicism does not reject any and all economic systems. Being present in the world is not condemned; on the contrary, the church's teachings prompt action in order to change the world, albeit partially. From this stance it is clear that no actual economy will ever be perfectly just, but some economic forms can lead to improvements. Not everything is equally sinful.

Besides prophecy, Christians are today involved in the broad movement toward restoring ethics. The radical lifting of restrictions on the economy— and on culture or politics—prompts a reaction. Movements are arising with the aim of reestablishing ethics in public life.

Having a broader base than the Catholic church, the movement for ethics in public life can have wider repercussions. The neoliberal model engages in advertising that tends to stamp out any independent thinking. Almost all the media—TV, radio, magazines, newspapers—are devoted to exalting the neoliberal model. In Latin America, there is practically no more diversity of opinion. A single kind of thinking is imposed, not by law, but de facto.

Freedom of expression has been nullified in practice. All the media have fallen into the hands of groups identified with the economic model that some are now seeking to establish. There is no more dialogue because there are no more interlocutors. Critics are, in practice, isolated from lines of communication. From the standpoint of communications, we have arrived at a totalitarian society in which there is only a single type of thinking and criticism vanishes.

Hence, it is time that there be developed a movement to critique established society in the name of ethics. We must also be aware that in this effort it will be hard to have access to the media.

The weakness of the movement for ethics is that it arose largely in reaction to the scandals of those who were involved in cases of corruption: the campaign to impeach President Collor and the campaign to castigate the members of congress who were involved in corruption cases. Such "cases" have stirred up public opinion more than the forms of immorality that are structural and ongoing. That is why involvement in movements for ethics in public life has constituted an imperative that runs against the current.

Is it enough to struggle for ethics? Most of the political programs of left parties seem to come down to a list of ethical values. In order to enter into reality, ethics must be embodied in political programs that contain a plan for being involved in the economy.

It is not our task here to propose an economic program. However, by way of suggestion, and without claiming any qualification for making concrete proposals, but simply in order to draw the attention of Christian readers, we are here going to present some guidelines suggested by Jorge Castañeda, who is surely one of the most qualified and clearsighted observers of the Latin American situation.

Any concrete program must take as its starting point the fact that Latin American nations are inserted into the world market. Even Cuba is striving to be brought in. Today, it is inconceivable that an economy in a Latin American country could withdraw from the market economy model. In practice, all left parties that are in any way representative and that aspire to come to power accept this starting point.

However, as the world is integrated into the market, the difference between different models of the market economy becomes more visible—the United States model is not the only one, although in Latin America the media tend to spread the conviction that there is but one model, the American one. There are notable differences between the North American and the European models, or the Asian model of Japan and Korea.[28]

In the European model, the government is deeply involved in the economy. The state generates almost half the gross domestic product. Through labor unions and other organizations, workers have a great deal of influence on decisions within companies and in the national economy. Inequalities are much less accentuated, and there is no great mass of poor people, as in the United States. In Japan and Korea, there is also a close relationship between the state and private business. Reciprocity between the company and its employees is deeper, and social inequality is not as great as it is in the United States.

Although the United States exerts strong pressure throughout the Americas—which they want to hold under their tutelage—Latin American governments can invoke certain arguments. They can link up to other continents of the so-called Third World in order to win concessions from the North. There is a danger that dire poverty will be globalized. The extremely poor of the Third World are increasingly going to threaten the First World. Sooner or later, they are going to cross borders—there is no way to close a border forever if some day a million hungry people want to break down the doors of the wealthy countries. The spread of dire poverty threatens the tranquility of the rich who could be ready to make some concessions. From the ecological standpoint as well, the rich nations need the help of the poor nations, which can place conditions and demand compensation.

Finally, the social explosions that an extreme poverty could set off can upset the whole world economy. The United States was terrified by the problems in Mexico. If the Mexican market were to close and if Mexico were to turn into a region in civil war, the United States would suffer the consequences. When extreme repression in Haiti hastened the flight of refugees who invaded American shores, the government in Washington reacted and had to demand that the Haitian military step down.

Hence, the countries of the South do have some means for pressuring to have the more powerful nations accept changes and stop imposing their exaggerated policy. Even in the framework of current international relations, Latin American nations can win a degree of autonomy and define their own model of a market economy.[29]

What should the main lines of the left's economic program be today? Castañeda proposes three points which seem quite obvious.

The Welfare State

The fundamental demand of a policy of the left will be the advancement of the poor.[30] Such a proposal is not proper to the left, but belongs to all those who assume the human duty of social solidarity. It is a priority of Catholics inasmuch as the Latin American bishops have proclaimed the preferential option for the poor. This does not happen to be a priority for the parties of the right—even if they proclaim it in their speeches, as it is useful to do in political campaigns today.

Certainly, in today's world countless criticisms are being raised against the welfare state, in both Europe and the United States, and the media are publicizing these critiques and spreading them in Latin America. As if the welfare state were an obstacle to economic growth! The effort is being made to blame the poor for world economic problems. Who "manufactured" the poor, if not the chosen economic model?[31]

The discourse against the welfare state comes from the privileged who, in addition to their privileges, still want to take money away from the poor. That the welfare state demands solidarity on the part of the privileged is obvious. Is not solidarity the basis for any ethical program for the economy?

The welfare state is being criticized in Latin America. However, there is still no welfare state in any country except in a very fragmentary way; it does not reach the very poor, and the services it provides are quite tenuous.[32]

The example of Cuba shows that it is possible to organize free high quality popular education and a health care and housing system that serves everyone. Besides that, it is possible to organize unemployment insurance and a decent retirement. It is possible to struggle against the corruption that diverts resources intended for social programs and to create an honest and effective management. Corruption comes from above, from groups accustomed to living like parasites by diverting public funds.[33]

To uphold the very purpose of welfare is now against the current; it runs counter to conventional wisdom in the media. However, the population as a whole can be convinced that it is possible and necessary. The churches must not allow themselves to be swept away by unfettered propaganda. Christians have the task of remaining clearsighted and resisting the suggestions of the corrupt.

Tax Reform

The point is not to set up any tax reform whatsoever, but a reform that forces the rich to pay. Any welfare program entails resources. Where are these resources to come from? A portion can come from renegotiating the foreign debt more resolutely.[34] Another portion can come from cutting military spending, which in today's world is becoming even more useless. But the bulk of such resources has to come from taxes. In Latin America the very wealthy use all kinds of tricks to avoid paying taxes. The main taxation should be direct: not only on income, but on wealth as well. Tax reform is a program of all parties, but the powerful know very well that it will not go beyond paper. Hence there must be a struggle for a government that has the will to carry out tax reform and provide itself with the means to apply it.[35] The reform must also cover the informal economy, which as a rule is nothing more than a means devised by merchants to avoid paying taxes.

A tax reform entails international agreements, particularly with the United States. In order to avoid paying taxes the rich will take their wealth out of the country and place it in other countries, especially the United States. Even now, the wealth of rich Latin Americans which is deposited in the United States surpasses the amount of the foreign debt. There must be special agreements between nations to tax capital that flees its country of origin.

The idea is not so utopian. Castañeda notes that at the Bretton Woods conference in 1945 the initial proposal that the United States Treasury made, through its assistant secretary, Harry Dexter White, included the following among the conditions for being a member of the IMF: "Countries must agree not to accept or allow deposits or investments coming from any of the member countries, except with the permission of the member country in question." Otherwise, capital will flee, as it is in fact doing. In order to avoid flight, governments close their eyes and do not collect taxes. They are thereby deprived of funds for any social policy.[36]

Industrialization

Industrialization is necessary. Certain countries have agreed to de-industrialize (Argentina and Chile) in order to devote their resources to developing natural resources. Nevertheless, only industry adds value to goods, and in matters of trade, anyone selling raw materials is always at a disadvantage. In addition, true participation in the present world entails learning the advanced technologies that are only used in industry.

Industry must produce for export. That is what the Asians have done, while Latin Americans made the mistake of undertaking industrialization in order to serve the domestic market. Producing for export means acquiring technologies, and that requires up-to-the-minute training, getting into scientific research, and preparing new generations who are able to compete with the most advanced in the world. Industry must accept the challenge of world competition.[37]

A small country cannot specialize in all branches of industry, nor in all realms of advanced technology. Each nation must choose certain areas for which it has more favorable conditions or greater chances of penetrating markets. Such an industrialization policy entails a joint government-private sector policy. A government has many means of promoting the kind of industry that it wants, but it cannot do everything by itself. It needs to have the initiative and aggressiveness of the private sector.

No economic program will change the social situation overnight. But that is no reason to cross our arms and wait for the coming of the Anti-Christ and the last judgement. Something can and must be done.

Such an economic policy can become engaged with the way a city is organized. It can provide urban liberation movements with the interlocutor that they need. It can aid urban action programs and complement them, after linking up with them.

Of course, such an economic liberation requires a new politics, and hence a political liberation. What does political liberation mean today? That is what we shall consider in the next chapter.

6

POLITICAL LIBERATION

Disenchantment with politics is widespread in Latin America and in the Western world as a whole; as always, Latin America is copying what is happening in the First World. We observe a kind of weariness, and among youth, a lack of interest. We need only compare today's university students with those of thirty years ago. Today's youth do not seem to be living in this world; they live in themselves, in their groups, in their youth culture which takes hold of them and removes them from the real world.[1]

The people have always been critical of politics and held it in low esteem. Today, however, it seems that criticizing politics is more than making conversation, and that politics and politicians have really been discredited. Is that the result of a systematic policy of the mass media which hold up the scandals of politicians and politics and turn such scandals into public entertainment? Or is it the nature of the media to ridicule everything governmental? It is hard to believe that the media are really innocent. Why don't they condemn just as vehemently the scandals that occur in private business, rather than always only those in politics? Why do they condemn what politicians earn, but not the earnings of CEOs and top managers? In any case, such campaigns contribute to the discrediting of politics.

People also feel a sense of powerlessness. The return to democracy created huge expectations; everything seemed possible. Ten years after redemocratization, little remains of that enthusiasm. The fact is that the return to democracy has been the result not of a conquest by the people, but of the skill of the same old elites. The elites judged that it was not a good idea to continue with military dictatorships which had in fact lost international support.

Redemocratization had to take place, but that did not mean handing power over to the people. The people, who had not conquered power by themselves, did not feel stronger after the return to democracy. They remain as they have always been—weak. The intellectual elites of the left, however, did have illusions about the shift to democracy. Many thought that it was they who had destroyed the military regimes, but that was not true. Realizing now where things are really heading under the new democracy, they feel a sense of powerlessness. Hence the limitation of the political weight of popular or leftist parties throughout Latin America.

Many have left politics to take refuge in their own selves. They have discovered their psychological problems and their personal needs. They have gone on to believe that political involvement has caused them to waste time, and they are striving to make up for that lost time. Military regimes left their imprint on many people who have no more energy for plunging into conflicts again. They want peace and contentment.

There is yet another aspect connected to Latin American culture. In Latin America, politics arouses enthusiasm when it becomes tragic and heroic.[2] Hence the myth of guerrilla struggle. The Cuban guerrillas—and later the Nicaraguan guerrillas—have had an incredible impact within the intellectual class. Even those who could never imagine themselves in a Sierra Maestra were thrilled and surrendered to such an idea. Any critical spirit yielded to the heroic exploit. Anything connected to the guerrillas was justified and made sacred.

At present—after the Nicaraguan election, after the peace agreements in El Salvador, after the inevitable decline of the Cuban revolution, a victim of its former dependence on the Soviet Union—there is no more guerrilla struggle. The left is convinced that guerrilla struggle leads nowhere and that is all there is to it.

Peru's Shining Path was unpersuasive because of its cruel excesses and its systematic lack of morality. The myth needs good guerrillas, defenders of justice, avengers of the poor, like the Tupamaros used to be in Uruguay. It is true that recently we have the Zapatistas in Chiapas and Subcommander Marcos, but this is something new that has still not been digested by the collective imagination. Marcos does not intend to destroy the Mexican state, take power, and establish a just and holy state; he has more limited objectives. His guerrilla warfare is not really a guerrilla war but a maneuver to attract the media, and especially to influence the United States. This is another type of politics that is still not well understood.

Now that the guerrilla myth has no embodiment and is in hibernation, what could arouse enthusiasm in politics?

The struggle against military dictatorships and for democracy has provided a tragic-heroic equivalent. Many were tortured, imprisoned, and exiled. Many died as martyrs. The masses were thrilled, and intellectuals even more so, with the "No" campaign in Chile (1988 plebiscite against General Pinochet) and with "direct elections now" in Brazil (1985). These were challenges to dictatorships and heroic acts.

Today politics has lost its tragedy and heroism. It has degenerated into farce, as seen in the legal processes against those who are corrupt. No one becomes enthusiastic over such comedies, which are briefly entertaining, but leave a bitter taste, making people disgusted over politics.

The guerrilla myth is so strong, and the need for the tragic so constant in Latin American history, that we can anticipate that violence will reappear. The myth of armed struggle will flourish again. Peace has never been an ideal arousing enthusiasm like guerrilla struggle. It is war heroes who are popular, not heroes of peace. The guerrilla myth, that is, the myth of the hero who avenges the humiliations of the people, who stands at the head of the poor to struggle in their name, is stronger than the attraction of daily involvement in municipal or federal political life and everyday activism.

Elections have never aroused real popular enthusiasm in Brazil (even the 1994 Brazilian election). Today guerrilla struggle is out of fashion. In view of this situation, it nevertheless remains the duty of Christians to be involved in politics, even though it is more bothersome and more routine, and its objectives are more limited than total liberation. How are we to engage in politics without heroism?

The three fundamental objects of politics—the nation, the state, and democracy—are all imported from Europe and the United States. Indeed, to this day they have never become well acclimated to Latin America. They have to do with projects—themselves the result of a long history—that do not exactly meet the aspirations of the population. Nation, state, and democracy constitute challenges. To what extent is it appropriate to plant these institutions on Latin American soil contrary to so many tendencies, especially those that are unconscious? Insofar as it is appropriate, what approach is most suitable for attaining them?

The Nation

Developments in Eastern Europe since the fall of the Soviet empire have shown how slow and difficult and full of obstacles is the process of building nations. Although the Soviet empire fell apart, all the stratifications built up over the course of history have reappeared. The entire history of Eastern Europe has been resurrected. Dozens of still unfinished nations, interrupted in the past by wars, conquests, and domination, have now emerged. The tragedies of Eastern Europe have been added to the tragedies of African and Asian nations.

The movement to form nations is very deep and seems unstoppable. It stirs up a vast array of problems, especially competition between neighboring nations claiming the same territory or the same populations. The result is conflict between irreconcilable expectations on the part of nations.

By comparison, Latin American nations seem more stable. Conflicts between neighbors are not so serious as they are in other nations, where they continue to lead to bloody struggles. The internal formation of the nation through the integration of all inhabitants is much further advanced in Latin America than in the cases just mentioned. Even so, there is much to be done in Latin American nations. Their models come from Europe and the United States. They have copied and sought to copy Western nations in all respects. Reality is resistant, however, and the result is a hybrid of a nation with the residue of the previously existing structures.

Latin America happens to be facing the task of building nations at a time when the more advanced nations are beginning to undergo disintegration.

The Nation and the Globalization of the Economy

In today's world no nation—with the exception of the United States—can control what happens to its currency. Thanks to computers, capital moves every day from one country to another for speculative purposes. Hundreds of billions of dollars are continually circulating in search of profit, and they can therefore destabilize a currency.[3] Under the pressure of neoliberalism, Latin Americans have learned how to attract speculative capital but they are now seeing the consequences of this game. The currency at their disposal can suddenly slip through their hands, as happened in Mexico.

The multinational industrial and service companies transfer funds from one country to another and no nation can monitor what is happening. The companies constantly seek those countries that offer them incentives and where taxes are lower—or can be evaded. They seek refuge in tax havens. Multinationals thereby avoid contributing to the nation as they ought. A great deal of the activity of these companies is removed from oversight by nations.

Indeed, multinationals make demands and claim privileges for setting up their factories. Because they provide employment, they ask for compensations and obtain exorbitant conditions. Nations cave in to their arrogance.[4]

The Nation and Dependence

The problem of the foreign debt has made the dependence of the nations of the South very plain. They are dependent on the IMF and the World Bank, agencies where United States interests always prevail. The IMF prescribes neoliberal remedies and pushes for drastic cuts in social programs. National governments that seek out these agencies are not free to plan their budgets, but need IMF approval.

Moreover, nothing can halt the invasion of American culture creating an environment receptive to whatever comes from the United States. The upshot is a climate of public opinion that will not tolerate any conflict with the United States. Thus, being on the side of the United States is a prior condition for any and every policy.[5]

For its part, the United States fears nationalism. It condemns anything that looks like budding nationalism and immediately attacks it, demanding that the government react immediately. Thus, a nation cannot mature and independently assume its destiny.

Citizenship

The greatest flaw in Latin American nations is the lack of citizenship. Only a minority follows the life of the nation; the vast majority of the popular masses in the countryside or the city are not informed and have no idea of what is happening. In elections they trust in their traditional elites. Real participation is very small. The illiterate, indigenous people, the unemployed or underemployed, regard politics as a television spectacle. They have no knowledge of the political game. They have no aspirations to politics, and hence do not identify with any party that might champion their aspirations.[6]

Transforming inhabitants into citizens—that is the challenge. Recently, movements such as that of Betinho* have sought to do that. The nation becomes strong and united when its citizens are able to understand and assume together the common tasks entailed in shared life, striving to get along with one another and thereby establishing the "national project."

In a dual society, the nation remains precarious. Nations that have either strong minorities or indigenous majorities have a particular problem: the indigenous never shaped the nation that was imposed on them. Under such conditions would it be possible to shape a political body that respects the rights of the indigenous peoples? What kind of nation would that be?

In Brazil, there is a split between the elites who belong to the developed Western world and the popular masses who belong to the Third World. How fashion a nation out of populations so different, whose cultures are so different? The nation will never be solid until this duality which is so sharp is overcome.

The primary political object is to form the nation, and that task remains unfinished even to this day.[7] Latin American nations are very unequal in this regard. On the whole Latin American nations are more solid than most African, Asian, or East European nations, but the task remains nonetheless.

The State

The biggest political problem in Latin America is the weakness of the state. In the First World in the 1980s there was a huge neoliberal campaign against the state, aimed at reducing its role, as though the state were the great obstacle to economic growth. As always, the ideology in vogue in the First World has disastrous effects in Latin America. Such is the case of the campaign against the state.

The Critique of the Entrepreneur State

Industrialization arose under the encouragement of the state or by state initiative, and under the protection of rigid protectionistic laws, except in Great Britain, where it began, and the United States, where the geographical distance meant that it had almost no competition. Currently neoliberals, the United States, and the IMF want those nations that are barely beginning the industrialization process to open their borders to all products from the

---

* Luiz Herberto de Souza, a highly regarded sociologist who in the early 1990s launched a movement whose immediate aim was to relieve hunger, but which was more broadly understood to be an attempt to harness a collective ethical sense to promote the common good. His moral stature was enhanced by the knowledge that he had AIDS (contracted from a blood transfusion). He died in 1997.

nations that have been industrialized for a long time. That amounts to killing them in the nest.

Government involvement in production has increased a great deal in the twentieth century. Not only has government taken responsibility for a good portion of infrastructure (highways, railways, aviation, maritime transport, communications, mail, telegraph, telephone, radio, TV), but it has also created basic or advanced technology industries, and has nationalized banks and insurance companies. In Europe the state has assumed responsibility for producing as much as half the goods and services, still within a capitalist structure. The socialist state took over production almost entirely.

The state also takes charge of economic planning, in some countries more, in others less. Its influence becomes decisive for the guidance of those countries. The state has planned, and continues to plan, a great deal in Europe, and even more in Japan and the Asian tigers, although always in conjunction with the private sector.

Criticism of state-enterprise began in the 1970s. That critique was applied by the Thatcher government in Great Britain and by the Reagan and Bush administrations in the United States (though government involvement in production has always been more modest in the United States). Since then, the cry for "less government" and the privatization of government enterprises has been unrelenting.

These critiques are aimed at an alleged inability of the state to run a business. On the whole, however, state-run companies operate well and run deficits only when they are obliged to offer services at low cost. Offering low-cost services is a way of redistributing national product; resulting deficits are not necessarily due to poor management. Some state companies may be poorly run, just as are some private companies. State monopolies are criticized, but those critics would simply transfer the state monopoly to a private company. That would worsen the situation. Interference of politicians in managing state companies is criticized, but that depends on the strength of the government.

With the exception of Great Britain, European governments have so far been very prudent in privatization. In Latin America, privatization has been taken seriously, and the neoliberal assaults have been followed literally. Chile and Argentina have privatized with gusto, as though privatization were a work of public salvation. Thus far, privatization has not demonstrated its validity. A number of the privatizations carried out in Brazil have been almost gifts to the private sector. What the future will bring is unclear, but there is strong pressure from business people—who, as always, want to take advantage of the state.

In the future, we cannot rely on having a national private sector, let alone multinationals or foreign investments, to carry out a coherent industrialization plan. Only the state can project and coordinate a long-term plan capable of significantly changing the economic situation of the country. That is true no matter what free market economists may be shouting; the future of the economy cannot be entrusted to economists.

The growth of the so-called "thirty glorious years" came to a grinding halt in the 1970s. Unemployment has been rising steadily, reaching 12% to 15% of the work force in industrialized nations. The state is blamed, but the cause of unemployment lies in the very thrust of capitalist society and in the technological changes wrought by the third industrial revolution. Private companies cause even greater unemployment. Hence Latin American governments need not consent to being blackmailed by economists.

Georges Clemenceau, who headed the French government during World War I, used to say that war was too serious a thing to be left to the military. Likewise, we have to say that the economy is too serious a thing to be left to economists. Politics defines the ends and economics chooses the means for the sake of those ends that politicians have chosen.[8]

Critique of the Welfare State

In the 1970s, the private sector and the wealthy began to criticize the welfare state. The critique began in Great Britain, which has the most comprehensive system, and in the United States.[9]

The arguments are not new. The welfare state is said to create people who are passive, who have no initiative and simply live off the goodness of the state, doing nothing. Social policy is not the remedy but the cause of poverty, because it separates people from work and from personal responsibility. Social insurance expenses are seen as a burden too heavy to bear, and so forth. Such arguments are repeated in Latin America where social security systems do not work well.

Problems have arisen primarily because advanced medicine is ever more expensive and unemployment has risen a great deal. Nevertheless, the welfare state is the only way devised thus far to translate social solidarity into practice—at least up to a point. Christians in particular cherish it. In practice—despite the critiques or political speeches and promises made to right-wing voters—First World countries have still not changed their social programs notably, although the threat exists, and their citizens are on the alert.[10] In Latin America, right-wing economists have more power and in fact have been able to cut social spending. Budget-cutting measures affect social spending first.

Latin America is in a situation in which the welfare state remains to be built. Neoliberal propaganda would like to replace it with a system of private insurance. The result would be that all those left out of the work world would also be excluded from social services. Neoliberalism trumpets the North American system, which has, in fact, created a mass of poor people incompatible with a state that regards itself as civilized.

Decentralization of the State

Federal states have always practiced decentralization and do not suffer so much the vices of centralization, but some federal states, such as Brazil, are so only on paper, because most of the individual states cannot survive without help from the federal government. Today there is a trend toward dividing the responsibilities of the government, and sharing them with regions and municipalities. However, in states still in formation, as in Latin America, a premature decentralization can prevent any change. For local governments are often more conservative than the central government; they are much more under the control of local bosses and much more prone to being plundered by the powerful.

In the First World, the aim is decentralization to respond to the aspirations of local diversities and to break down to some extent the anonymity of the central government. By contrast, in Latin America the great problem is the weakness of the central state, and the weakness of the very meaning of the state.[11]

Strength and Weakness of the State

Thirty years ago politics was at the center of the concerns of the intellectual class in Latin America. Politics was understood to be primarily the conquest of "power"—and power lay in the government. People had the illusion that whoever was installed in the government held "power"—and that this power would enable them to change the world by pointing society in whatever direction they wanted.[12]

Through practice people have learned that government does not mean power. Power is more diffused and hidden; it is identified more with resistance than with change. The strong power in society is the combination of forces that tend to keep and consolidate the balance of forces in society. Consequently, any change entails confronting a mobilization of all the conservative forces.

Revolutionaries think they can change everything at once, face all their adversaries at once, and present all their objectives at once. They accordingly either quickly fall to the combination of all the forces resisting change, or they are forced to set up a totalitarian state, that is, one based on secret police terror and permanent inquisition.

Those who are in government know that they can deal with only one problem at a time, and in order to resolve it they put together a combination of forces so as to isolate a single adversary. Thus any change is costly. In addition, those in government have to deal with an administration that can bring to a halt any change simply by not carrying out orders, and so everything remains on paper.

Contemporary society is so complex that any change causes an infinite number of repercussions and many reactions that are often unforeseen. That means that any change brings a series of new problems. You move one piece, and you have moved all the pieces, and so you have to refashion a new equilibrium.

Currently, the state has been weakened by the weakening of the nation.[13] To all of this must still be added the weakening resulting from the deterioration of democracy, even—and especially—in the older democracies of the Western world. In Latin America, the state is weak because it has not yet been fully established. The first challenge remains that of fashioning the state.[14]

Clientelism is still thriving: the elites think that the government is there to serve their private interests. They choose public officials to carry out their orders. They make no distinction between public good and private good. They plunder the state—as though it existed to solve the financial problems of their companies, to finance works on their properties, to nourish their political followers with favors and positions. They pass out government jobs as though it were their booty. All the powerful create around themselves a court of "maharajas" and parasites paid by the government. At the moment, they have enthusiastically gone over to the privatization ideology; in it they have discovered a new way to appropriate public property for themselves.

The facade of a state under the rule of law is maintained. In appearance the state is governed by laws that serve the common good; it is free and independent, subject only to the popular will expressed through democratic means. Facing the outside is a facade which to some extent can conceal the real power plays. In reality, laws are drawn up in such a way that there is always provision for the exception that allows the powerful to be exempt. If the law is a burden, an amnesty need only be issued and the problem vanishes.[15]

The masses of the people do not amount to a force sufficient to force the government to be rational and objective. Most people believe that stealing is just what politics is about. Why would anyone become involved in politics except to steal? That is how they think, and that is why they are so indifferent. They think that the government steals no matter what: whether it is one party or the other is all the same. They only become aroused when there emerges a populist leader who stirs up hope of being able to struggle against the traditional elites. Even then, how often they are disappointed!

The state is poor because it cannot summon the capacity to collect taxes from the powerful. Far from paying for their share of social solidarity, the wealthy draw on the state's meager resources to serve their own personal politics. Lacking contributions from those who hold wealth, the state seeks to sustain itself through the sale of natural resources (oil in Mexico and Venezuela, copper in Chile) or through indirect taxes.

That is why the state is still largely a fiction in Latin America, a Potemkin-like facade. Seen from outside, everything works along the lines of the modern theory of the state: the government drafts and promulgates laws and decrees and prepares a budget and balance sheet; the congress discusses, votes, and examines; the courts apply the laws, the police seize criminals and the law is applied.

In practice, however, the laws are applied to the poor, while the wealthy pay government officials off or phone the minister. The budget is not followed, and no one knows where the money goes. The corrupt are amnestied; the innocent are in prison while the criminals pass as upright persons. The powerful do not pay taxes. Any of the latter who have any problem with the authorities need only say the magic words, "Do you know who you're talking to?" and everything is settled.

Under these conditions the Marxist critique of the state is very often true: the state is the means by which the dominant class exploits the poor. Marx was commenting on mid-nineteenth-century European governments, but the critique is still largely valid for Latin American governments.

In conclusion, let us reiterate that in Latin America the state is weak. Strengthening the state to free it from the feudal powers that hold it captive to their private interests is the great goal of politics. But a state can be strong only if it has behind it an ongoing popular mobilization. European states became (relatively) strong because governments were backed by strong political parties that were engaged in permanent vigilance. Without strong parties there is no strong state in a democracy. Thus, we come to the issue of democracy, which is actually a new problem, because today's Western democracy is no longer what is described in political science textbooks.

Democracy in Crisis

One point on which there is unanimity in Latin America is democracy: whether left or right, everyone wants democracy unconditionally. Democracy has become a myth beyond discussion; praised and worshiped, it is an absolutely fixed reference point. Behind such enthusiasm, of course, lies the memory of the previous National Security military dictatorships. In Latin America, democracy means the end of torture, arbitrary arrest, secret police, being underground. Certainly, as Churchill said, even with all its flaws, democracy is still better than all other systems. It has its flaws, nonetheless, especially now when it is going through a deep crisis to which it could succumb—at least in a number of nations.

The Crisis in Western Democracies

As always in the twentieth century, the United States is leading the way. In the present phase of Western culture, the priority of the economy has become absolute. Democracy is in crisis because politics has become empty. There is no more politics because there is no more discussion, and no option to be made freely. The economy takes over as the sole norm, sole absolute value, and sole ultimate reference point. Neither the state nor the people are free to choose goals. The state and politics no longer have their own goals; the only goal is economic growth, the health of the economic system, and the salvation of capitalism. Never has the economy enjoyed such a radical dictatorship. We have here a problem of culture inasmuch as this is not only an imposition by economic elites, but indeed the people as a whole ratify the choice: the only goal is economic. Thus all parties end up with the same program. That is very obvious in the United States, but in Europe since 1970 the difference between socialists and liberals has gradually been erased, and they all want the same thing. They all feel constrained. Operating here is a will that is stronger than a political will, a collective will rooted in the culture.

Thus weakened and deprived of its supreme authority, the state no longer has any overall project, and it does not have its own goals. Parties lose their raison d'être—which used to be to draw up a program for governing, a program with goals. The people are no longer mobilized for great causes. Politics has fallen into disfavor, since it has accepted simply serving the economy. The weakened state is deprived of its authority and it is surrounded by lobbies, interest groups, and influential groups pressuring to make their interests prevail. The government is condemned to continually negotiate agreements with these groups, and is continually losing its authority. The common good and common objectives retreat to make way for private interests. Conglomerates are especially voracious; if they have a great deal of influence in Washington, one can imagine the weight that they have with governments that are much weaker. The state is gradually becoming a captive of pressure groups.

Freedom of expression, as embodied in freedom of the press, has always been the foundation of democracy. It makes transparency possible, and enables citizens to know what those governing them are doing, and to criticize, react, and bring about desired changes in direction. That is how so-called "public opinion" came into being. Public opinion is the government's interlocutor, the voice of the citizenry vis-à-vis the state, the condition for the political dialogue that gives shape to democracy.

The direction taken by the economy has led to a concentration of the media in a few hands. The number of newspapers is declining. Radio and TV stations form networks. Information has gotten to the point where it depends on a few conglomerates controlled by a few individuals. The behavior of the media has changed; they have also become pressure groups. In addition, they are dependent on the economic conglomerates that finance them. They are also lobbies vis-à-vis government bodies; they are no longer the voice of the people but the voice of the economic conglomerates that they represent. They work to achieve agreement between the economic powers and the state, thereby helping subordinate the state to economic patrons. The public opinion that they guide is no longer the spontaneous opinion of citizens. The media, especially television, manufacture public opinion and shape it to their own desire.

In this regard, TV helps destroy any capacity for critical thinking. It presents not arguments, but constantly repeated slogans that end up penetrating people's minds. Ultimately, rather than being the people's voice, the media have the effect of making the people declare themselves incompetent and, hence, submit to the dictates of those governing, who are themselves subject to economic conglomerates. This is a simplified sketch but in overall terms it represents what is actually happening. The media make and unmake governments, and no one really knows what is happening. The upshot is that public opinion and accurate information vanish. Citizens receive the news that will dispose them to accept the desired direction but what is most important remains hidden. The media serve primarily to hide what is happening; they disinform more than they inform.

Those in government lose the ability to undertake any government program because they are constantly under the eye of the media. Once in office, the only object of the administration becomes winning the next election. It is held in thrall by opinion polls, such as Brazilian Institute of Public Opinion and Statistics (IBOPE), and by the picture of the situation drawn up on a daily basis by the media. The administration watches out for its image. Instead of governing, it is continually adjusting its makeup. Its guiding principle is: how will public opinion react? What is going to come out in the media? Hence the dearth of long-range politics. Governing means surviving and giving the impression that you are governing. Politics is becoming utter narcissism: politicians taking care of their image. To be means to appear.

Meanwhile, technicians and managers run the state. Problems are so numerous and so complex that elected representatives are no longer capable of checking the facts, understanding what it is about, and knowing what is behind proposals. Technocratic politicians and administrators draw up laws and decrees, and apply them if they wish. The representatives of the people think about elections and deal with their own image. What counts is not what they actually do but what people think they are doing.

Television turns politics into a big game. Politicians line up to say a few empty words. They all say the same thing, leaving people confused and regarding politics as a contest like any other. The content doesn't matter; it's about rivalry between persons. One wins and the other loses; it's all a matter of luck. Television has thereby helped make politics more of a show than a reality. There is no way to become properly informed, since the information itself is manipulated. Each candidate says, "Vote for me because I'm the best." Being "best" means being more photogenic, or fitting the ideal model of man or woman. Moreover, time passes quickly for TV; what happened yesterday has already vanished. No one recalls the candidate's promises or platform. Speeches are filed away and forgotten after the election. Projects have no continuity. What counts is winning today; seeing what has to be done can wait until tomorrow.

Those acting in the government are on stage and they try to please the audience. Even if they are doing little or nothing so as not to create enemies, they have to give the impression that they are doing something. Government representatives travel a lot, talk a lot, and create news. What counts is making the news. Democratic politics has become a show, and it does not tackle any of society's problems because it is unwilling to displease anyone.[16]

Even so, the game does not always succeed in entertaining the public. There are more interesting games. The result is that politics has lost favor. The Greeks would say that democracy has become demagoguery: the only thing politicians want to do is please the crowd. The more traditional Western democracies are heading toward demagoguery. Moreover, given the weakening of the nation and the state, democracy is becoming empty. Hence it becomes empty demagoguery, while the multinational economic powers establish new worldwide feudalisms that challenge the authority of states and seek to subject peoples to their will.

Democracy in Latin America

After two decades of dictatorships that affected almost all nations in Latin America, democracy has become sacred. It is an absolute value, to be defended unconditionally, despite all its corruptions. The fear left by the military is so strong that no one dares question the new democracy. People shut their eyes to its problems, or perhaps attribute the flaws that they fear they might uncover in the system itself to the personal failures of those in power.

Fear of the military is not a sufficient basis for establishing a true democracy. Actually, the political heritage of Latin American countries is not very favorable to democracy, except in Chile, Uruguay, and Costa Rica. Moreover, the educated classes are very alert to developments in the West, and so to the traditional weaknesses of democracy in Latin America must be added the new weaknesses of Western democracies. All this is sufficient to show that democracy is far from having triumphed. It now faces very serious obstacles.

The fact that the armed forces have returned to their barracks does not mean that they have given up the role that they have always played of being the ultimate backup. In Brazil, they are called the "moderating power" (alongside the executive, legislative, and judicial powers or branches of government). Not even in Argentina, where they were discredited by a shameful defeat in the Malvinas/Falklands war, have officials of the armed forces given up their political role. They will no doubt return when democracy plunges deeper into crisis. As in the past, when the ruling classes have perceived that the democratic system might grant a modicum of real power to the workers, they will ask the army to step in to maintain their traditional control. They have always done so in the past, and there is no reason for them not to do so in the future.

Drawing inspiration from the executive class in the United States and Europe, the ruling elites of the nation are less interested than ever in a democratic state. What might interest them is a weak state. But should democracy mean a strong state, they would rather dispense with democracy.[17]

In the past, elites plundered the state. Today, they regard the state as justified insofar as they can divert public resources to their private interests. Because the middle and lower classes mimic the game of the elites, clientelism is still the basic structure.[18] The elites have always wanted a weak state, and so they are thrilled by neoliberal theories that have given their traditional practice the appearance of greater economic rationality.

In any case, if democracy means greater participation of the lower classes in the government, the elites want nothing to do with democracy. They want a democracy where companies can impose their own conditions on workers, with no government interference.

It can be argued that in the nineteenth century the Western democracies were also aristocracies and remained so until 1914, or to some extent until 1940. True democracies with popular participation really came into being after World War II. The democracies in Chile, Uruguay, and Costa Rica are older than most of those in Europe. Hence, we could think that we need only wait a while and allow Latin American democracies time to mature and solidify. Indeed, such an interpretation could be sustained. It may be that Latin American democracies will solidify just when Western democracies are going into crisis. But that would be more likely if Latin American elites were less attentive to the fluctuations in the Western society that they wish to emulate. If the elites had national or patriotic sentiments, the likelihood would be even greater. Currently, however, they are imitating the new ruling class of the Western world, and mentally they live in a cosmopolitan world: TV, radio, the press, private education, advertising—everything exalts and fosters cosmopolitan culture and makes not only the elites, but a good portion of the middle classes, foreign to the rest of their own people.

The mass of the people are not in a position to be actively involved in political life in such a way that they can stand up to the interests of the dominant class. They are not sufficiently educated, nor do they have the organizing ability. They do not have their own media. When the democracies arose in Europe there were people's newspapers, people's sources of news. Today the media are at the service of elite control, and inculcate a culture that for the mass of the people is sheer spectacle without any active participation.

A "public opinion" takes shape spreading an ideology of consumption which promotes the possession of goods that grant comfort and status. Thus, even the very poor increasingly nourish the desire to have a TV set, refrigerator, appliances, their own car (or at least a motorcycle). Political involvement is not a priority in this ideology. Having the impression of involvement through the electoral game is enough.

Elections are of little help toward a true rise of the popular masses, because constitutions are fashioned in such a way that one of the branches of government can cancel a decision made by the others when such a decision might threaten the status quo. Moreover, the state has few resources. After subsidizing companies by granting them countless breaks, paying their debts, rescuing failed banks, and providing city services for bourgeois neighborhoods, there is nothing left for local development projects that could really change the situation.

Without economic democracy, political democracy becomes appearance—as has been the case throughout history. This is the biggest obstacle to the unfolding of a true democracy.

Attempting to imitate institutions that have emerged elsewhere under other conditions inevitably leads to formalism. From the very beginning, intellectuals in Latin America have split into two opposing camps: those supporting imitation of the West and those protesting against such imitation.[19]

The political institutions defined in constitutions are particularly artificial. Taken literally, Latin American constitutions are generally much more advanced than the constitutions of more traditionally democratic countries.

They are, however, constitutions devised to be appreciated esthetically rather than practically applied. A primary formalism is that of congresses. In theory, members of congress represent the citizens, but in practice, in order to be a congressional deputy, one has to have the support of major political machines that can amass millions of dollars. Most congresspersons represent leagues of elite groups. That is why congressional representatives are not responsive to their people.

The executive branch is surrounded by all the traditional and modern economic powers which are connected to the great traditional families; thus, the modern is allied with the antiquated. Both get along very well inasmuch as the whole point is promoting and consolidating privilege. The executive branch can do anything provided it defends elite interests; it cannot do anything that departs from that direction. It cannot have popular support because support depends on the media. The media are now engaged in an unrestrained propaganda for neoliberalism, which is presented as the only rational model. Those who do not accept the official ideology are derided as though they were out of their minds.

With regard to the courts, poor citizens are unlikely to have access to them. They will never be able to win a case against the powerful. Lawyers are prohibitively expensive. Thousands of poor people spend years in prison without ever coming to trial simply because they cannot afford a lawyer.

Imitation of the West now enshrines technocrats, especially economists, who are regarded as infallible, even when their predictions turn out to be completely wrong. So great is the worship of economists that they have reached the point of exercising a real dictatorship in the name of economic science. In recent years, Carlos Salinas de Gortari was venerated in Mexico (until he fell precipitously from grace), as were Domingo Cavallo in Argentina and Hernán Büchi in Chile; Fernando Henrique Cardoso won the election in Brazil as the wizard who produced the Real Plan.

In the short run, servile imitation of the wealthier societies of the West is arousing illusory enthusiasm. After a few years, any small incident can cause the imported system to implode, resulting in disillusionment, until the next illusion comes along.

All this formalism is the reason why democracy is so weak. That is why new authoritarian populisms are bound to appear. After a certain amount of disillusionment, the country is willing to sacrifice formal democracy and to place its hope in a charismatic leader. For the moment, after the very harsh military regimes, people remain attached to democracy. Even so, however, one can foresee that it will not last long.[20]

From the standpoint of the lower classes, almost all improvements have been the work of the various instances of populism. The popular masses have little reason to be grateful to democratic governments, and so, in this regard, the masses are not so attached to democracy. A shrewd observer said that the Chilean people—regarded as the most democratic in Latin America—are basically monarchists: they want a good and just king who is attentive to the needs of the people; they want a chief who gives orders. The traditional masses prefer an active and effective boss to a democracy that makes many promises but does little or nothing to fulfill them.

From a rational standpoint, it is discouraging that democracy is so weak, but in the actual unfolding of history, de facto realities prove more decisive.

Civil Society

The notion of civil society has lately reappeared and attracted notice in Latin America, and especially in Brazil. This has happened as a result of the new citizenship movements that have attained a certain magnitude. These new movements have raised the question of whether they are not a new expression of civil society. Might this civil society provide the basis for a real democratization of political life? Might citizenship movements be the political expression of the popular masses, something that has always been lacking in Latin American democracies?[21]

First, we must specify what civil society means. Sociologists and political scientists generally present a concept of civil society on the basis of their overall system. They start from a comprehensive interpretation of society and attribute to civil society a role flowing from their overall theory. Thus, notions of civil society vary depending on whether they are proposed by Hegel, Marx, Gramsci, or Habermas, and so forth. We are not going to enter into a discussion of these theories, because, in any case, there remains the question of determining whether they are relevant or not in Latin American society.[22]

We take civil society to be simply the totality of relationships between citizens, whether institutionalized or not, insofar as they are independent of the state and the market. Civil society arose in the West in the medieval cities which struggled against the power of the emperor, kings and the church—and everything connected to them.

In the West, civil society was able to restrain absolute powers and force a degree of participation by the forces of the people. Civil society has been able at particular moments to influence the state for both good and ill. At certain moments it has been able to dominate the state and almost bring it to a halt.

Liberalism and capitalism were opposed to all civil society; their ideal would be complete freedom of the market vis-à-vis the state. There would be no intermediaries between citizens as sheer individuals and the state—only the give and take of the market.

However, neither liberalism nor capitalism has been able to achieve that project; they have encountered a great deal of resistance. A new civil society became reorganized even against the liberal constitutions established by the liberal revolutions in France and the United States. Labor unions and other workers movements achieved real power to discipline the market and influence the state—at least in Europe and in the states emerging from the British empire.

In the twentieth century, it can be said that civil society has succeeded in democratizing the states of Western Europe to some degree. It has been widely noted that in Eastern Europe the working class participated in the struggle against the communist system. That helped weaken the will of the communist party elites. Even so, after the fall of the communist regimes, civil society has not proven so effective for setting up true democracies, and hence it is clear that civil society by itself is not enough.

In the United States—the primary point of comparison for Latin America —civil society has always been strong locally and weak nationally. Grassroots organizations have a powerful impact on determining who governs locally. Nationally, the market has always been more free than it is in Europe. In the United States, civil society is increasingly composed of powerful lobbies which primarily represent economic interests. These lobbies reach the point of paralyzing government power. Hence, civil society is often evaluated in negative terms: it is the manifestation of private interests, especially of the most powerful. That is why people are completely indifferent to politics in the United States. Why vote if the president will be forced to do what the lobbies want? In this instance, civil society is inimical to democracy.

It is not enough that there be an intermediate organization between the state and citizens. If that organization is nothing but the sum of private interests, nothing will be left of democracy but a facade to cloak the pressures of powerful groups. The latter can even reach the point of canceling out popular representation achieved through constitutional channels.

And in Latin America, what is the situation? Latin America was born almost without civil society. The institutions deriving from medieval cities were not established on the Latin American continent. Citizens were not organized and the colonial government struggled systematically against any kind of organization of civil society that might be a starting point for independence. Even so, independence came about—and indeed it had to happen. Independence was nonetheless achieved without much popular organization. The state remained weak and dependent upon the lords of the land. A small middle class arose in the cities but it was very dependent on the state and on those same great families. Such was the case in the early twentieth century.

Outside of Chile, Uruguay, and Costa Rica, no powerful civil society could take shape among the popular classes. Labor unions did not succeed in creating a force capable of standing up to the state, let alone to the business class. On the contrary, they became very dependent on the state or on economic forces. The same thing happened to other popular movements.

On the local level, neighborhood associations have succeeded in organizing certain kinds of aid, but they have not established themselves as permanent bodies for monitoring political power. Indeed, they have often been coopted by the political class.[23]

What about the citizenship movements that have emerged recently? Certainly they are movements independent of the state, although their scope is quite limited thus far—if we consider the practical results achieved. They are, moreover, essentially middle-class movements. The same is true of parties that are seeking to be forces of opposition to the state, which hope to carry out a different kind of policy: e.g., the Workers Party in Brazil,[24] the Frente Grande in Argentina, the PRD in Mexico, and so forth.

Civil society encompasses a certain sector of the middle classes ("lower middle classes" as they are called in Brazil, since in Brazil the rich call themselves middle class, just as conservatives label themselves leftists). There is no really effective civil society within the popular masses. No extensive popular organization has yet been achieved. There are certainly strong organizations among the indigenous, but they act as movements for indigenous autonomy, not as movements of civil society within the nation. Black people and mestizo people have still not established a democratizing civil society. There are many groups and associations among the ordinary people for cultural and athletic purposes and for games or entertainment. But they are not groups with a political capability and so they are easily coopted by the elites.

In short, there does exist a civil society in Latin America that has been active since the beginning of this century. It took a great step forward after 1930, another one after 1950, and yet another step after the redemocratization of the 1980s. Nevertheless, it still does not involve the majority of the people, and hence it is condemned to feel frustrated very often, inasmuch as the traditional elites know how to manipulate the popular masses and legitimize themselves in the process.[25]

Moreover, imitation of the new ruling class model coming from the United States tends to bolster the traditional elites and make them even more impervious to any change that could limit their privileges. This new ruling class exerts so much pressure on governments—demanding privatization of the public sector, lower taxes, the withdrawal of the government from setting wages, and the dismantling of the little that exists of the welfare state—that alongside such power citizenship movements look very frail.

Conclusion

With regard to high-level politics, that is, relations between states and worldwide forces, the world of the poor cannot do much. We are far removed from nineteenth-century proletarian internationalism. There is not even the shadow of an alliance of peoples to deal with the globalization of culture, the economy, and politics.[26] This is a task for those elites who still retain some solidarity with their people. These minorities among the elites can do much to prepare future paths. Not all elite governments are equal. It will be necessary to discern what is valid and what is counterproductive from the standpoint of the poor. Not all governments deserve to be rejected apocalyptically. Within current structures and relationships of forces, governments emerging from the present democratic system cannot make big changes, but they can help their nation to a greater or lesser extent.

On the national level, the goal of the popular sectors is a truly popular party that is embraced by the masses and can count on their support. That is a long-term goal. It would be a party able to support a strong state for the sake of an aggressive national policy in the contemporary world and could mobilize people domestically.

That is a long-range task because populist parties will emerge to occupy the space of the true people's party; because it is difficult for a party of intellectuals to become accessible to the masses; and because political consciousness-raising has to work uphill in the depoliticizing consumer society.[27]

In the short run, urban politics offers a more open field. It will be easier for mayorships to be won by a popular or left party than state or federal governments. It will also be easier to mobilize the people in neighborhood struggles than in national struggles. Everything said previously about urban politics could be repeated here. Although changes in cities are piecemeal and do not change worldwide structures, they are a starting point. Cities can constitute important poles of influence in the future. A unified force of cities can counterbalance the power of lobbies and prevent the national state from being completely subordinated to dominant economic forces. Urban and municipal politics is a school of political apprenticeship for poor people. The poor can win strong positions in the fabric of cities, even though the elites are abandoning the cities.[28]

The immediate objective is to form a popular civil society. There is a great deal of ferment in cities today. Many groups are emerging to solve immediate local problems. As they become consolidated and take up some shared need in an ongoing way, they are forming civil society. They are engaged in an act of citizenship. A person who regularly becomes involved in public life becomes a citizen. There is a strong movement in this direction today. Besides the Catholic church, many other churches are committed to such action.

The experience of efforts at political and economic change in the twentieth century has shown that everything depends on cultural options. A people is not going to make social, political, or economic changes if it does not want to, if it is uninterested, or if it is seeking something else. Everything depends on culture. There are some basic cultural options that have the effect of making all their consequences accepted, no matter how irrational they seem. There is no such thing as pure rationality; rationality only exists within a particular culture. Hence, it must be stressed—and this is increasingly obvious—that underlying all social liberations is a cultural liberation. That is the topic of the next chapter.

7

CULTURAL LIBERATION

The economy, politics, and social life are three components of a single culture, and it is culture that unifies them. The politics, economics, and social life of the West are intimately connected: one and the same culture underlies the three dimensions, and that unity is reflected in all aspects of daily life, and in the arts and expressions of the West. Today this culture is often called modernity; modernity is thus, nothing other than Western culture.

Western culture started with a rather sharp break in the sixteenth century. The well-known trial of Galileo clearly displays the two cultures in conflict. Galileo was seemingly defeated because he was forced to accept silence, but in historical terms he was the victor, because after him the movement that he was expressing has advanced continually. Since the seventeenth century, the new culture, which today is Western culture, has grown uninterruptedly, little by little permeating all aspects of public and private life. It had to struggle because the previous culture defended itself—until the nineteenth century it was not so clear that the modern was going to defeat the ancient.

The fact is that the church was deeply inculturated in the previous (premodern or medieval, the name does not matter) culture. It was so inculturated that often it did not know how to distinguish what was Christian from what was proper to medieval culture. Despite attempts to reconcile the new culture and Christianity, the prevailing trend was to systematically defend the old culture and how Christianity was expressed in that old culture. Until Vatican II, the deep inculturation in pre-modern culture was an almost insuperable obstacle to evangelization. Even after Vatican II, most Catholics still cannot be said to have understood what was at stake. But the result has been that little by little people of the West have been leaving the Catholic church.

The biggest surprise of this history is that today the church is now seen as a bearer and transmitter of a Western culture that it combated desperately and that it has never accepted. The fact is that Christianity has traveled through the world as part of the baggage of the Western powers and has been confused with them.

Today Western culture is invading the entire world and causing conflicts, clashes, divisions, wars, and revolutions everywhere, and yet all indications are that we are still only at the beginning of a history of cultural conflicts. Modern Western culture has still not done away with all pre-modern culture in the West. There are still some islands of medieval culture, although they are ever less important. At the same time, modern culture is being subjected to harsh critiques at the hands of a program that is called post-modern, although it is quite doubtful that it is the harbinger of a new culture. The major thrust is still the conquest of the world by modern Western culture. And the church's main challenge today is the confrontation with modernity. Worse yet, as Western culture penetrates further into other cultures and on other continents, the conflict with the church is spreading further.

The drama lies in the fact that Western culture presents itself as the culture of liberation. The economy and politics and the new society are all regarded as ways to modernity. And so the church, which is opposed to modernity, looks like the great enemy of freedom; indeed, that is how the church has appeared since the seventeenth century. Today, especially in the South, Western culture is condemned as oppressive. But that does not mean that the church's pre-modern criticisms are right. What constitutes the liberation of culture? An accurate answer requires careful discernment.

Modern culture has a starting point clearly located in history. It began by adopting a new priority: the priority of the economic, i.e. the priority of production of material goods and services to transform material living conditions, and the priority of action to change the material world. That was the prospect of the scientific spirit that laid the foundations for the new culture.

With this new priority, everything began to change. The priority used to be contemplation and the order of the universe. The church has still not entirely put off that culture, even as it has been discovering the modern.

What can the cultural liberation of the poor mean in today's context when modern Western culture—which claims to be liberating, but whose claims are very much in question—is triumphing?

The Option for the Economy

This option is, as it were, the point where all the misunderstandings and all the ambiguities between the church and modernity converge. With rare exceptions, the moderns, whether liberal* or socialist, are not opposed to Christ or Christ's message; they condemn the church for being incapable of translating Christ's message into reality. They say—both liberals and socialists—that with its preaching and sacraments for two thousand years, the church has failed to put real charity into the lives of the various peoples; it

---

* Liberal in the European sense of those favoring capitalism and individual freedom, as opposed to conservatives, who favored tradition and were often linked to the church. Liberals tended to be anti-clerical. Trans.

has not changed anything. As their positive response, both liberals and social-ists offer modernity—that is, material production—as an effective means for saving human beings from their ills. They promise to accomplish what the church has not been able to bring about: a just and happy society.[1]

Today it would be easy to reply to the liberals and socialists that they have not fulfilled their promises[2]—even though it is not so clear that they have done any worse than the church; in some ways, they may have even done things better. The practical discernment question is this: what is liberating in modernity? What is oppressive? What has been worthwhile in the economic options made? What has been mistaken?

In the Hellenistic culture in which Christianity was so deeply inculturated, especially after Constantine, the supreme value was the order of the universe reflected in the order in human society. The supreme moral value was sub-mission to the law of the universe, the natural law. The human being's supreme achievement was to contemplate the order of the cosmos and accept it lovingly. There was no room for transforming activity. For each being had its calling marked by the place it occupied in the universe: certain humans had been born to be slaves and others to be free—there was no discussion. Indeed, wanting to change the order of things was the sin of pride, that is, of revolt against the eternal order. Even when freedom was recognized, it was more of a drawback than a benefit. The stars in the heavens were the exemplar; the model science was astronomy inasmuch as it could describe an immutable and perfect order. Human freedom was flawed when com-pared to the perfect order of the stars that never rebelled.

It is clear why Galileo aroused such passionate opposition; for his trial two cultures were in conflict. Galileo was delving into the stars, which were the foundation for the whole edifice of culture, the value system, and the order in the universe. Galileo was threatening the foundation of all moral-ity and all religion when he touched the order of the heavenly bodies. In the Hellenistic culture adopted by Christianity, the only options open to free-dom were either to submit or not to submit to the order of the cosmos, that is, to God's will. In this context, there was no possible way to ground a con-cept of liberation. The only possible liberation was liberation from sin which consisted in submitting once more to Order or to God's Law inscribed in nature.

Hence, all the modalities of transforming action and social change pre-sent in the New Testament were concealed or repressed; there was no place for them in the cultural framework in which christendom had placed Christianity. Much is said in the gospels about social change, change in the relationship between rich and poor, people and authorities, and so forth. The Hellenistic cultural coating prevented all that from finding expression. There was no place for liberation in the history of Christian theology from the time of Constantine to the Reformation, which questioned the way Hellenism and Aristotle held christendom in thrall.

Fortunately, culture could never completely envelop all Christians. Even when christendom seemed completely static and the world seemed to be living on the basis of the most perfect "order," there were always minorities who did not submit and who discovered in the gospels different motivations and energies for action and for changing the world. They were the "mystics" or the "spirituals," who were almost always viewed with suspicion because they were not content simply to repeat what was said by the learned. There were some who, like Bartolomé de las Casas, challenged the inculturated theology of Sepulveda. As a rule such prophets were defeated. They are being rehabilitated only in recent decades when the church's traditional alliance with Hellenistic culture has been considerably shaken.

Today modern Western culture is beginning to be confronted and condemned in the name of liberation. It would be a very serious illusion, however, to think that the future of culture will be a matter of returning to christendom's past.[3] Post-modern aspirations are not intended to renounce aspirations toward liberation. On the contrary, they are heightening the claims of freedom. Modernity is not being accused of having sought freedom, but of failing to pursue liberation consistently.[4]

The Option for Science

The seed of the option for the economy was already present in the option for science as the core of culture. Science has radically shaken the credibility of the culture of christendom, to the point of destroying it. Science has discredited the teaching authority of the church and of its anointed teachers; it has destroyed the argument from authority and dissolved all the symbolic constructions by which human beings previously understood the world. Thus science has broken down barriers and has opened the way for unrestrained social forces, such as capitalism, which had been kept in check during the middle ages.

Science has promoted acting in the material world to put it at the service of human beings. Transforming the material world would enable people to struggle more successfully against the traditional evils afflicting humankind, and so be the driving force of its liberation. This idea has been present since the Renaissance. For the ancients, liberation meant bringing the body under the control of the spirit. For modern science, liberation means improving the body through material things.

The science of the material world was developing throughout the middle ages. The architects who built the cathedrals, castles, palaces, and monasteries had very sophisticated scientific knowledge. Monks, too, developed scientific knowledge as they developed agriculture, water systems, and artisanry. The church raised no objections as long as science did not touch the foundations of the culture of christendom: astronomy, the world of the spirits, the relationship between body and soul. Thus the problem was not science in itself but rather the conflict with the ideals of culture with which the church was identified.

This is not the only case where a dominant culture opposed the movement of science. It has been noted that at the beginning of the Christian era, the

Greeks had everything that would have made possible an expansion of science, but society chose other values and the advance was halted. The same thing happened in the Arab world, and prior to that in the world of Chinese culture, where many inventions remained unexploited because the dominant culture was not interested in them.

It was not scientific discoveries that constituted a novelty in the West between the fifteenth and seventeenth centuries, but the fact that they aroused interest in society and became part of the beginnings of a new culture. They served as a foothold for creating a new culture after the old one was destroyed. Galileo's trial was nothing new: that was common, one more repetition of the age-old story. The new element was that Galileo's trial caused a stir and became a banner in the uprising against the church's teaching authority. It was the signal that the ancient culture was being rejected in its core, and that a new culture was emerging.

Scientific Reason

Science gives priority to observation of facts. It therefore has to isolate "facts" and dissect the world of perception into millions of particular "facts," each of them an object to be observed. To be truly scientific, observation must be confirmed by experimentation. Such is analytic reason. In the event of a conflict between observation and deductive arguments based on comprehensive ideas about the world or life, science sticks with observation and rejects arguments from unifying reason—that includes a rejection of the argument from authority.[5]

The visible accordingly becomes the supreme authority and disqualifies the invisible. The huge mass of symbolic and imaginary speculations stirring in people's minds for thousands of years collapses. The symbolic vision of the world and life that reached its culmination in the Baroque culture of the seventeenth century comes tumbling down.

The church saw the threat: it felt that the entire edifice of material and spiritual culture was going to be annihilated if the scientific vision were to be victorious. It could not let go of a culture that had produced so many works. It was unwilling to let go of a theology that seemed to it to be inseparably united to dogma. It resisted—and it organized resistance. It mobilized Catholic kings and princes, although it found them ever less enthusiastic. The kings recognized that forging an alliance with a backward church could only undermine the credibility of their power.

Scientists had a powerful argument: their science produced effects, and their predictions came true. Many began to imagine the benefits that the scientific method might provide if it were to develop. For a long time, scientists continued to combine fragments of the former world-view with its symbolic reasons with their new analytic knowledge. It may be that a purely scientific kind of thinking with nothing from the previous "imaginary" is impossible. In any case, analytic methods spread faster and faster. Since 1950, that expansion has been so rapid that more things are discovered in one decade than throughout the entire previous history of humankind.

Today there is nothing untouched by science. Everything comes from science, everything is artificial. There is no longer any natural food or drink, there is no longer any natural water or rain. The air we breathe is no longer natural. Scientific knowledge has advanced to the point where it occupies the entire earth. Science brings change, sets things in motion, and causes things to interreact.[6]

In the twentieth century, science has gone into industry, thereby enabling it to develop without limits. The only limit to science is time: the time needed to invent something new. This time is ever shorter, however. By the time new discoveries are made known they are already out of date. In the time needed for them to be communicated, new knowledge modifying the previous knowledge has already appeared.

Science and Power

Science seeks and attains power; that is how it has been since the outset. Scientists sought not to contemplate the world but to conquer it, to achieve new effects in order to better the human condition. Science has obtained what it sought. Yet, for a long time its effects were limited, and scientists themselves did not become rich with their inventions. Since the turn of the century, however, scientific discoveries have had ever more important applications in industry, medicine, and now in communications.

Today, science offers a great deal of money and grants a great deal of power, but that money and power are increasingly in the hands of the great economic conglomerates. The universities themselves enter into agreements with economic conglomerates. Scientists work for large companies. The power of science is part of the power of a company, and profit from scientific discoveries increases capital.

Not only does science create power. Many observers of contemporary society believe that science is becoming the primary power. In the competition between multinationals, science is increasingly the decisive factor, and the companies that want to win have to invest increasingly in scientific research.[7]

In their initial intention, scientists were seeking the power to improve human life. Today they no longer have control over their own power; the power of science is largely subordinated to economic power. Today inventors and discoverers increasingly need expensive devices, costly infrastructure, and expensive means of communications so that their discoveries can enter into the scientific circulation of the world. Scientists can no longer do research alone and at their own expense. They are cogs in a machinery that they do not control.

Nevertheless, from the outset science has been pursuing economic purposes. It did not anticipate that it would become so much a part of economic life to the point where it is becoming the main economic actor. What is happening today was inherent in its first aspirations. In short, the scientific option was an economic option.

In their own private lives, most scientists have continued to hold on to the traditional symbols and the symbolic representations of the world, and have been faithful members of their churches. However, the scientific movement as such runs up against this traditional culture and casts it out forever. Taken as a group in history, scientists establish a power that they do not control. Science has an inner drive that is independent of the intentions of its main practitioners.

Economic Science

For centuries physics was the reigning science. It was in the world of physics that the analytic method was best applied and where the most spectacular results were obtained. In the last century, the aim of making economics a science was announced. Today economics claims the status of a science, and economists are highly respected; they are entrusted with governing society. Economics seems to be a summation of all the sciences, the science that grants each particular science its role in the evolution of humankind. Economists are garbed in the prestige of science, thereby enabling them to present themselves as specialists in society, capable of guiding societies scientifically. Today's societies appear to have achieved the hope toward which the ideologists of the last century, whether liberal or socialist, were pointing: the hope of a society run by science, the science in question being economics.

This would seem to be the end point of making the economy the core of the culture, but there is no consensus on this point. Many scientists are unwilling to recognize that there could be a comprehensive science capable of providing a model for the entire society. All sciences are continually subdividing, and the condition for their success is their particularization; thus, there is no such thing as a science of the whole. Contemporary "economicism" would hence be the expression of an ideology—one more ideology among the countless others that have arisen, and hence it would live outside the scope of science.[8]

Production

The great myth of the bourgeoisie was production.[9] The abundance of material objects would resolve all ills, save humankind from poverty, and create equality between all human beings. Freedom and equality were to be the result of the abundance of material goods. Scarcity was regarded as the cause of domination and inequality. Thus, the economy would bring about what Christian charity had never succeeded in fashioning: a society of free human beings, equal, and all one family. That is why industrialization found support in society, despite the horrors of the factories, and likewise why the battle for productivity is also accepted by society and is the inspiration for a consumer society. Today the productive machinery can produce much more than is necessary, but in doing so, a strange dynamic is created: producing for the sake of producing. If needs are satisfied, new needs have to be created so that the products of industry can be sold.

Socialism claimed to be the system that would produce best, by creating the conditions for a society of free and equal human beings. The notion was that the contradictions of capitalism would thereby be avoided. Socialism therefore had to win: its greater economic efficiency would assure it of victory. But that was not how things turned out, and faithful to their principles, the socialist leaders have withdrawn. Now capitalists think that capitalism is the only route toward achieving vast production.

Indeed, capitalism has been able to produce a quantity of goods that no one, even in the nineteenth century, would have dared to imagine. And it produces ever more products that compete on the market. Today, no one doubts that production can be increased unlimitedly. The question that arises is this: is such ever-rising production still a valuable goal? Does it still provide meaning for a culture completely oriented toward it? These questions arise alongside the perennial contradictions of capitalism, namely that despite the bounty it produces, it does not provide everyone with what they need.

The Reign of the Market

Until the great migration from the countryside to the city, only a small portion of what was produced, few goods and even fewer services, went through the market. Almost all services were free since they were performed within the family. In the urban environment it is almost impossible for a person to live off what he or she produces; everything passes through the market. City dwellers need to buy almost everything they consume. They have to purchase more and more services. They have to buy or rent their house or apartment (even if they live in a shantytown). They have to pay for the preparation of food and drink. They have to pay for cleaning services and trash pickup. They are ever more dependent on other persons and have to pay them. The simplest recreations, games, and sports: you have to pay for everything. Thus, everything enters into the market.

Money thus becomes the measure of all things, and everything is assessed in quantitative rather than qualitative terms. Despite attempts to react by seeking "quality of life," it is quantity that prevails. Goods and services are of value not because of their intrinsic qualities, but because of their market cost. A famous soccer player is worth so many million, a model so many million, a house so many million, a dress so many thousand, a meal in a restaurant so much, and so forth.

The trend is toward the one-dimensionality of life that Marcuse condemned years ago, but which has been growing ever more. Economic value is the ultimate norm. This one-dimensionality must bring advantages; after all, it is accepted by the vast majority of people. Many women, for example, experience their entry into the labor market—instead of doing household tasks for free—as a liberation. They would rather prepare meals at a lunch counter all day long than prepare a meal for the family at home. Entering the market grants status. In a culture dominated by production, a person who is not paid for production feels devalued.

The option for the market, the option for the economy, and the option for production are all-embracing options of Western peoples and increasingly of other peoples who are entering into this same circle. The older generations initially resist and defend their traditional values. Then young people join the new culture and become its promoters.

A few minorities raise criticisms. But their critiques cannot conceal the massive fact of the option for the consumer society made by all social classes. What is the dream of the poor in Brazil? To also be able to buy, to use money for buying. It is not so much the usefulness of the objects that they are seeking as the act of buying and owning the things, because they have understood that owning is what the new culture is all about.

Globalization of Culture

The option for the economy has had one initially unanticipated consequence: culture itself has become part of the market and has become an economic good. Culture is ever more subordinated to the economy. Indeed, as technologies and artificial production processes advance ever more rapidly, culture has begun to use more and more tools created by technology. The culture or culture-communicating industries are the most important in the world today. The second greatest export of the United States after aircraft is the export of the objects of the cultural industry (recordings, films, videos, cassettes, etc.).

Music is distributed through a huge recording industry. The plastic arts are reproduced in photographs. Literature reaches the popular masses through the films that it inspires, and film brings together all the plastic arts. Today commercialization invades culture to such an extent that there are few locations where there still remains a spontaneous culture—one not driven by the market (whose advertising takes place primarily on TV).

The reduction of culture to the market is having grave consequences: in the market the strongest emerge victorious and their weaker competitors are eliminated. The fact is that over the course of the twentieth century the United States has been at the forefront of all techniques for industrializing culture. Since World War II it has conquered the market, and has to share it only with the Japanese. Americans and Japanese now dominate the culture market; they decide what is going to be sold on the market. They are the distributors of culture, now that spontaneous culture with a personal imprint occupies less and less room.

The economic power dominating the market has many ways to control culture itself. Whoever dominates the form, dominates the content. People speak of a globalization of culture; it is an extension of the globalization of the economy. Today's world culture is not something new: it is not a new creation inherently universal, superior to all particular cultures. To this day there has never been a universal culture in the sense of an expression of the human being as universal. Nor has there been a universal culture in the sense of a cultural merging fashioned by combining all particular cultures. Globalized culture is a particular culture: North American culture. It has even managed to largely invade its Japanese competitor. It is eliminating the old European cultures and invading the entire world.

How account for the triumph of North American culture in today's cultural world? The reasons are primarily economic. In order to understand this, one would probably have to take into account certain features inherent in North American culture.

European cultures were aristocratic and elitist. The people themselves used to take part in aristocratic culture—all worked at the service of the aristocracy as domestic servants, artisans, or peasants. They were involved in elite culture, acting in it as servants. They were present in the dining hall of the aristocrats—even though they did not eat the same meals.

When the new masses took shape in the urban industrial world, European society had nothing to offer them. Quite the contrary, in the twentieth century, aristocratic culture has become increasingly elitist. The United States has created a mass culture, that is, a culture adapted to its "middle class": the class of industrial and service workers. And that culture has spread around the world. The greatest symbol of American culture is Coca-Cola. For European cultures, which have thousands of brands of wine or beer, Coca-Cola is an abomination, an anti-beverage, a beverage for uncultured people. But Coca-Cola is nevertheless invading the entire world, and all nations are giving up their traditional drinks in order to take up Coca-Cola. Sheer propaganda? Simply the result of advertising, a sign of the power of those who have enough money to conquer the world? Or is Coca-Cola perhaps the kind of drink that ordinary people enjoy, something exactly suited to their sensibility?

In any case, the culture that has become global is United States mass culture. It has conquered the middle classes in the Third World, and is reaching the urban masses of the poor through TV—which is simultaneously mass culture's best advertisement.[10]

United States Mass Culture

This culture is invading private life, displacing the firmest traditions of ancient peoples. Ways of eating and drinking and preparing meals are changing: fast food is ever more the norm. For example, the traditional noon meal is disappearing, as are family meals. Foods are increasingly following American taste: the hamburger, which to European traditions is odious, is winning out in all countries—with American seasonings. From the standpoint of traditional culture, American cuisine is a non-cuisine. Even so, the new generations are making it a symbol of emancipation and progress. The same thing is happening with beverages. American mixed drinks are eliminating people's traditional drinks. For alcoholic drinks, whisky is the obligatory status symbol, not because it is Scotch, but because it is American.

In housing and city design, American models are the pattern for anyone who has money. Cities are planned as though they were auto racetracks. They are made to facilitate automobile traffic; any other considerations are secondary. Clothes and fashions are also American. People's clothing everywhere is becoming alike: North American fashion is taking over. This is generally justified on the grounds that it is more practical—even when it is not well suited to the local climate.

The use of English is inexorably making its way everywhere. Setting up computers in all services forces users to learn English words. Similarly, almost all technologies require the use of English. The kind of thinking and expression proper to the English language is tending to spread everywhere.

The Americans have created a television style, a way of communicating on television, and almost all the programs (the various genres) made for TV. They also dominate the film market, spreading throughout the whole world the myths, problems, and way of life of the middle class in the United States. They have created popular literature, the kinds of magazines (and malls) for men and for women, for youth and children.

The prevailing leisure, games, and sports are all American—with one glorious exception: soccer. The United States has not been able to replace soccer with their own baseball except in the Caribbean. What does that failure mean? Is it not simply an isolated exception?

Thirty years ago American travelers could be spotted immediately; they were different from everyone else. They looked so outlandish that people used to smile with amusement as they watched them go by. Today tourists around the world mimic Americans so well that their nationality can no longer be recognized. What seemed outlandish has become the norm.

A sign of the times is the obligatory pilgrimage of the middle classes to the Disney World shrine in Orlando, where the whole mythology of North American culture is presented. The crowds go not out of curiosity, but as though to a shrine, in order to learn the art of living, to learn how to be American; it is a true initiation. Of course, the poor cannot go there; that remains a dream deferred until later. Meanwhile, TV shows provide a substitute.

There is a style that is becoming universal, a set of means of expressions. When people have parties, even little parties out in the bush, they always try to imitate the American style spread by TV. There is no musician or singer who does not try to draw inspiration from American stars. What is leftover for other nations is very little. The quixotic tirades of the French in the Uruguay Round cannot halt the juggernaut: the Americanization of universal popular culture. Hence the uprising of religious integralisms, such as that of Muslims. Once the gates are opened, American culture conquers all.

Far from merely extending its mass culture to all, the United States also dominates scientific culture. Most scientific discoveries are made in the United States. That is where most of the scientists of the world are concentrated. Almost all Nobel prizes in science are won by Americans—or Europeans and Asians living and working in the United States, many of them now U.S.

citizens. Ninety percent of scientific publications are in English and those not published in English are disregarded. Something similar is true of artists.

The dream of most talented people is to head toward the United States, and it is their aspiration to emigrate there. That is the greatest triumph of the United States, greater than its military power or economic power: it has the power to attract the most creative people in the human race—from all continents and from all races. Obviously, this attraction of the best talent is just what makes it different from everywhere else.

Turning Other Cultures into Folklore

All those who enter into the new culture find that traditional culture becomes something external to them; it becomes incomprehensible and loses all attraction. Converts to the new culture initially reject their past with a feeling of liberation. Entry into the new culture gives them the impression that they are freer—and more themselves. They experience the older cultures as a constraint and do not perceive what is confining in the new culture. Later on, they return to the old culture out of curiosity. For all other cultures are henceforth objects of curiosity, objects to observe, perhaps to study. All cultures have become, at a more elevated level, objects of scientific inquiry, objects of anthropology. Little by little, all peoples, seduced by worldwide culture, are discovering their own culture as something alien, something that can no longer be lived.

In the most vulgarized form, cultures are turned into objects for tourism, since tourism is becoming a major money-making activity. Millions of tourists are continually looking for new things and soon they will number in the hundreds of millions.

These tourists are seeking new things in other lands. But that is not enough. Cultures are also the object of curiosity. Anything that peoples produce culturally can become an object of tourism: religious and sacred objects, philosophies, traditions of family, tribe, and peoples, celebrations and customs, clothing, food, and so forth.

Facing this avalanche of tourism, some peoples attempt to close their doors, or at least their hearts. They do not look and do not allow themselves to be seen. They do not want to be photographed by tourists. Temptation is strong, however. Many sell their culture to tourists. Indigenous people sell religious objects as though they were profane—and they know that they will be profaned. They sell their celebrations, their ceremonies: they become a spectacle in order to get money from tourists. They turn their culture into a merchandise—just like the Dutch who on holidays put on their traditional clothing to give tourists the impression that they are faithful to their customs. Likewise, any Brazilian display for tourists needs its women from Bahia all dressed up for folklore—for the sole purpose of selling tourists an illusion. That is how culture is turned into folklore.

At the end of this path peoples present the roots of their own past as a folklore show, with the illusion that they are descendants of their ancestors.

(People from São Paulo or Paraná playing at being Italians or Germans.) But such shows are really dead. People cherish the illusion that the culture of the past is being maintained, but they are deluding themselves. They are tourists to themselves.

A good portion of the Catholic church has become folklore: museum churches, liturgical ceremonies that attract tourists, the assault of photographers or TV that reduces everything to the condition of being an object of folklore. What do the millions of tourists think in the presence of the material remains of what used to be christendom? What is worse is that they don't think anything.

Consumer culture is something all peoples want to achieve. The invaders are now welcomed as liberators. Precisely because the new culture seems to be liberating, it is harder to resist. What can peoples confronting such a situation do? Can this trend which is so strong be modified in any way? In the name of what?

Consumer Culture

In traditional culture, most people, if not all, were actively involved. There were many people's poets, many people's musicians. All artisans were artists in their own way. There were many painters and sculptors, and there were many theater groups: every town had its own. Each village had its band and its singers.

Once culture becomes an economic value, the culture market eliminates anyone unable to compete. Since culture entails investment, and hence capital, competition eliminates the weakest. Few have access to mass distribution. The rest are left without an audience. Culture industries manufacture and promote some stars. The various companies compete trying to push their stars as far as possible.

There has to be a continual turnover of stars, new productions, an infinite ability to attract the public: they are selling culture and they have to conquer the market. They have to create their market by attracting attention. They are taken in by their own advertising. Ultimately culture is advertising and advertising is culture.

Individuals among the masses realize that they aren't stars, and their cultural production is of no worth. They become discouraged; they are abandoned. Popular artists become objects of local folklore, at best; they are one more thing for tourists to see. Some popular artists accept this humiliation in order to survive. But that isn't culture. From being producers of culture, the multitudes become consumers. They pay to go to the show, for the show never stops, and TV makes it available to everyone.

There accordingly occurs the dissociation between objectivity and subjectivity, so much trumpeted by modernity. Until this century, this affected only a tiny portion of the population, those who had access to money. In the twentieth century the economy has invaded the culture of entire peoples. Now all are invited to provide the consuming public. They have to have something to consume. The figures measuring audience are fundamental for TV or radio stations, and for the entire culture industry. There have to be lots of buyers; failure to create a sufficient number of consumers forces one out of the market.

The culture items consumed on the world market are increasingly the same: they come from American industry. Naturally, each people consumes these products in its own manner: it introduces imported products in its own subjective way. Even so, a subjectivity that does not elaborate its own things gradually loses its identity. Its subjectivity becomes unsure, and restless, and begins to doubt itself. That is why peoples today, especially the weaker ones, are going through a great identity crisis. Their response to cultural invasion is to aggressively assert their own personality. However, that assertion is lacking in solid content and becomes ever less tangible, a sheer claim of a subject with no content. The person turns into a claim, seeking to be recognized as a person. Since the subject cannot even see or show its own works, it can at least aspire to be a person. It thinks that it will attain personality through acknowledgment by others. That is why cultural rights are asserted.

The separation between producer and consumer has invaded all areas of culture. If persons do not hold onto an area of life where they can salvage the unity that used to exist in the older cultures, there will be no remedy. On the one hand, we will have the triumph of the culture market, and on the other, millions of restless consumers seeking their lost personalities. What is true of peoples is also true of individual persons.

Critique of Globalized Culture

Globalization is a process; it is the consequence of the subordination of culture to the economy. The new globalized culture is able to work its way into all countries because it succeeded in arousing people's enthusiasm, starting with the young. The fact that the young are a majority in the countries of the South makes penetration easier. Even so, the market's conquest of culture does not take place with no resistance or critique. We are spectators—but also participants—in the struggle between traditional cultures and the new culture. Let us examine the forces opposing cultural conquest.

Resistance

Socialism

Paradoxically, and contrary to what it sought to do, socialism has helped maintain traditional cultures. Its fall unleashed the invasion of globalized market culture.

Socialism sought to be "scientific" and professed a radical economics: the communist revolution was to issue from the abundance of material goods. In principle, economics had absolute priority. Socialist development, however, fell far short of expectations. In practice, it kept peoples at a rather low consumption level. It wanted to impose a common ideology, the ideology of the party, but the means used to impose it on everyone were completely counterproductive. People became all the more attached to their traditions. As a rule, until 1989 the culture of the socialist peoples was far more traditional than that of capitalist countries.

Beneath the official culture there survived an underground culture in which religion, not economics, was the core. Although persecuted, religion resisted communist regimes better than it did while enjoying privileges in capitalist countries. We need only recall the example of the Catholic church in Poland. As soon as socialism fell, the confrontation with globalized culture brought greater havoc than forty years of persecution.

The cultures of more primitive peoples

To some extent poorer peoples are protected by their very poverty. That is the situation of the indigenous peoples of the Americas and of the cultures of the tribes who are still living by themselves in Africa, India, and Oceania, and in the more remote locations in Asia. They are not very concerned about the market (and vice versa). They still live largely in a closed economy. Under such conditions they can maintain their customs.

The problem is that in such regions from the moment that something (e.g., oil, minerals, wood) begins to interest the market, the people can put up little resistance to invasion, and destruction comes swiftly. They find themselves in a cruel dilemma. Such peoples often believe that their future lies in independence and so they struggle to remain isolated, protected against destructive contacts. But as they continue along these lines, they become weaker and weaker until the moment of an encounter that is almost inevitably bound to occur. Yet if they adopt the other alternative and try to assimilate, the white man arrives, and they run the great risk of being "absorbed" and of being placed on the lowest rung of industrial society. Does the solution lie in adopting something in between? But what must you do to remain in an intermediate position—one that you can control—as you maneuver around the danger of falling unintentionally into what you were striving to avoid?

The great Asian religions

The strongest barrier to the conquest of the world by American culture is constituted by the great Asian religions: Islam, Hinduism, Buddhism, and Confucianism. These religions are not centralized organizations like the Catholic church. By that very fact they do not seek to draw up strategies or plans for conquest. Islam sometimes goes back to the dream of the caliphate, but it is unlikely to reestablish it in the current political context. Nevertheless, these religions penetrate so deeply into the everyday life of peoples that they are able in fact to form strong barriers. Political or cultural movements emerge within them, seeking to block the entry of the West's cultural goods— and with some degree of success.

That is true only to a limited extent, however. The world religions themselves are suffering from deep internal divisions. Integralist movements seek to close all doors and defend traditional culture in its entirety. They fear any kind of contact with the West as a risk of contamination. Yet, other tendencies are more open to dialogue. The traditions of these religions themselves are more open to dialogue than the integralist tendencies. Within each religion, the "liberals" can invoke testimonies, texts, and antecedents that favor communication and even the assimilation of things from outside. Others realize that Western culture has positive aspects: science for overcoming superstition, production for overcoming dire poverty, and democracy for overcoming traditional patriarchal authoritarianism.

Christianity

Christianity could offer guidance to other religions if there were more dialogue, since it has experienced the confrontation of the new culture within the West itself. Christianity has acted in two opposite ways. In Europe, the Catholic church and the churches that emerged from the Reformation generally took up a defensive posture. They increasingly sensed that the new culture was a threat to their historic inheritance, to their message and their presence in the world. Actually, the moderns have usually not been opposed to Jesus Christ. As a rule, they have sought to carry out the message of Jesus either without the churches—which they accused of betraying their founder—or, when necessary, against the churches. Hence, the resistance of the churches to modernity encountered systematic persecution in only a few instances. That was what happened in the French revolution and its expansion in Europe and in the former Soviet Union and its satellites. However, the struggle has been constant since the mid-seventeenth century, when the victorious culture began to move away from the church and the church from it. Baroque culture was the last hurrah of a Christian culture, the last great manifestation of christendom. After that, the history of the church became the history of a long defensive action. The Catholic church struggled step by step to defend christendom; it lost every battle. The other churches sometimes thought that they could benefit from the losses of the Catholic church, but they ended up taking the same positions (except for churches rooted in the people, like the Methodists).

Vatican II brought changes. This Council was prepared for by theologians, intellectuals, popularizers, and Catholic politicians who had struggled for three hundred years for a more positive alternative vis-à-vis modernity. For three hundred years, they made up an ever suspect minority, and were often condemned. At Vatican II, they were finally able to present their alternative, and it became part of the conciliar texts to some extent. Yet no really radical change took place: the spirit of Vatican II survives only among a minority in the Catholic church, even though it can call on conciliar texts for support.

The upshot of this struggle is that the percentage of the baptized who actually follow the guidelines of the Catholic church or take part in the activities that it proposes has fallen and continues to drop. The vast majority of Catholics retain certain ties to Catholicism, but in their everyday practice they make no commitment. They remain critical and mistrustful toward the church, even while they respect Christ, with whom, however, they are increasingly unfamiliar. The other churches have developed along more or less the same lines in their respective countries, while making more concessions to modern culture. They have also lost many members—even more than the Catholic church.

In the United States, Christians have taken another path: they have identified with their society. Most Christians belong to churches that started from below, the self-described free churches. These latter have set the tone and others have followed. The result is what is called American "civil religion." Christianity has shaped itself to fit North American culture to such an extent that being American and being Christian (or Judeo-Christian so as to include Jews) have become almost the same thing. The emphasis is on the moral aspect of religion, that is, its practical aspect. Differences between denominations do not matter much because the central message is the identification of the American way of life with the gospel. Christianity has become the idealization of the American dream and American myths.

This is how Western Christianity has lived out the dilemma of the great world religions: stand in opposition and risk losing every battle, or enter into the new culture and risk being assimilated by it.

Science vis-à-vis the Critique

Before considering the critiques, it must be emphasized that for its practitioners science has been and is experienced as a movement of liberation. All science arises from the critique of previous systems of knowledge. Scientific work frees people from the domination of illusions and superstitions that have dominated human beings throughout history. Until modern science, human beings took their bearings from symbolic reason. They accepted systems of ideas or images that were incompatible, and whose practical applications only augmented the ills of humankind. We need only recall the bizarre things done by traditional healers, the use of magic rituals, or invocations to the gods to resolve the ills of humankind. It is the vocation of scientists to break away from a world of human ignorance and stupidity. Hence, they have often had the idea that they are the vanguard of humankind in the conquest of truth over error, of justice over exploitation by the strong, and of the true good over all illusions.

Indeed, millions of scientists have been devoted to science as if it were the new priesthood. The practice of science requires rigor, discipline, and self-denial in order to accept what observation reveals, and not to delude oneself and others when experience runs against the desired outcomes. Scientific work during the past three or four centuries is one of the most extraordinary and fascinating achievements in the history of humankind. The Western world rightly thrills with the epic adventure of science. Many have even imagined that the adventure of science could replace the adventure of war in the imaginations of humankind.[11]

Nevertheless, as science has developed, critiques have been forthcoming. The critiques have come first from the resistance put up by traditional religions and older philosophies. In this century, the crises arise from the heightened awareness of scientists and other persons who are more aware of where society is going. The critiques are not merely yearnings for the past, but warnings about the direction taken by the scientific movement as a whole.

Critique of scientism

In view of the success achieved by physics in the seventeenth and eighteenth centuries, the Enlightenment reached the point of conceiving what St.-Simon and Comte in the nineteenth century would call the scientific age of the world. They imagined that science could fashion an overall representation of the world, and would provide a substitute for the previous philosophical or theological visions. Henceforth science would provide what was sought in religions and philosophies: knowledge of reality. The difference would be that, while theologies and philosophies had told falsehoods produced by the imagination, science would provide the truth about the world, based upon observation of reality.

Throughout the twentieth century, however, it has become ever more obvious that science cannot provide an overall vision of the world. Nor does it claim to do so. First, there is no single science. Sciences keep subdividing in a seemingly unending process. Making progress requires analyzing more deeply and defining objects of observation that are ever more multifaceted. If science is to make progress, it must continue to be fragmented. The result is a huge accumulation of fragments of knowledge. No one could have even a superficial knowledge of all the sciences. No one could know all of physics or all of biology. A good scientist is one who is completely familiar with a thousandth or even a millionth of what is to be known scientifically. There is no longer any such thing as a scientific view of reality. Science is no longer interested in reconstructing a single world view. Henceforth there will be no single view of the world. If some sciences convey the impression that they are presenting a view of the whole, they do so only by wrapping their data in fragments of the old mythologies, thereby creating the impression that they constitute an overall vision.

Sciences identify relationships between objects of experience and make it possible to foresee certain effects. That enables them to achieve spectacular effects. However, they are not in a position to say why that is so.

It is true that scientists elaborate hypotheses on the basis of certain experiments in order to be able to experiment with other effects. Hypotheses are always provisional, however. They exist in order to be subjected to criticism. Hypotheses are made to be refuted and replaced by others that are more all-encompassing or less conditioned by residues of mythology, and they are always attached to the concepts of those formulating them.

Until the nineteenth century, physics seemed to be the queen of the sciences. It seemed capable of encompassing in itself all beings in the world, so that some day it would fashion a single grand science of physics. In the nineteenth century the role of being the reigning science was conferred on political economy, the human science that garbed itself with the features of scientific rigor. Naturally, political economy will never achieve the rigor of physics. It will never be possible to isolate its objects in the same way. It will never be possible to find two economic facts as similar as two molecules. Never will it be possible to have economic facts, which are always so complex, be repeated. Never will the human sciences have the predictive capabilities of the sciences of dead matter.

Hence, the scientism based on political economy was the most fragile of all. To the extent that anyone sought to make political economy a general theory and a vision of humankind, the actual result was that ideologies were created in pseudo-scientific guise: Marxism, positivism, and liberalism. The writers of post-modernity have proclaimed the death of the great ideologies. But that death did not affect the sciences. Indeed, the sciences have continued developing ever more. Scientists have not lost their prestige. They are sought out and the media have made oracles out of anything they have to say on any topic.

Science and power
The debates among scientists over building and using the atomic bomb by the United States after World War II were a first signal. Science could apparently make a decisive contribution to military power. Since then the problem has grown: even today, after the fall of the Soviet Union, an impressive cohort of scientists is dedicated to the pursuit of new weapons.[12]

Scientific discoveries used to occur by chance and reflected the vagaries and inclinations of individual researchers. Today scientific research entails large amounts of capital. Capitalists direct the pursuit. Research cannot be directed at any object whatsoever; discoveries are aimed at conquering the market. Researchers are increasingly employees of companies; their research is governed by the company's goals.

Many scientists are concerned. Researchers have lost control over what they invent. They can no longer anticipate what will be done with their discoveries, and they cannot guide their use. Once the discovery is put to use, scientists can no longer control its consequences. It is clearer today that the effects of new discoveries are not always benign.

The sciences increase the virtual powers of humankind and it is good that that happens. But who harnesses these powers? Who transforms science into technology and that into industry?

The sciences are good and are always valuable. The critique is prompted by the use made of science. In today's society, who could take charge of directing scientific research? Because of the option for the economy, the owners of the economy take that control for themselves, and most people remain indifferent or even think that that is fine. In fact, the sciences are subordinated to economics. Any discovery that is not of economic interest is not going to be picked up. Problems connected with science are now recognized as problems of the economy.

The Critique of Political Economy

Critique of production

Capitalism and socialism have shown themselves to be two variants of the same cultural option, the option for the economy. Indeed, in the West there is a basic consensus in the dynamic portions of society: the goal is production. The supreme criterion is growth of production. Nations are valued in terms of their GDP. TV, radio, and periodicals continually offer data on production. Statistics are the basis for assessing worth.

Production is the great myth of the bourgeoisie; the work ethic was created for no other reason than to foster production. Certainly, production has increased astonishingly throughout the twentieth century, reaching levels that no one would have imagined. Societies are governed in such a way as to increase their production.

All this is true, but production—at least as it is presently being implemented—does not resolve the problems of dire poverty, the basic needs of a good portion of the population, or unemployment, which affects up to 25% of the work force in Spain, for example. This emphasis on production enables a minority to accumulate ever greater wealth. Any reforms, any proposals for redistribution, are considered impossible because they would keep production from rising. Production has thus become an idol to which the lives of whole peoples are sacrificed.

To these considerations we must add the ecological argument, which demonstrates that production at any cost does not make sense. Production is not about simply bringing new things into the world. Production comes from transforming material goods that were once in nature. In past centuries it was thought that people could take from nature whatever was there; nature's bounty seemed to be infinite. Taking things away from nature did not seem to harm anyone. Materials were first taken from nature, and then returned to it in the form of trash and toxic gasses. Nature seemed able to absorb them without limit.

Ecology has now come to the fore, enabling people to become aware of the earth's limits. But production has already expanded to the point where it has begun to seriously disturb the balance of the earth. The changes are so grave that they could harm the earth's inhabitants. Industry corrupts nature. Production is also destruction; there is no production without destruction. Production entails a cost that economics has never taken into account. It assumes that production does not destroy anything, but in fact it wreaks havoc.

Ecology has made it possible to discover that the current "American way of life" cannot be extended without thereby rendering life on earth no longer viable. Production cannot continue at its present pace; it has to cease or change. Unless changes are implemented, the earth will become uninhabitable. Today's excessive production remains as it is only because of the criminal indifference of the privileged, who are unwilling to lose any of their advantages.[13]

From now on, in a rationally governed society, production will have to be limited and guided according to the possibilities of nature and the primary needs of humankind. We are far, infinitely far, from such an awareness. Meanwhile it is the poor who are the primary victims of ecological disasters and imbalances in production. Hence they are probably the only ones capable of struggling for a rational guidance of the planet.

Critique of political economy as science

In its origins political economy was the science that sought to organize how goods are shared in the population. Over time it has become increasingly the science of production. Production has become the primary economic function.[14] After World War II, when the economy of the warring powers had to be reorganized, economists assumed a major role. Economic science was finally being given the priority that its devotees had hoped for in the nineteenth century. The neoliberal offensive, to which the third wave of industrial transformation opened the way, has anointed the economists: they have taken over the IMF and the World Bank, and have become the obligatory advisors to all of the weaker states. Economics is imposed on nations as an obligatory guide. The goal is always production. Science has become a government program imposed by international agencies, in practice serving the needs of the great multinational conglomerates.

Within postmodernity, a revolt is taking place against the dictatorship of an economic science that legitimizes the program of particular groups and confers on them a diploma of rationality.

Third-world countries are particularly sensitive to the prestige of economic science, which to them looks like the secret of the power of the more industrialized nations. Their economists study at American schools and rigorously apply the recipes taught there as though they were the revelation of the truth. They do not realize all the ideological aspects included in so-called "economic science," nor the fragmentary nature of the observations on which it is based. As a rule there is no discussion of the extent to which economics is really scientific. Moreover, a theory worked out in a particular social and cultural context cannot be applied just as it is in other conditions.

Ethics and Religion

What is happening with ethics and religion in culture today?

With regard to ethics: the culture born in modernity—rooted in North American culture which is becoming global—presents itself as the embodiment of ethics; it is regarded as the basis for a society finally founded on ethics and liberated from the many forms of corruption found in traditional societies. Modernity ought to be the liberation of ethics or the advent of ethics in society.

With regard to religion: modernity is not opposed to religion but seeks to keep it confined to the world of private life. Indeed, neoliberalism has recently been offering religions a more active role in society. How are we to view such a situation?

Bourgeois Ethics

The bourgeois ethics that has little by little conquered the West until its culmination in the 1960s, when it managed to embrace almost all of Western society, has also penetrated into Latin America and in the petite bourgeoisies of the Third World. In Latin America, however, it has never succeeded in unseating the aristocratic morality inherited from the conquistadors nor the family morality of the poor. That is why the present crisis of bourgeois morality does not have such a great impact on Latin America, which is shifting from traditional morality to a post-bourgeois morality almost seamlessly.

The fundamental principle of bourgeois ethics was the clear distinction between private and public ethics. Indeed, women were always tied solely to private ethics since they were kept out of public life. For the bourgeoisie, the two types of ethics ought to have nothing to do with one another: each governed in a sovereign manner its own sphere.[15]

In private life the bourgeoisie wanted to maintain traditional values: the absolute value of the family (gradually reduced to its basic nucleus), the Ten Commandments, and honoring one's commitments. In public life, however, those same principles were subordinated to other values.

The supreme value is work. Work is supposedly the source of property. Hence, attachment to work is extended in the defense of private property. For the bourgeois, laziness is the worst vice and the source of all evil. Poverty is regarded as the result of laziness, and hence it does not deserve any compassion. For the bourgeoisie, public life gains strength especially in the market, and the market is a struggle. People all defend their own interests, that is, what they regard as the fruit of their work and as their legitimate property.

Public life is also the basis of the nation. The bourgeois identifies himself with the nation and helps it to prosper. He believes that the taxes he pays grants him the right to monitor government spending. The bourgeois struggles to break free from the lords of the land, and from the large families that live off the country and off their money, i.e., that of the bourgeoisie. The bourgeois stands in solidarity with the nation, not with the aristocracies who only know how to spend money that comes from the work of other people, nor with the very poor who are regarded as lazy, who don't want to work but "prefer" their miserable situation.

This bourgeois ethic finds expression in the "Declaration of the Rights of Man and Citizen." It is expressed in the form of rights rather than duties, as was the case in traditional morality. The bourgeois claims rights and defends rights. His ethic is, first and foremost, the defense of his own rights.

The national state sought to somehow extend the bourgeois morality throughout the nation. In the industrialized world it has succeeded to some extent—except for marginalized social classes, such as unemployed blacks in the United States or immigrant workers.

In Latin America, bourgeois morality was adopted by the middle classes and by intellectuals, who imitated Western society, as was bound to happen. However, they did not succeed in imposing it on the ruling classes, and hence this morality—even though it is inscribed in constitutions and law codes and stated in public speeches—has never been fully accepted.

What have been called violations of human rights result from the clash between the traditional morality of the elites and the bourgeois morality of the right of the citizen. During the military regimes, awareness of human rights violations stimulated the rise of strong movements struggling for ethics, that is, for bourgeois ethics.

During the military regimes repression also hit young intellectuals and middle-class political activists. For example, torture—a routine practice of the police when dealing with the lower classes—was also used on members of the middle class. This was what aroused indignation. There never was a demand for human rights among the popular classes, and the change of governments does not affect customary practice. Even so, a popular awakening is now taking place as a result of migration to the cities. Consciousness-raising is beginning among the poor and they are starting to react against traditional forms of oppression.

Consciousness-raising activists, non-governmental organizations, and also church-related organizations for the defense of human rights have recently set in motion a process that seeks to awaken a new popular consciousness. The popular classes are beginning to discover that sometimes the bourgeois ethic of human rights can be useful to them as well.

Of course, human rights are abstract principles—by themselves they are powerless. What gives them impact is social and political power, which, even in a limited way, serves the middle class. When it comes to the popular classes—which have almost no social, political, or economic clout—human rights remain on paper only. Those who trample the human rights of the poor are not in danger of being brought to justice.

To the extent that the poor manage to form active organizations that are recognized by the media, they will be able to make use of bourgeois ethics, and begin to invoke some human rights. Until that happens, they will prefer to have the protection of local chiefs, politicians, gangsters, traffickers, etc.

To this day, most poor people do not have the backing of strong organizations able to sustain an action on behalf of human rights. The ethic that remains is the residue of the traditional ethic of the rural world: the absolute value is the family, no matter how tattered and broken up. Loyalty to family is the highest virtue. Beyond the family, there are ties of dependence on those who have replaced lords and bosses and who in case of need can solve the problem. Loyalty to local leaders is the second principle of popular ethics.

"Christian ethics" by itself has no specific content. In the minds of the people it is identified basically with the ethics of family solidarity. To it is added the rule of hospitality, taking in wanderers or traveling beggars. But this is part of the family ethics in all traditional peoples, and is not specific to Christianity.

Evolution of the Bourgeois Ethic

Just when bourgeois ethics is making a timid appearance in Latin America it is in a deep crisis and real decline in the First World, where the moral crisis is much deeper. The moral crisis comes not so much from the masses; it is a crisis of the elites, that is, of their own moral degradation.

In recent years, there have appeared a series of scandals to which the media had previously turned a blind eye. The scandals in Italy lifted the veil covering the secret ties between politics, the mafia, and large corporations. There have been scandals in Spain, and then the huge scandal of the Crédit Lyonnais bank in France, one of the largest in the world, as well as the scandal of Barings Bank, one of the oldest institutions in England, and pension fund scandals in the United States. Billions of dollars disappear in such scandals—to be recovered through taxes. Some scandals have reached the point where they were condemned, but one can imagine that many others have managed to remain hidden.

Such scandals indicate how corrupt the ruling class is. It practices the morality of pirates and corsairs, thereby joining the traditional elites of Latin America, and the new elites who have taken power in the new nations.

Another sign of the disappearance of the bourgeois ethic is the spread of financial speculation. Every day more than a trillion dollars cross borders and change hands. Most of this capital is no longer for investment; it is for speculating. Speculation can be so strong that it destabilizes currencies and governments, destroys budgets of whole nations, ruins millions of small investors, and thrusts millions of workers into unemployment. Speculation itself has become a huge business. Meanwhile, it is claimed that there is no money for the most urgent needs of billions of people who are in a state of extreme poverty.

One more sign: the complicity of governments and of large manipulators of funds and of organized crime (drug traffic, for example) is obvious in tax havens. That is where everything is legitimized, everything is laundered, and all the immorality in the world can be piled up with impunity and can defy all those who still believe in ethical values. A huge amount of corruption by the elites is being uncovered little by little, but the corruption is reaching extremes now at the close of the twentieth century.

The decline of bourgeois ethics

Until a few years ago the bourgeoisie maintained a double morality. While practicing radical individualism in business and public life, e.g., never sparing the weak ("business is business"), in private life, they retained the traditional rules, and solidarity extended as far as the nation, in the framework of national legislation, according to the so-called "rule of law." Today the parents of the bourgeois ruling class are discovering to their horror that young people, including their own children, have abandoned all these traditional ways. They also are practicing radical individualism in private life as well. From now on there is only one morality: the morality of self-promotion. No more solidarity; the sense of the nation is disappearing. The new elites are withdrawing from the nation, enclosing themselves within the walls of their Edens (Alphavilles, beaches, tourist cities, dream cities—Miami, Las Vegas, the Pacific islands, Monaco, etc.).

Their elders are horrified and wonder how it is possible that such a "development" toward barbaric customs could have occurred in a generation that has received the most refined and sophisticated education that has ever existed. Horrified by this "development," they look for help and resources: who might restore ethical values to a class that has lost even its ethical sensibility? Indeed, this very shock and surprise prompts some observers to think that the elites themselves are the major problem.[16]

In public life, the traditional bourgeoisie was attached to two values: work and nation. The new generation has learned that wealth and social status come not from work but from information. Those who are in the know learn how to manipulate capital, sell their information for a very high price, get into the market at the right time, and always find someone else to do the work. From now on, it is knowledge that is valuable: knowledge enables people to engage in speculation and to defeat a competitor who got the information a few hours later. Indeed, work is now discredited. Increasingly, for the lower classes, work is becoming only a way to have holidays. You work so that you can have access—one month in the year and on weekends—to the situation of those who can "enjoy life without working."

With regard to the nation, the older generation used to feel solidarity with others, and they devoted their wealth largely to foundations or to aiding the less fortunate classes. They felt the call of social responsibility, albeit in a deeply paternalistic way. By contrast, the new generation has lost the sense of nationhood; they have no compassion for losers. What John Kenneth Galbraith calls the "culture of contentment" reigns. Among the elites, each individual pursues his or her satisfaction: comfort, welfare, security, tranquility, no troubles—utterly insulated from what might be happening to others. This is selfishness turned into an absolute norm. Of course this situation is a privilege that is only possible thanks to a very complex system for repressing and holding down the population so that no one will disrupt the peace of the secure areas.

Human rights

Human rights arose in an individualistic context and can be applied in a variety of ways. Primarily, they are tools for defending one's own interests. Whoever has the most power and can pay the best lawyers finds in human rights a powerful weapon of self-defense against competitors—or any person who arouses their disgust. Hence the vast amount of litigation in the United States and the ever growing number of lawyers.

The elites invoke human rights to struggle against a government seeking to collect taxes; to demand the freedom of the market, that is, the opportunity to dominate the market; to demand privatization, in the name of the superiority of private property, and so forth. In the name of human rights, they compel weaker countries to open their borders, all the while lobbying to keep the borders of their own country closed.

The defense of the human rights of the weak is a different matter: their human rights can be invoked only if powerful institutions or well-known prophets are ready to speak out to defend them.[17]

Games instead of ethics

For 90% of the population, everything that goes on in economics, politics, and social life is a big show. They never come physically close to the elites— the people who actually do what is shown on TV. TV turns everything into a show; everyone can watch the show.

Television's system of communication shapes consciousness. What do we actually see broadcast on TV? A series of selected facts (for a particular time of day), without any apparent order: a minute of war, a minute of an earth-quake, 30 seconds of a fire, 30 seconds of a political scandal, 30 seconds of a business scandal, 30 seconds of a big freeway accident, 20 seconds of a statement by a government minister, 20 seconds for a deputy on the oppos-ing side to say the opposite, and so on. No logic, no way of knowing what this parade of images means.

The TV message shows that an incomprehensible game is being played in the world, a game in which no one understands anything, because there is nothing to understand. These are games between adversaries, about which you never know exactly what they want or don't want. No explanation of the fight is provided; it is sheer rivalry between individuals. Ultimately, every-thing happening in the world is shown as though it were a game. The best image of this is found in TV game shows, where millions are given away for no apparent reason, where a person can gain millions simply for having said the winning secret word by chance. Sheer chance; sheer arbitrariness—that's the way the world is. In the end, if you win, it's because you're lucky, and if you lose, it's because you're unlucky. There is no rationality to it. Just another show that, if nothing else, is entertaining. How long can this go on?

Young people thus learn that life is all a matter of luck. Some win and oth-ers lose. Some have lots of money and others nothing: pure luck. It's the same thing as what happens in beauty contests: winning is pure luck. Elections are the same: pure luck.

In any case, the poor know that they are out of the game. At least watch-ing the game offers them a way to while away the time. They cannot distin-guish well what is shown as fantasy and what is a real event; there's not much difference.

In television news, time is all chopped up. New events are shown each day, a fleeting episode in a story. But you can never know how the story begins and how it ends. Quick scenes of something that has happened are projected. The next day there are other scenes, about other matters. You never know what is really happening and how things end. Everything goes passing by, nothing is solid, and there is no continuity. What is shown is devised in order to arouse a moment of curiosity—and not so that there will be any chance to reflect. Everything goes passing by and nothing remains. When time is dissipated in this manner there can be no ethics. For ethical reflection can take place only when people can know how things began, how they developed—and what the consequences were.

True, there is always an anchor person to guide the spectator's view, but it is quite clear that the concern of the anchor is to sell the product that is going to be advertised after the talking; the show is there merely to lead to the advertising. The most important thing is the advertising, because the station operates on the money it earns from advertising.

In the midst of such confusion, older people look for something that can restore moral values to a society that has lost its ethics. They believe that the churches could play a role—at least that is what they believe in the United States; and Latin American elites look toward the United States. The elites are willing to offer much more room to the churches on the condition that they are able to once more provide a moral education to a generation lacking in it. That anticipates the next section, in which we will consider religion in the world today.

Ethical reaction

An initial reaction to the decline of moral conscience is now emerging, for the dissolution of the old moral values reduces life to a succession of static moments with no continuity, meaning, or direction. The sensation of the moment seems to be the only reference point. This can be seen in holidays. Holidays used to serve as milestones over the year to give meaning value and, in particular, to give meaning to one's work over the year. Today there are more and more holidays. Carnival lasts for a month; there are several carnivals during the year. In a way, every weekend is a holiday and nothing will keep that from continuing: at the end of this "development," every day will be a holiday and life will be a succession of holidays, as it was for the aristocracy of the *ancien regime*.

An ethical reaction is gradually taking shape, as has been attested in Brazil by the success of the campaign led by Herberto de Souza (Betinho). Such movements are no doubt going to spread. They express the reaction of millions of people to a social "development" that is out of control.

Of course such an ethical reaction will have to get at the roots of the moral disintegration of the West, namely in the option for the economy. It involves reversing a movement several centuries long. Certainly the popular masses retain ethical reserves. The problem nonetheless lies in the elites. Convert the elites? Prepare new elites from the world of the people? How long will that take?

In the short run—and probably for one or more generations—the reaction will have to be taken up and led by groups of middle-class intellectuals (in the Brazilian sense of the word).* The transformation of the popular

---

* In Latin America the term "intellectual" often includes professional people, including teachers, and roughly all those with university degrees. Trans.

masses is a long-range process. Out of it will come a new ethic—what it will be we cannot yet know. It will have to be different from the horrifying option for economic growth, even though the latter is deeply rooted in the minds of all.[18]

Religion in the Hour of Crisis

Just as modernity was a process of emancipation from traditional morality, family morality, and aristocratic morality, it has been a process of emancipation from christendom. In Latin America as in Europe, the struggle against christendom was led by the bourgeoisie and by the children of the bourgeoisie who created socialism and led social struggles. Traditional religion has been able to hold out longer in Latin America than in Europe. Even so, it is far along the way to disintegration. We are witnessing a religious revival far beyond what is happening on other continents. In the midst of this "development," what is happening to that part of the church that made the option for the poor in Medellín?

Bourgeois religion and its fate

The bourgeoisie sought to apply to religion the same distinction that operated in ethics. The principle is that religion is a private matter. Religion cannot govern public life. That means the destruction of christendom, which Luther had already provided to some extent with the doctrine of the two kingdoms. The reformed churches established various kinds of compromise with the bourgeois doctrine. The Catholic church fought back every step of the way, retreating only when it had no other alternative. The Catholic church defended its involvement in public life, and did not willingly give up any of the kinds of presence that it had in Christian society, thereby bringing upon itself hostility, struggles, and various kinds of persecution. Even so, it did not completely break with the bourgeois world, and in the twentieth century it reached various forms of accommodation. It did not come to any reconciliation with socialist regimes, inasmuch as the Communist Party of the former Soviet Union was intransigent to the end. The communists radicalized the liberal doctrine to the point of prohibiting any external manifestation of religion.

In Latin America, the bourgeois doctrine was applied in a wide variety of ways. Hostility against the Catholic church reached its high point in Mexico, where separation between church and state was more radical. In other countries separation took place in a more or less violent or peaceful way. A common characteristic is that separation between church and state had little impact on the rural masses; they continued to practice their traditional religion under the protection of traditional aristocracies.

Even in Mexico, opposition to the Catholic church never went as far as it did in almost all of Europe. That is why there is no anticlericalism in the popular masses except in some of the older sectors of the working class. The representation of the bourgeoisie was weak. Many preferred to join one of the

Protestant denominations that entered Latin America at the end of the last century: the Presbyterians, the Methodists, and to a lesser extent, the Baptists. Freemasonry defended liberal ideas, but, except in some localized instances, it never played the role that it did in Latin countries in Europe. Little by little it became a club of local notables.

Even when the ruling classes were anticlerical, they were content to see the church continue to play an important role in the countryside. They feared social revolts more than the church. They entrusted to the church the role of maintaining calm among the rural masses, the indigenous, black slaves, mestizos, and landless peasants in general. The clergy played this role almost unfailingly until 1960. The bourgeoisie made sure that liberal principles were limited to their own class and to public institutions. They wanted the church to retain its traditional role among the poor classes and women.

Popular religion

Looked down on but tolerated by the liberals, treated with condescension by the church which lived off it but found it an embarrassment, popular religion enjoyed a consensus until the 1970s. The liberation church saw in it a collaborator, perhaps unconscious but effective, for changing of society. The traditional church saw in it the promise of a support that would last forever. Popular religion provided the basis for the hope that Latin America would not undergo the anxieties of secularization and abandonment by the masses, as had been the case in Europe. That is the sense of the Puebla texts.

Even at the time of Puebla (1979), however, popular religion had begun to break down, and that has been happening ever more rapidly since that time. The process is irreversible because it is tied to urbanization. Although the former peasants bring the Virgin of Guadalupe and some traditional religious symbols when they come to the city, their religious behavior changes. TV does the rest. Religion used to be culture; now TV is culture.

Paradoxically, those most faithful to popular Catholic religion are the indigenous peoples. Even though this religion was imposed on them, they have assimilated it and adapted it to their religious needs to such an extent that now it has become a sign of their identity (except for a minority of indigenous groups that were not brought into Christianity).

As is the case in Europe even today, some fragments of traditional popular religiosity may be able to survive for some generations. But they will be marginal phenomena of no great importance to the way the world is moving. We will have to accompany this popular religion in its manifestations until they die out, but we cannot expect them to provide what was expected in Puebla. Today people are looking for a new popular religion.

The grace of Medellín

It has now been almost thirty years since Medellín. Officially Medellín is still alive. It is still obligatory to refer to Medellín, although less so than ten years ago. If the decisions made there had been taken to their ultimate consequences, there would have been a radical revolution in the history of the

Catholic church in Latin America. Some people, some dioceses, some parishes, and some religious communities, took the Medellín options as far as they could. Others stopped half way, and some applied 10% of the Medellín decisions, others less, and others changed nothing at all.

The option for the poor is really an option against the entire movement of globalized western culture—it is an option against christendom. That was a lot! It was a complete about-face. It meant starting along a lonely path, against the prevailing direction in society.

And after almost thirty years, where are we? Taken as a whole, the Catholic church still does not have the "face of the poor." It is still not the church of the poor—even though it speaks of them a great deal. Some dioceses—less than 5% of the dioceses in Latin America—restructured themselves in terms of the option for the poor, even while still not taking on the features of the poor. Altogether they do not amount to 5%.

Indeed, quite the opposite is happening. The church continues to devote an enormous portion of its human and material resources to the service of the most privileged: universities, schools, hospitals, and prosperous neighborhoods in cities. Its culture has ceased being archaic and patriarchal and has become modernized. The clergy now have the characteristics of middle class, cosmopolitan culture. Moreover, priestly training consists of transmitting this culture to young men who for the most part come from a popular culture (now in transition).

Alongside this, the church has moved into the world of the poor with Christian base communities and with pastoral agents committed to popular liberation. Some pastoral agents have become involved with political struggles. A prophetic stance by a group of bishops—a stance multiplied and applied locally by some tens of thousands of priests, and men and women religious—has been especially significant. It has been this prophetic word—accompanied by prophetic deeds—that has most drawn the attention of society at large, and has been widely made known, whether in a positive or negative light. On the whole, the mass media have reacted negatively and have waged a defamatory and belittling campaign to this day.

Unfortunately, the direction of Medellín did not fit into the worldwide strategy of the Roman church, and so it has been sacrificed. Especially since the 1984 and 1986 instructions by the Congregation for the Doctrine of the Faith, it has become more obvious that most church people have moved away. Anyone following the line of liberation was isolated and marginalized, until finally almost none were left in ecclesiastical institutions. What happened was the same thing that happened in Europe in the time of modernism. Modernism was hounded and isolated; finally, some of its main representatives were pushed out of the church. Something similar happened in France with the progressive movement and, indeed, anything that had a progressive flavor between 1945 and 1955. Many were reduced to silence, and a number were pushed out of the church.

The movement survives, but it has no voice in the church. It is there in reserve, until new changes create new situations. In any case, there has now appeared in the church a new generation that was not involved in the events of the sixties and seventies; they cannot even imagine what those times were about, what the hopes, struggles, dreams, pains, and tragedies were.

Is all of this simply going to be an episode? Will history go on its way completely ignoring it? That is not likely, because the options and great debates of the sixties and seventies were not simply minor episodes. In their way, and within the Latin American context, they raised the question of the church vis-à-vis the new culture, i.e., vis-à-vis globalization, vis-à-vis a culture that takes as its priority the option for economic growth, money, and consumption. It is not enough to preach against materialism or consumerism; preaching will have no effect on the behavior of Catholics, let alone of society. Something more radical most be done.

Today the challenge is more serious than it was at the time of Medellín. We have a better idea of where the world is going and of the winds that are blowing us too.

The resurgence of religion

Practically all sociologists of religion and the classical masters of sociology concluded that religion was coming to an end. Their analyses always converged toward the same point: the disappearance of religion. But their analyses were wrong. Indeed, nothing better demonstrates the frailty of the concepts of social science and the large role played by ideology in social science. They offered myriad reasons why they believed that religion was going to die—mainly because they wanted it to die. And yet religion has reappeared vigorously, particularly in Latin America.

As was bound to happen in a people so divided culturally and in all realms of life, religion is returning with a different face in the elites and in the popular masses.

A worldwide market of religions has opened up among the elites. What has proved most successful, however, have not been the great traditional religions, which in some fashion tend to absorb their members. Rather, people are gravitating toward esoteric sects, the traditional sects in the West and sects from the East.[19] These sects offer varied religious experiences with a rather vague doctrine, a strong emotional content, and a rather undefined morality. They all provide a higher "knowledge," albeit quite poor in content, that is reserved to initiates. They offer an appeal to a universal and total love that is also quite undefined in its concrete expressions. They leave a great deal of room for each individual's imagination. They offer spiritual direction and advice in wisdom.

Ever since the Renaissance, such sects have existed in Europe alongside official orthodoxy, taking advantage of openings for freedom. Ultimately, they derive from ancient Egyptian wisdom, which was gathered by the Greeks and transmitted to the Christian West by the Arabs. Indeed, they were always present in the Byzantine empire. Today Asian religions also draw people, especially those who have become more westernized.

Among ordinary people, it is the pentecostal churches that are growing most rapidly. Brazil stands at the forefront, followed by Chile, but Protestantism is entering all countries in Latin America and the Caribbean. In Guatemala it has absorbed a good portion of the population for twenty years.[20]

Recently, the Catholic church has become aware of the challenge posed by pentecostalism. The pentecostal churches provide more powerful religious experiences: an experience of conversion, a fervent welcome, integration into a strong community, strong leadership by pastors, return to an uncompromising traditional morality, liberation from vices, and healing of the sick. That is just what suits the needs of the majority of the people, who are poor. It is true that they are moving against the current of Western society and the dominant culture. For their members, however, that is not a great sacrifice; after all, they are offered only a tenuous participation in the dominant culture. And what they see in that culture is primarily the occasion of sin: immoral parties, drinking, drugs.

By becoming involved in pentecostalism, the Latin American masses are engaged in their own modernization. Pentecostal churches reject modernization—as did rural religion.[21] Yet pentecostal churches permit and stimulate personal religious experiences, i.e., modernization. Pentecostal churches are likewise emancipated from the Catholic hierarchy.

Most of those who belong to pentecostal churches unquestionably find there a cultural liberation. They feel that they are more active, more involved in creating culture, and more truly participants than they were in popular Catholicism, where they repeated solely out of custom ancient rituals that they did not understand.

For people who have already experienced liberation, what can a new discourse on liberation mean? There lies a challenge for the Catholic church.

The charismatic renewal is increasingly playing a role in the Catholic church like that of Protestant pentecostalism.[22] It also presents a challenge, because the charismatic renewal attracts, persuades, and converts using means that practically bypass the traditional Catholic heritage. The rapid expansion of the charismatic movement shows how much it responds to contemporary culture; it provides just what people want. It is the expression of the inculturation of Christianity in globalized culture.

Toward a Conclusion

This chapter on culture and the liberation of culture shows to what extent the theme of inculturation is loaded with ambiguities and how many problems it raises (or conceals).

History shows that the greatest difficulties of the Catholic church in evangelizing come from its inculturation into medieval culture. Inculturation was so complete that it became almost impossible to separate Christianity from the culture of christendom. For that reason the rise of the new culture has taken place in the midst of repeated, harsh, and often bloody conflicts with the church. That problem still stands today: the greatest obstacle to mission is this indissoluble link between medieval culture and church, the upshot of which is that in order to be a Christian one must accept the so-called "universal" catechism, the Roman ritual, and the Roman code of canon law—an entire culture that is inseparable from the Christian message.

Might it not have been preferable to have been less inculturated?

The new globalized culture offers the church some room: to provide the new generations with an ethics, console the victims of progress, welcome those defeated in the market, and offer moral compensation to those who have not been able to have access to the market.[23] The axis of the new culture is not religion but rather economic growth. What does it mean to be inculturated in this culture? Does it mean accepting the priority of economics, fitting into the secondary function that the culture offers? That is what many are in fact doing. They become integrated into the dominant culture with the idea that they are going to be able to dominate it when actually the role reserved to them is that of taking in the defeated.

Indeed, there are two cultures: the new globalized culture that is actively practiced, the culture of those who know how to handle the tools; and the culture that is passively received like a show, with no chance to be actively involved. The first side of the culture offers an ultra-privileged status and a way of life that the royalty of former times could not have imagined. The second side is made up of constraints, desires repressed, satisfactions ever incomplete, and many problems. What does it mean to be inculturated? Where does evangelizing inculturation lie?

We know well that throughout history there has always been a range of options. One portion will be absorbed by the dominant culture. One portion will try to convert the dominant classes. One portion will go to the poor. One portion will stick with ancient christendom and its remains to the very end. Our intention here has been simply to understand what is happening and what these options mean.

Before pondering the presence of the church in the world today, we still want to consider in one more chapter the aspiration for a personal liberation. This perspective was almost absent thirty years ago. Today, as a result of the new culture, people's concerns are increasingly centered on the "self." How can there be a true personal liberation in a world fascinated by the "self"?

8

PERSONAL LIBERATION

A few years ago, a theologian very much involved in liberation theology wrote,

> This is where we have to start: by recognizing that Christian activists are in a period of personal crisis, and it does not seem to be superficial or something passing. It is not the crisis of one activist or another, but is something much deeper and more widespread. This crisis, even when not manifested explicitly, can be seen in many ways: discouragement, apathy, departure of important leaders, major existential crises, which frustrate the sense of meaning in life, the loss of a sense of struggle, a crisis of ethical values, and so forth.[1]

In that same article, the author went on to indicate that "another risk is that activists will be absorbed by that crisis, becoming so bedazzled with the new discoveries about themselves and their subjectivity that they will be kept from moving ahead and building a more integrated personality, where personal demands and social commitment will be in balance."[2]

Faced with the growing complexity of the liberation of the objective world (culture, society, economics, and politics), many become weary and feel drawn to the other side of the movement of liberation in the Western world: the liberation of the person, or the growth in affirmation of subjectivity. Indeed, we now witness an avalanche of "made-in-USA" subjectivity. Particularly since World War II, there has been an outpouring of techniques, formulas, methods, doctrines, wisdoms about developing the person, and this entire vast production is now expanding to the rest of the world.

Modernity separated object and subject: the objectivity of the outer world, which was handed over to science and technology for the sake of production, and the subjectivity of the "I," which involves the search for one's self. In modernity the self is no longer discovered in the world, and no longer situated in the world. One discovers oneself through introspection. Science and knowledge are dissociated.

In no other country has this dissociation gone so far as in the United States. Nowhere else does the economy unfold with greater autonomy, and nowhere else has individualism been so affirmed or have so many formulas for treating the self and the problems of the self-arisen. This entire outpouring is now inundating Latin America beginning with the upper classes and intellectuals.

Hence the danger of bedazzlement. Some people who used to be involved in social struggles have exchanged socialism for capitalism: they are now working for neoliberal governments. Others have left the objective world and discovered their own subjectivity. Or rather, they have discovered that alongside the history of the objective world there is a long history of subjectivity and a vast huge cultural world that offers endless resources to those who have just recently discovered their own subjectivity.

In Latin America, a great deal of the room occupied ten years ago by objective liberation struggles (political, economic, etc.) has been permeated by the culture of subjectivity. Many used to be unaware of this world of subjectivity or paid little attention to it. Now in the 1990s, it is clear that subjectivity is more relevant to the middle and upper classes than is the objective world. That was already the case in the United States and Europe, of course, since the proclamation of the postmodern era (approximately 1975).

Many activists, especially Marxists or those influenced by Marxists, used to regard the whole world of subjectivity as irrelevant: for them it was an alienation, or a mistake. Many of those who then used to deny the subject and personal problems have now become bedazzled by subjectivity.

The issue of personal liberation runs through the history of the West at least since the fourteenth century, and probably, in its roots, since the twelfth century. The pursuit of the liberation of the subject, of the self, of the person, has been threatening the church since that time. Spiritism, esoteric sects with the new sciences, New Age—and also in another sense Catholic and Protestant pentecostals—are part of this history of the human subject's pursuit of liberation.

Given the temporary setback of political movements for liberation, movements to liberate the individual are taking on some importance and are going to give the church's teaching authority more "headaches" than movements for political liberation, which actually have never constituted a real threat to the dogma or structure of the Catholic church. Now things are going to change; the problems are on their way.

We are far from a possible reconciliation between subject and object. The world of subjectivity needs to be taken up as it is, after expanding for centuries. If Christianity does not offer a valid response to personal concerns, it will be swept aside from the West and Latin America, because the challenge is much greater. The challenge is not only to a theology of liberation, but to the whole world of the traditional churches which can no longer rely on a majority of absolutely loyal peasants but have to survive in the world of the cities.

How are we to practice a discernment and pursue sure paths in the midst of the extremely complex history of "spiritualisms" and all the esoteric sciences which have not been displaced by the scientific sciences but in fact seem to have multiplied? We need to situate present debates in their historical formation in order to avoid the "bedazzlement" effect. For centuries the church has been challenged by esoteric religions that sought to draw Christianity into a supposedly more all-encompassing or more universal higher spirituality. The church has often responded by issuing condemnations. Today condemnations have little effect and drive away those attracted to these new movements.

The Rise of Personal Liberation

We cannot provide here in a few pages a history of struggles for the affirmation of the person since the middle ages. We merely want to situate the contemporary developments that have surprised many and disconcerted some.

Historically, the subject or person as asserted in modernity emerged out of a centuries-long struggle against christendom. The church defended christendom until Vatican II, and thus the struggle for the emancipation of man or woman as subject or person often sounded like a struggle against the resistance of the church, that is of the clergy or the magisterium, who were defending christendom.

In christendom each person has his or her place in society and must be identified with his or her social role. Being or doing something other than one's defined role is not allowed. No one may allow himself or herself the luxury of having personal problems. There is little, if any, room for an individual consciousness. Even marriages are arranged by families and imposed on young people. Hence, any affirmation of personal freedom is interpreted as rebellion, possibly even as revolt against God, an act of pride and a sin of refusal to accept God's will, inasmuch as God's will is expressed by the place that the person occupies in society. For centuries the clergy would require Christians to go along with such a situation and would treat any effort to break the established social order as a sinful revolt. The movement toward personal emancipation starts from this situation.

Origins

By the fourteenth century there are signs that some people are no longer content with a particular identification or with their social role. First, there are the mystics who continue the line of spirituality practiced in the Low Countries and the Rhine. All are marked by Meister Eckhart who was able to articulate themes and aspirations that were quite universal in this world of free cities or communes. Despite papal condemnations, it seems that for the most part this widespread movement (among the Beguines and the Beghards, for example) remained orthodox. The mystics did not want to split away from the church, and they accepted all its dogmas. Even so, the living power of their religion was no longer in the external religious gestures imposed by Catholic discipline (Fourth Lateran Council).

Mysticism draws life from a search for God that does not go by way of scholastic theology (which is closed to lay people), the sacraments, or the church's teaching authority. There is a direct relationship between God and the mystic's soul. The notion of a soul as a created spirit that can communicate with God without going by way of matter (that is, the church of sacraments and priests) develops. A "spiritual" life emerges and becomes independent of official worship. A current of spiritual life is born and develops on the margins of the official, sterile religion; it dissociates itself from official worship. Religion and spirituality split apart.

Alongside the mysticism that intends to be orthodox (despite several condemnations) there is a heterodox movement of the "free spirit" spread through the Empire, the Low Countries, and northern France. There, the human spirit is emancipated from the body and becomes divine or quasi-divine. Human beings become part of the divine in their whole spiritual life; they are composed of an energy that is the only energy in the entire world. Once the spirit recognizes itself as divine, it has the same freedom as God; it is above any law and acts out of sheer spontaneity like God. It is above sin. The "free spirit" owes no submission to the church, and does not have to make any material religious gesture, for that would mean falling away from relating with God or in God in a purely spiritual way. Any external religion vanishes.[3]

Of course, people can be burned at the stake for advocating such ideas, and so the "heresy" circulates underground, thereby making repression more difficult. Thus, there arises an environment of religious persons who challenge the power of the clergy in religion and fashion a spiritual religion where no institutional element of the church has entry.

Parallel to this mystical or religious world, there develops at the courts of monarchs or princes the poetry and music of the troubadours, who sing of the new love, a heretical love that challenges the strictly family love of christendom. Wandering around in the courts and even more in the free cities are architects, artists, poets, and writers who no longer draw their inspiration from scholasticism but who pursue other, generally semi-clandestine, sources (books from the East through the Arabs, for example). A new social class arises there, one that the church is unable to control.

The Renaissance

The Renaissance extends the environment of the courts of princes and the circulation of ideas much further. From Constantinople (which eventually falls) and from the Muslim world come new documents from antiquity. Gnosticism, the hermetic writings, the writings of the neo-Platonists, Plotinus, and Proclus are mixed together with the sciences of astrology, alchemy, and the resources of ancient medicine and ancient magic. At this time there is no clear distinction between real science and science fiction and no border between the real and fantasy. What is happening is the manifestation of a world of thoughts breaking free from the control of the church and scholastic theology.

What arouses people is not so much the content of these things as the possibility of thinking for oneself. Thinking is no longer merely invoking scholastic authorities; it no longer means subjecting one's own thought to that of the theologians or the church's magisterium. What is being asserted within the whole swirl of ideas is the desire for the emancipation of individual thinking.

Since that time, the tendencies of that new thinking have been clear. First, it tends toward a pantheistic idea of God and the world. God, humankind, and the world are fundamentally united. A single energy, a single force, unites everything, so much so that in order to communicate with God and the world, the human being has no need for the mediation of the church, christendom, or authoritarian scholastic theology. Human beings need only look within themselves and there they will enter into contact with the totality of Being.

Second, soul and body are distinct. The soul has an autonomous life, independent of the body; it can act by itself. The mind can think independently. Thus, the mind, the soul, the personal spirit do not need the mediation of matter. The matter that they seek to avoid is once more the institutional church, priests, sacraments, the entire setup of christendom: starting in the Renaissance, the individual consciousness proclaims its independence from christendom. It cannot say so clearly, but its emancipation takes place in a disguised manner through adherence to all kinds of spiritualist thought.

Third, energy is said to be circulating among all beings in creation. Hence, there are resources everywhere. Everything has an influence on human life, everything can be used: stars, extraterrestrial beings, plants, stones, and animals endowed with special qualities. Judeo-Christianity had affirmed the distinction between God and creation; this new way of thinking returns to the unity of all things. Everything is divine and God is in everything. Pantheism does not dare to declare itself openly but from now on it is present. Naturally, the "authority" of the magisterium now loses its foundation: there is no more revelation because there is no revealing God. Revelation is in everything and everything is revelatory.[4]

The Reformation

The Reformation stands in both continuity and discontinuity with the Renaissance. In any case, it was a decisive step that had a radical influence on the subsequent development of the person. The reformers attacked the magisterium and scholasticism head on. They highlighted the individual subject, not on the basis of ideas foreign to Christianity, but in the very name of Christianity. They invoked the Bible against the magisterium and scholasticism. They made faith not an act of submission to the church, including christendom, but rather an act of submission directly to God. Henceforth,

Christianity becomes centered on the human individual, and all ecclesiastical mediations will lose their value.

The reformers themselves were afraid to leave the individual truly alone before God. They surrounded the individual in a kind of christendom that was not so solid as that of the Catholic church, but even so, they maintained or restored a number of traditional institutions, albeit under other names. A weaker equivalent of the magisterium appeared in synods and consistories and especially in the class of pastors—which became very similar to a Catholic clergy. It has been said that Lutheranism replaced the magisterium of the bishops with the magisterium of theology schools. Actually, in a few decades there was created a Lutheran scholasticism and a Calvinist one as well, and the Bible was read through the prism of these theologies, as was bound to happen.

The Reformation was nonetheless the high point of the expression of the human subject, and it is no wonder that during the sixteenth and seventeenth centuries, the bourgeoisie and the literate elites were continually drawn toward Protestantism. Despite the new orthodoxies, the Protestant principle continued to operate: new movements emerged within Protestantism tending toward an ever stronger affirmation of individual faith as the only path of salvation and of encounter with God. Despite the reservations of orthodox Protestants, we cannot fail to see in twentieth-century pentecostalism a new embodiment of the Protestant principle: a new affirmation of the believing subject vis-à-vis new magisteriums. We need only observe how the Assemblies of God and other denominations were born.

Because the faith of the reformers is further removed from christendom, it becomes more spiritualistic than medieval faith which is tied to christendom. It will be one of the roots of modernity in the sense of the separation of subject and object.

The breaking away of the reformed churches had very strong repercussions in the Catholic church. It prompted the Council of Trent, which, in reaction to the freedom of the Protestant believer, exalted the objectivity of the Catholic faith. Trent objectified and enshrined scholastic theology. It turned the faith into a vast array of propositions on objective things in christendom: the sacraments, the clergy, the magisterium, the means of salvation, that is, the whole set of mediations established during christendom. The object of faith had more to do with mediations between God and human beings than with God. This kind of reaction to Protestantism had the effect of placing the Catholic church in an even worse situation for dealing with modernity in the following century. The church became identified with scholasticism, and the latter entered into conflict with the new science.

Moreover, the Reformation emphasized the transcendence of God in the biblical sense, and thus raised a barrier against the "neo-pagan" or pantheistic tendencies of the Renaissance. It presaged the future conflicts with the esoteric movements and the "New Ages" of all centuries. The Protestant principle also has its fundamentalistic side.

Modernity and the Subject

Since the critiques of postmodernity we can see more clearly the diversity of "modern" tendencies. We are also learning to locate it not as the end point of an evolution, but as one more stage in the history of the Western world, and a complex stage that retains residues of earlier stages within whatever is new.

Modernity made possible the liberation of the person. It was prepared by earlier phases, but it is clear that the emancipation of the human being as subject was a second constitutive aspect of modernity following upon the establishment of the objective world of politics, economics, and culture now liberated from christendom. This was also an instance of the subject's self-conquest through the struggle against christendom considered as an all-embracing whole, where each person was fated to accept his or her role.

Descartes' philosophy is the traditional symbol of the emancipation of the person. Descartes' starting point is the thinking self. For him the thinking self can be regarded as a reality in itself, independent of the world of christendom in which it lives. The self is the starting point for thinking, and from the outset it prescinds from everything said by christendom. Descartes thus expresses theoretically what scientists do practically; he expresses in theory how Galileo acts.

This is the beginning of a path leading to freedom of thought, freedom of expression, freedom of the press, and freedom of teaching. The "self" wants to express itself fully with all its means, independently of any magisterium, Inquisition, or censure.

The subject, which becomes free thought, achieves its expansion in the world: it becomes the citizen, emancipated from monarchs and from divine right, and it creates a political order that emerges from free thought and admits no criterion other than that of reason. The same subject becomes property owner and producer, creates or expands the market and sets up an economy in which individuals behave in accordance with their own rationality, i.e. a rationality independent of social rules imposed by christendom or the lords of the earth. In a word, the free person establishes politics, founds the economy, and founds a culture which seeks to be rational.

Science, which is an expression of personal, free, and rational thought, tends to gradually break away from older ways of knowing, not only from scholasticism but from all esoteric kinds of knowledge. Little by little a distinction emerges between the real and the imaginary, between observed reality and fantasy, and hence the distinction between astronomy and astrology, physics and magic, chemistry and alchemy, traditional medicine and experimental medicine, and so forth, is gradually refined. Esoteric sciences, along with older philosophical systems and the whole legacy of the previous millennia of magic and superstition, are forced to retreat before the advance of pure rational thought. The separation is clear by the mid-seventeenth century, although for some time scientists continue to be attached to the residue of esoteric representations in their scientific works.[5] While those who are

solely devoted to research engage in a work of reduction and systematic elim-
ination of the esoteric imagination, the general reading public remains
attached to a mixture of science and esotericism, regarding it all as science.

We need only recall Freemasonry, which, from its origins in the eighteenth
century, wished to be the standard bearer of science and continued to include
esoteric elements in its ritual and ideology, believing that they went back to
the ancient wisdom of the Egyptians. Nevertheless, the scientific movement
moved further and further away from esotericism and all kinds of magic
thought.

Even though they founded the separation between subject and object, and
between the individual mind and the order of the world, the moderns were
very concerned to create something to replace christendom, that is, to restore
the unity of subject and object on a rational basis, and to refashion a world
of "order and progress" (the national motto of Brazil). They could not conceive of "progress" without "order," the order that had been the principle
of Christian society.

How to reconstitute an equivalent of christendom? First came the attempt
of the Enlightenment: reason could be the foundation of the new order, inasmuch as reason was simultaneously individual and universal. The same reason that is the light of the individual is present in all human beings. How
could this reason not unite humankind and serve as the basis for a new
order? Reason would provide the principles for a new religion, natural or
rational religion: such attempts were made during the French Revolution.
Reason would also create a political society, the rule of law, and an economic
society based on freedom of ownership and the free market on the ruins of
feudal rights and the property of the church and the traditional lords of the
nobility.

The French Revolution showed that the Enlightenment's effort to create
a human society based on universal reason was a failure. Its supporters could
claim that the times were not yet ripe, and that the forces of opposition were
still so overwhelming that a victory of reason was not possible.

The nineteenth century was born under the sign of the great German ide-
alist philosophies, which were attempts to reconceive an equivalent of christendom starting with reason and the subject. They were pure theories,
ideologies with no one to embody them in history. There were no human
minorities to realize such dreams. Christendom was resisting and was unwilling to succumb. The structures of the *ancien regime* were still standing.

Then came various nationalisms and efforts to make the nation the lost
unity of subject and object, but, like christendom, the nation showed itself
to be oppressive insofar as it sought to be as totalitarian as the former christendom. Positivism strove for a scientific religion of humankind in order to
build a society governed by science. At that time, however, science was not
yet part of the lives of most people. The republic and the ideal of the republic could reconcile individual freedom with the realization of a collective
order. But how could the republic be established among people who for the
most part remained loyal to christendom? It was imposed by force. Individual

freedom was imposed by law, and Catholic peasants were persecuted (France, Spain, Portugal, Mexico, and so forth). Throughout the nineteenth century, esoteric sects proliferated, coming out from underground to proclaim the message of total reconciliation and of unity between object and subject. Freemasonry itself, as we have seen, maintained ties with the esoteric sciences. However, the triumph of science and the victories of scientism are such that the esoteric cannot achieve much success. Besides that, scientism creates a kind of science fiction that projects the utopia of a world completely humanized by science. Science itself offers better prospects than esotericism could imagine. The real overcomes fiction, and there is no room for fiction.

We accordingly reach the twentieth century, which begins with a frightful drama, the First World War, which destroys most of what remains of christendom, such as the great empires. The West is opened to individualism. The subject now stands facing societies that have been destroyed. The liberals begin to doubt: will the subject be able to refashion a social order in which it will retain the freedoms that have been achieved? At the same time, the churches lose control over the popular masses.

Up to 1914, only about 10% of the population is involved in modernity. The rest are peasants or domestic servants still living in dependence on the church and the nobles, that is, on christendom; and they are not involved in the market, and have no citizen rights. They are loyal to their churches.

In the twentieth century, the rural masses migrate to the cities and to industry; they learn to read and write, acquire rights, and begin to take their place in public life. From now on, the opposition between the reigning individualism and the need for a stable social order becomes an unavoidable problem. How are subject and object, individual reason and social necessity, freedom and sacrifice for society, to be reunited?

The various totalitarianisms, whose history is so well known that we need not rehearse it again, now come on the scene. Their starting point is always that christendom is in ruins and that a unified humankind must be refashioned, one in which freedom and solidarity, freedom and progress, submission to a common good and individual liberty, are reconciled. In practice, the appeal of order is such that totalitarianisms end up subordinating the freedom of the individual to the order of the whole. Freedom remains as a utopia, a promise for after the revolution. Totalitarianisms ultimately come tumbling down (e.g., Soviet communism, in 1989).

Were totalitarianisms modernity? They were modern phenomena, but they did not express people's deepest yearnings. What was deepest was the emancipation of the individual, along with the liberation of the economy, politics, and culture from the control of christendom.[6] Yet the moderns were afraid and sensed that the breakup of the old society entailed a danger: everything could fall into anomie. The bourgeoisie accordingly looked for substitutes for what used to be christendom, seeking foundations in rational values. In practice, there were no such rational values, and totalitarianisms were guided officially by ideologies, which were nothing but a façade. They entered into the dynamic of generalized fear and the pursuit of security, namely, the preservation of the regime at any price. They fell into the trap that Hobbes had condemned.

The fall of totalitarianisms was not the fall of their ideologies, because these latter never really existed. It was liberation from dominations based on fear. Thus, people did not believe in Nazism, fascism, and communism—they were afraid. We Christians have no right to be shocked at this: in christendom people also lived in fear.

What has become obvious with the fall of ideologies is that fear was not something proper to christendom, but that it is present in all societies that seek to impose unity and to impose the reconciliation of the person with society. This suggests that the fundamental problem of human life and of human community may be the problem of fear. How are we to be delivered from fear?

Postmodernity

Our concern here is not the philosophy of postmodernity, which reflects the new situations that have emerged since the 1970s. This philosophy is very much connected with specifically French situations, such as the predominance of Marxism among the French intelligentsia from 1945 to 1975. Here we are concerned rather with the new way men and women are feeling and thinking, the new way they are seeking personal freedom.

What is most often and quite correctly highlighted is the rejection of ideologies, of the great "narratives" that have deceived the twentieth century. Marxism as an ideology died around 1975. But American "liberalism," which did not survive the Vietnam war, has also died. The ideologies of development and authenticity have died, as have populisms, and so forth. People who had placed their hopes for freedom in these ideologies have gone on to condemn them as disguised forms of domination or oppression.[7]

But this same rejection is directed at institutions: it is a rejection of politics in its institutions, a rejection of the school, the hospital, the prison, the police, the churches, and philanthropic institutions. A secret or unconscious will to power and domination is uncovered everywhere. Nothing deserves loyalty, dedication, or sacrifice anymore. Everything comes to be seen as a hiding-place for falsehood. Even business companies are discredited: they go from one capitalist group to another, move to other countries, and split up or join larger conglomerates.[8]

The result is that human beings are reduced to the level of individuals isolated in the world. This is happening at the same time as the third industrial revolution. Postmodern man is the new executive; his life is a permanent struggle because economic life and the market do not allow for a truce. The game is all against all; whoever is left behind loses.

Executives do not work with matter; they work on human beings. They have to convince, seduce, stimulate—in short, they have to win. Each day is made up of victories or defeats. Executives are afraid of losing. They do not have their own thoughts, and cannot have their own feelings. The pace of life is such that each day is different from the last. The past disappears; the future is the next day. Human life comes down to a point or a moment; no past, no future, nothing solid.

No wonder executives have deep identity crises. They are subject to stress, to psychoses and neuroses caused by a feeling of emptiness and meaninglessness—what is called narcissism.[9] Executives do not know who they are. They seem to be the freest people on earth, but they do not know why they are free or for what. They have to win; if they lose, their lives have no more meaning. They live running after illusions so as not to have to realize that their life is slipping away without meaning. They have to compensate for this lack of meaning with a continual representation. They have to play a stage role.

In the United States this new category of people is far advanced. It is being rapidly imitated in all countries around the world. The *ens executivum*, which is the highest reference point in the West today, is the endpoint of modernity. The executive has been freed of all the fetters that the moderns had placed on themselves as a defense against the dangers of total individualism. We have now arrived at complete individualism.

The first cries of alarm are now being heard. How can such a class of individuals guarantee the future of humankind? In reality, it cannot. Today's economic conglomerates have no sense of responsibility. They are aware that they are rushing toward planetary disaster, but the law they follow is to earn money and eliminate their competitors; what happens later does not matter. As for the governments of nations, their aim is to win the next election. What happens later is no concern of theirs. There are no more comprehensive proposals, and no more answers. Some international congresses are simply puppet shows; every participant gives his or her little ten-minute speech. The whole ritual of congresses takes place and then everyone goes home wondering how to use the event for electoral purposes.

No one feels responsible for the future of humankind anymore. Everyone is playing a role—poorly concealing their emptiness. Everyone seeks help from psychologists who tell them how to overcome the feeling that their life is empty: in effect, they are asking the psychologists to tell them a lie, and to make them believe that their life does have value. Upon reaching this point the person has acquired greater freedom than ever—in the sense of independence—but it is an empty freedom that has no idea of why it exists.

A new factor has been added since the 1960s, the decade of sexual liberation. The last barrier of christendom as traditional civilization was the family, by far the most resistant of all structures. The family has been shaken. The sexual revolution of the sixties proclaimed the end of all taboos and prohibitions, both outer and inner. It coincided with the discovery of much more effective means of birth control. It was also the revolution of women, who became free of close dependence on men in sexual matters.

This sexual revolution has had very strong repercussions in the West. It has gradually become clear to what extent people were concealing repressions, fantasies, and taboos—an unconscious or semiconscious world that had never been brought to awareness. For many people, and especially for many women, the sexual revolution was—and still is—experienced as the most visible, and most vital manifestation of personal freedom. This fact cannot be underestimated—except in the Catholic church, probably because it is headed by celibates and males.

The family has been shaken. It has become more difficult for men and women to approach one another. Nevertheless, the advent of the human person as a subject of his or her existence has unquestionably been a decisive step, although even in the West, sexual life is still outside the field of consciousness and reason.

The sexual revolution highlights the individual, but that individual is also thereby isolated. It thus extends and accentuates the effects of postmodernity. It has arrived late; the bourgeoisie was afraid of shaking up the family, which it correctly perceived to be the supreme defense of social order. The new class has no fear of disturbing order, but it leaves human society quite anguished with regard to its future.

What has been said about postmodernity does not apply to all human beings. As noted previously, the contemporary age is the first in which an internal separation within peoples has taken place. The culture splits: the experience of freedom is granted to the privileged classes whose daily needs are met. Their problems revolve around what is superfluous, not around survival.

In the contemporary situation, it has been the outcast who have become visible, and they are a majority in most countries on earth. The outcast also have their experience of freedom: a freedom without support, a freedom of nothing and for nothing; it is the freedom of those about whom no one is concerned and who are superfluous. They have freedom but can do nothing. It is a negative freedom. They are in the big city, which offers them no more than a precarious refuge. They survive and each day again take up the struggle to survive. Such freedom is so poor that if a charismatic populist leader comes along, the urban masses will happily sacrifice their freedom. For sacrificing their freedom would not amount to sacrificing anything. The family is still the last salvation, the only reserve of values. Looking toward the future, this threat cannot be underestimated.

The Return to the Esoteric

In reaction to the crises of the objective world and the emptying out of freedom, a return to religion is plainly taking place. Postmodernity has rejected all attempts to refashion the unity between object and subject, and has condemned any long-term project, but it has left the world with nowhere to go and the person utterly alone. Clearly, such a situation ought to be reflected in a strong yearning for the unity that has been lost. How refashion a unification? How unite what is separated?

The sciences have become more diversified. They have multiplied and no longer seek to represent reality. They offer an immense dispersion of data that make it possible to multiply effective techniques, but are ever further away from the project of making the world known. The sciences have lost any intention of pulling things together; hence the sensation of an immense void. All this helps explain the return to religion. Religions have always offered a global knowledge, an overall vision of reality, a vision of all reality as a whole.

There is new interest in Christianity. In the West and in Latin America, most people say they are Christians and think they are, although their ties with the Catholic church or the other historic churches are ever more tenuous. Neither the Catholic church nor the reformed or so-called historic churches benefit from the return to Christianity. The churches have not recovered from the critiques that they have suffered since the twelfth century—since Joachim of Fiori, the spiritual Franciscans, all the medieval heresies, the Reformation, and all of modernity.

In the eyes of large numbers of people, the Catholic church still appears to be an obstacle to freedom and not energy for freedom. This can still be said, despite Vatican II, Medellín, and the action of the Latin American churches on behalf of the liberation of their peoples. That has still not been enough to demonstrate that a radical change has taken place. The changes brought about by Vatican II have not been decisive enough in the eyes of the great masses; they were so balanced that the message did not come through clearly. Many of us read our desires into the texts of Vatican II, but the Council itself fell short of those desires: it did not break with christendom and did not proclaim the message of freedom that would have begun a process of rapprochement with the peoples of the West.

Indeed, this is not a matter of official documents but rather about the daily life of the church, the day by day contacts between clergy and their people. At that level the church still appears to be the defender of traditional morality and traditional social relations. It is little involved in common tasks. It is not identified with the struggles for the liberation of the person.

That is why many, Catholics included, are looking for answers in other religions. For Christians, however, it is very difficult to adopt one of the great Asian religions: Islam, Buddhism, Hinduism, Taoism, etc. With some exceptions, these religions do not offer a cultural model accessible to Western people, and so the solution is sought in the esoteric which has always paralleled Christian history, since gnosticism in the early centuries. Gnosticism has always existed, even in the periods when it suffered the greatest repression at the hands of christendom. It has always been a way to live a Christianity independent of clergy and magisterium.

The esoteric is found in the form of theosophy, the hermetic tradition, the kabala, alchemy, theurgy, astrology, anthroposophy, Rosacrucianism, freemasonry, spiritism, and so forth.[10] Recently in the United States, during the 1980s, a kind of amalgam of traditional Western esotericism and a number of messages from Hinduism were fashioned into what is being called "New Age." It does not offer anything new beyond what is already found in the Eastern and Western traditions.[11]

New Age claims to refashion the unity between subject and world, and so to rebuild the unity lost by the sciences. It claims to be a science, a comprehensive science of the whole, a "holism" on the basis of which everything acquires meaning. New Age is not an organized movement, and has no fixed doctrine. It is rather a tendency, a set of some basic positions that individuals interpret in their own manner. It is unlikely to be a complete system, like a religion in the traditional sense. It seeks to form new people. Actually its entire hope is placed in the coming of the Age of Aquarius, which has replaced the Age of Pisces. If it were not for this, and if it were to rely simply on inner conversion, it does not seem that it could be more effective than previous religious movements, and would probably have less impact, since it is completely unorganized. It seeks to rely on the good will of some other type of human being.

New Age has not been the first attempt to refashion the lost unity. Earlier there were the Oxford groups, and gnosticism in Princeton. Such phenomena abound in the English-speaking world. However, it does not seem to be succeeding in really opening up a new era in the history of the world, or even in the history of modernity. It may be a contributing element, but the dispersion of its followers very much hinders it from acting on society. Things would be very easy indeed if individual religious conversion were enough. We will have something to say about its religious message in the next section.

The return to the esoteric is one of the manifestations of renewed interest in religious matters in reaction to the widespread critique of modernity. In Brazil, the esoteric movement is stronger than spiritism, which performs useful activities in many circles but cannot claim to be an overall response to the challenges of modernity.

The subject of esotericism is the same subject as that of gnosis (i.e., knowledge), namely the person who through knowledge is seeking to reach his or her salvation. Such a subject is withdrawn from his or her material or historic setting. Through gnosis the subject enters into the world of true reality which is spiritual: knowledge of the single energy that encompasses God, human beings, and the world, including extraterrestrial beings. God, the world, and humans are a single reality. All is in all, and exists in all. When human subjects enter into their own selves and reach their deep self, they discover that all is one. In this unity, they find peace, health, and salvation.

The problem lies in the fact that human beings are not pure spirit; they are body, tied to an entire evolution of the material world and to an evolution of human societies. They may possibly engage in an experience of interiority and find individual salvation, but that does not necessarily help others, or automatically correct their relationship with others. If the person seeking salvation in pure interiority is a member of the privileged class, as is often the case, it may well be that his or her experience is a flight from responsibility toward the world. In any case, the subject of the esoteric is a subject diminished by its non-involvement in the dramas of the outside world; the esoteric does not succeed in reconciling subject and object in the outer world.

Religion and Personal Freedom

It seems paradoxical: Christ's message is a message of freedom, but even so, not even Christians always live in that manner. Some even think that being Christian requires giving up freedom, even if the sacrifice is worthwhile. Others bear the loss of freedom with resignation but they think it is absolutely necessary in order to enter into eternal life.

Since Trent, the Catholic church itself has not regarded membership within it as a call to freedom, as a path open to freedom, but rather as a duty in obedience to God. From this standpoint, freedom is necessary in order for obedience to be meritorious, but it is always a freedom in which consent is a matter of obligation. It is not really about enhancing freedom.

Over the ages of christendom, many have left the church in the name of freedom. It may have been in the name of a false freedom, but it has happened so many times that it has to be alarming. If religion is not inherently an expression of freedom it is unlikely to promote liberation and unlikely to convince our contemporaries. Let us look at some decisive aspects of humankind today, especially with a view to Latin America.

Freedom and Experience of God

People experience freedom when they can have a personal religious experience, a certain experience of God, or something that they experience as God.[12] Most traditional Catholics have a faith and a religion that comes from somewhere else, and is something simply accepted: the catechism tells them what they have to believe, the priests provide the sacraments, and commandments of the church tell them what they have to do. They are passive recipients and passive executors. It is no wonder, then, that even many men and women who are practicing Catholics display so little enthusiasm and almost no missionary outreach. When dealing with pentecostals or members of other religions, they remain silent and almost feel ashamed of their religion.

What are they lacking? A personal and immediate experience of faith.

The object of faith is God revealing, not the mediations by which this revelation reaches us. Christians have faith in God; their faith is not directed toward the Bible, church documents, the priest, or the catechist. Yet it is precisely the latter that most people experience. They have not been educated or prepared for a personal experience. A faith that is not based on a personal experience can only be alienation, and can only be lived as alienating.

The primary reason for the success of pentecostalism, whether Catholic or Protestant, is theological, not psychological; it is the very nature of faith. In rural culture, Catholicism was transmitted like the rest of culture: there was no need for a personal option based on a personal experience. People experienced miracles or God's goodness in the rain or in cures performed by the saints, but they did not experience God in faith.[13]

In pentecostalism, people say, "I have now accepted Jesus, I now know

Jesus, I have now chosen Jesus." No doubt such experiences may be complex psychological phenomena, not made up of sheer faith alone; any experience that can be felt has a psychological component that may not be authentic. However, the frequent results of moral transformation and dedication to family or community show that it is not something purely esthetic. Many of these experiences display the character of true faith that is missing in the routine of traditional Catholicism, even when it is using theologically correct formulas. The most significant thing is that the persons who undergo this experience feel that they have advanced, that they are more human and have developed their personality further. This experience has a liberating effect.

The urban world demands greater personalization. From now on, faith must be grounded in an experience of God and Christ. Some get to that point on their own, but they are the exception. One is normally educated or prepared for this, or is directly and decisively challenged by a missionary.

Among the poor, the place where religious experience is encountered is pentecostal churches, or in the charismatic renovation, once it has reached the poor classes. At one time, socially committed Christians used to condemn and reject pentecostalisms as forms of "alienation." The poor, however, do not make such a judgement, and in fact they judge that that is where they have experienced their liberation. We need to keep in mind that for many poor people, the first and most important liberation is liberation from their religion; everything else then follows.

Who are we to demand that they change the order of their priorities? It is very significant that in Nicaragua, as well as in El Salvador and Guatemala, pentecostalism has grown much more than elsewhere at the very time when the Catholic church was most committed to social action. One might think that it was in order to find a refuge from the risks of social action—but that was not the case in Nicaragua. For the situation was very much the same in Nicaragua, where social action was protected by government authorities, as it was in El Salvador, where government authorities were against it. Is it not because at that time, for ordinary people, freedom of religion—the discovery of personal freedom in a religion that made such an experience possible for them—was what was most important?[14]

Pentecostalism presents to the masses the traditional God as he was taught by the first missionaries. For the middle class and intellectuals this idea of God has lost all credibility. They see this God as anthropomorphic, associated with images of childhood and dependence on the family, a moralistic and distant God. Esoteric or New Age groups present a more plausible idea of God; God is present in everything, God is everything; God is the energy of the universe and the source of all life. God is the life in everything that exists. God can be reached by plumbing one's own depths; we find God within ourselves. The experience of going down into the depth of the self leads to the experience of God, which is also experience of the self, experience of the world as a whole, and experience of the relational knot tying God, self, and world together.

In any case, what is sought in this religion is a direct experience of God, without going by way of the ecclesiastical system, which most people do not understand because it is completely alien to contemporary urban culture. It is interesting to note that many Catholics who discover this religion feel relieved, as though they had been delivered from a great constraint. They used to feel the Catholic system as a meaningless imposition with no purpose, because the mediations (sacraments, worship, doctrine, clergy, moral precepts) did not lead to an experience of God, offered nothing to the person, and seemed to operate magically, or indeed in a purely administrative way, as though salvation were to come at the end of a series of formalities.

Certainly the desire for liberation in religion has become more universal and more insistent. The church cannot assume yearnings for liberation in all areas of social life and remain dead to yearnings for religious liberation. Indeed, there is a long tradition of Christian mysticism that is perfectly orthodox and has been part of the history of Christianity parallel to the heterodox tradition, although in christendom it was very suspect for two reasons, one valid and the other dangerous.

The mystics were often placed under suspicion of allowing themselves to fall into heterodoxy and of wanting to free themselves from the institutional church in order to form a purely spiritual church. That was why the mystics of the Low Countries and the Rhine (in the thirteenth to the fifteenth centuries), the Spanish mystics of the sixteenth century, including St. John of the Cross, and others in various places, were persecuted. The church has condemned many of its best members out of fear of a threat of heterodoxy. Today the mystical tradition provides a great deal of material for a spiritual orientation suited to the individual person.

Another reason lies in the danger of confusing psychological experience with true spiritual experience. There is such a danger in both the esoteric (spiritism, theosophy, and so forth) and in pentecostalism. Some experiences can be produced artificially with the right psychological means. Some experiences are nothing but pure feelings, and others are purely ecstatic. Nevertheless, such experiences are not necessarily an evil; the evil would be to think that they are real experiences of the true God. Genuine mystics embody the long journeys that lead to a true knowledge of God in the "dark night," but those paths must be taught.

Even thirty years ago, when liberation theology first emerged, traditional popular religion was still strong.[15] It was judged to be a sufficient foundation on which to build a praxis of liberation. People thought that the problem was to show Christians that to be consistent with their own religion they had to enter into a praxis of liberation, and that is what was done. Today among the urban masses and even in the most distant hamlets, everything has changed. Traditional religion has been weakened a great deal; it is no longer so solid. It has been shaken by the new urban culture and it is no longer a foundation for a praxis. It is necessary to first reaffirm religion and bring about a true conversion. If Catholics do not manage to do so, other religions will—as they are in fact doing.[16]

Interreligious Dialogue

People used to be familiar with only one religion and only one church. No option or choice was possible; there was no doubt or hesitation. Now we have a true market of religions. People who live in cities can quite easily become familiar with and compare various religions.

Actually, many make efforts to learn, they make comparisons, and they have doubts. Particularly in Brazil, many take items from several religions, or they try out a new church. Many are Catholics, but also spiritists, and they are interested in New Age, and go to an umbanda center and they also put some stock in macumba as well.

Many are satisfied to have a number of religions, each of which can help them deal with one area of life, while other areas are left for other religions. Others are seeking the religion that seems to them to be truest, but they have still not made a choice. These persons bring interreligious dialogue into their own persons. They engage in internal ecumenism, inasmuch as various religions are present in their own minds.

These persons are often afraid of Catholics, because they think that the Catholic church is intolerant; it demands a choice and does not allow them to pick and choose. Pentecostal churches are even more intolerant. But the Catholic church also bears such a reputation—even though there have long been Catholics who have known how to practice the art of concealing their multiple religions.

There are persons who are afraid of falling into a trap. The Catholic church is quite "soft" for pulling people in, but once someone has entered, the doors are shut, and one can no longer attend other religions. To preserve their freedom of choice, many prefer to keep their distance from the Catholic church, or at least from its visible structures.

Certainly, there cannot be freedom to choose between truth and error. But who can say what is true and what is false? Can a person allow another to come and tell him or her what is true and what is false? Religious freedom is freedom to seek for as long as one finds necessary, freedom to choose, and freedom to decide when the moment is right.

On the Transcendence of God

In polemics and apologetics, in order to defend the church's authority and decisions, the hierarchy often invokes God's "transcendence," as though that transcendence were the basis for such expressions of authority. Whatever the intentions of the authorities in such cases might be, the people understand transcendence to mean exteriority. They understand that it is outside me, something other than the self, that thereby places limits on the self; something that is conceivably a threat to the self. Almost all the arguments of modern or contemporary atheism result from a false interpretation of God's transcendence, as do almost all relations of mistrust toward the Christian churches and particularly toward the Catholic church.

God is transcendent in the sense that God's being is of another level: God is creator and we are creatures. God is source of life and, we, a life deriving therefrom. God is not Other alongside us, or exterior to us. God is Other enveloping us and independent of us. God's transcendence and immanence cannot be separated. God is in us, in the depth or root of our being; more present in us than we are ourselves, inasmuch as God is source of our self. Transcendent, accordingly, does not mean alien.

Even Karl Barth, who so emphasized God's otherness and put forth the notion that God is "Other," toward the end of his life had to recognize that he had exaggerated: he had taken transcendence to such an extreme that immanence disappeared from his theology. He had to acknowledge the "humanity of God," that is, that the "Other" as applied to God does not mean exterior, and that the "Other" God is also more deeply human than human beings themselves.

Among the people, God's transcendence is often expressed by the notion of the "will of God." In the Catholic church the "will of God" is constantly invoked. What do the people understand by the "will of God"? In most instances, it is invoked to legitimize something that comes from outside, that is imposed, that is not understood, that goes against one's own desires, an arbitrary decision, the exercise of sheer power, in short, the manifestation of a will quite like a human will. God's will comes to be confused with the will of the church, or that of the pastor or a religious superior. God's will thus comes to be seen as a will contrary to that of the person, as a more powerful will to which one can only yield, because it is more powerful. Thus it is imagined that God wants to affirm his power by humbling the freedom of his creature.

This is all blasphemy, but one that is constantly repeated. The church's documents themselves are not exempt from it. For example, in the Vatican II Decree on the Religious Life, we can read in paragraph 14: "Under the influence of the Holy Spirit, religious submit themselves in faith to their superiors, who take God's place." How can a creature take God's place? How can the will of a finite human being take the place of the transcendent and immanent God? Are superiors somehow transcendent? Are they not part of the same world in which their subordinates are present, and are they not motivated by passions of fear, envy, love or hatred, rivalry, and so forth? And how can they be immanent? Are they perchance in the depth of the personality of their subjects as the source of their life and their freedom? This may have been a slip on the part of the Council fathers, but it is a deeply significant slip, because in practice that is how people behave in everyday life.

God's will is the source of the deeper, more authentic human will. What God wants of a person is what that person feels at the deepest level of his or her being. Certainly we are all divided and we fail to do what we will, as St. Paul says. However, that which we will deep within ourselves, even without doing it, is precisely God's will, which is not alien to our desire. On the contrary, it is our most intimate and most personal desire, even though we are resisting.

God's will cannot be opposed to our deepest desire. What happens is that persons do not immediately identify their deepest desire. They can go for years struggling and wavering back and forth. If an external authority is hasty and orders a person to obey before he or she has recognized his or her deepest desire, the result is a revolt because freedom has been wounded. We cannot in God's name impose a behavior that the person does not recognize as coming from the depths of his or her own being. Anyone so acting is nourishing the idea of an arbitrary God opposed to human freedom, a God who fears the creature. Now God's revelations show that God, who was all-powerful, became weak and impotent in order to allow the full development of human freedom. Instead of the God who liberates the human person, the false image of a despotic God is reinforced. Christendom, which was based on Roman law and on a vertical structure of society, did not see that as unfitting. It invented theologies that legitimized an arbitrary will of God and a sheer affirmation of power, as though that power were the assurance of order in the world. In the mindset of that time, everything that served to maintain the order of the world or of society was legitimate. All arbitrariness in individual cases was excused and on a more general level was simply ignored. We no longer live in those times.

Given the image of the arbitrary and despotic God, it is no wonder that many prefer an almost pantheistic God, a God completely in tune with us, as found in the esoteric.

The Liberation of the Self

In their traditional rural setting, people used to be poorer but they were happier and more balanced. They had more wisdom, and fewer personal problems. They worked harder and suffered more, but their lives were happy and they were more thankful, more reconciled to their life. Some fragments of that old society still remain in Latin America, and so we can make comparisons with the situation in the cities. Even so, young people are moving out. What they want is not happiness, but the utopia of a new culture. Ultimately, they hope to find happiness, but for now they face many problems and yet, this is what they want.

Life in urban culture makes people more vulnerable, insecure, and anguished. Hence, we see a pursuit of tranquility and peace, a pursuit of inner equilibrium, a pursuit of meaning and value, a pursuit of identity. People go running around, become tired, become exhausted, and in the end, do not know what they are and what they are doing. They live in a state of continual dissatisfaction, attempting to overcome it within the endless means of entertainment offered by the market. That becomes possible because there are so many means of entertainment on the market that they can fill every moment of people's lives, not allowing them any time to ask themselves what they are doing and what is of value in their lives.

The dominant culture is one of satisfaction or contentment.[17] This is not, however, a satisfaction that has been reached, but one that is being sought, questioned, anguished over. People are all seeking their happiness—that was not what their elders and those in the rural area did. Because they are not happy, they are running after happiness, and there is no lack of prescriptions for it.

To begin with, they place the blame for their unhappiness on the feeling of guilt instilled in them by society, that is, by their education. Once they have "gotten rid of guilt" there are prescriptions for happiness which are brought together in a huge market. All areas of the world have prescriptions to offer. Meanwhile, violence is rising in the cities, and there is a risk of dangerous explosions. Where does the solution lie? Where is true wisdom to be found?

Getting Rid of Guilt*

Throughout almost all the twentieth century, psychoanalysis has symbolized the movement to rid society of its guilt. It has been the symbol of psychological liberation. Psychoanalysis was not alone; other psychologies have also taken up this question, as have most moral philosophies in this century, which has really been the century of the struggle against sin.[18]

Sin was said to be the cause of all human unhappiness. People were educated to think they were sinners. Instilled in them was the feeling that they were sinners, that they had a debt to pay. They went through life with the feeling that they would never be able to pay the whole debt, and hanging over them was the threat of a vengeful power that was coming to collect the debt. Besides that, churches claim that payment will have to be made in the other life if the debt has not been paid here on earth. To expiate guilt persons accept suffering and privation and they devise such things if they do not have enough imposed on them by their circumstances. People punish themselves in order to avoid God's punishment. They go through life pursued by guilt feelings.

Guilt feelings do not come from the awareness of one particular act or other. Indeed, those who feel most guilty are the very people who would be incapable of committing any transgression. What they have is an overall impression, a confused feeling of being a debtor, of not being what one ought to be, and of not fulfilling one's duty.

Where does the feeling of guilt come from? We leave it to specialists to seek a satisfactory explanation. In any case, there is no doubt that the church, missionaries, and preachers used and abused sin in their preaching. There is no doubt that since the Middle Ages, the sense of sin has occupied the forefront in the pastoral activity of the church (all the Christian churches). Because the feeling of guilt was strong, it was easier to keep people submissive to the church by nourishing a consciousness of sin. For the church also

---

* In this section Comblin uses the terms *culpabilização* and *desculpabilização*, which are used by some scholars (see note 18) but do not have English cognates. Trans.

held the remedies: confession, indulgences, meritorious works (especially alms, including alms to mendicants).

The church used the instilling of guilt as a preferred procedure in Christian education, and families took the same route. It used guilt feelings in the realm of sex. The family was defending itself and the church was defending the family. A feeling of a very grave sin was cast over anything done outside the discipline of the family. Sex was systematically connected with sin. This was easy pastoral work; one needed only arouse the ever-latent awareness of sin.

After almost a thousand years, the instilling of guilt ultimately provoked a huge revolt that exploded during the twentieth century. Men—and women even more—began a struggle against sin, that is, against the awareness of sin that they found in themselves. They condemned the church's message of guilt. They sought ways of being liberated from the sense of sin. They wanted to live without punishment or threat or debt to pay.

The church offers the sacrament of penance, but that sacrament has become the symbol of the pastoral work of instilling guilt. It horrifies most Catholics: the number of confessions today is not even a thousandth of what it was thirty years ago.[19]

Certainly in the more industrialized countries of the West the struggle against sin is over. People have gotten rid of guilt and it is no longer a concern. The new generations are no longer being told what people were told for the previous thousand years. In Latin America, the situation is different. Only since 1950 have the psychological disciplines begun to make their way in. The traditional education held sway until then. Hence the struggle to get rid of guilt is still going on.

In Brazil, it was particularly the literate classes, those who received a Western-style education, who actually internalized guilt. As a rule, blacks were not affected and did not share in this sense of sin, nor did the indigenous nor a good portion of the mestizo people who were little marked by the impact of the Christian imparting of guilt, because they had little contact with the clergy.

Liberation from guilt, the revolt against sin and the sense of sin is a challenge to the church. The message of Jesus is the forgiveness of sins. How does this message reach the mass of those baptized? Is it not, in most cases, with the idea that God does not forgive but punishes, and that the conditions for forgiveness are so complicated that there is practically no forgiveness? There are some people who say that God is different, and is not like what the priests say. They put God on one side and the church on the other, like two contradictory voices.

In christendom the clergy showed anxiety over sin because they felt responsible for the order of the universe. Priests did not regard their mission as forgiving sin but preventing it. Thus, they took on a task of publicly assuring morality. Should that be the mission of the church? Ought it to be preventing sins at the risk of projecting onto society a general feeling of guilt and appearing in the eyes of the people as a police enforcing customs and morality? In any case, it would be unwise not to look for a response to the revolt against the sense of sin that keeps so many people away from the church.

Liberation from Inner Discontent

Today it is not the sense of guilt—particularly of guilt linked to transgressions in the area of sexuality—that disturbs our contemporaries, but a general feeling of malaise or of discontent. To the extent that people's material welfare improves, their psychological discontent also increases. Material problems diminish, but interior problems increase. Such dissatisfaction has to do with lack of meaning in life, lack of personal identity, and failure to find those values that are worth pursuing.

Some are criticizing a narcissism that is becoming the way of life of the new generation. This criticism is raised especially in the United States, but also in all classes around the world that have taken on that way of life. Lacking any fixed reference point or secure set of values, people look for masks, they invent little dramas, they run from one fashion to another, they momentarily adhere to any passing novelty in order to conceal their inner emptiness.[20]

For mental health, since ancient times, there have been kinds of knowledge that can be transmitted: from theosophy to astrology, transcendental meditation, positive thinking, spiritism, and so forth. All these ways lead not only to truth, but to mental health. Among the middle classes everyone practices at least one of these treatments that promise equilibrium and happiness. All these methods, which could be listed for many pages, have at least one sure effect: they draw attention to the deep imbalance and profound insecurity of men and women who have entered the new urban culture.

In this regard, moral and spiritual counseling are now very appropriate to our age. Priests used to provide counseling through the sacrament of penance or on house visits. Today this ministry has declined a great deal. Most Christians seek out other counselors: a spiritist medium, evangelical pastor, *pai-de-santo* or *mãe-de-santo* [Afro-Brazilian men and women mediums], astrologer, or someone else. In large cities there are many counselors. Only the Catholic church is neglecting this ministry. Yet among Catholics there are many people willing to provide this service; they would have to be given an official mandate so that their ministry would be officially accepted and recognized.

Certainly personal attention is the great need of people today. Everyone is concerned about problems of immediate survival and problems of community life in a society still in formation. Emotional and practical personal support will often be felt as the primary need.

The social activists of thirty years ago failed to appreciate everyday life, and hence they have not won the confidence of the multitudes. Only one who is integrated in his or her personal inner life as well as home and family life can be confident of having support in times of struggle and difficulty. Liberation also exists and is built in everyday life.

Liberation from Violence

For forty years, more or less from 1956 (the attack on Moncada, Cuba) to the end of the guerrilla war in El Salvador, the problem of Latin American violence was the problem of political violence, i.e., guerrilla-style armed insurrection. That problem still exists in Peru and Colombia, but it is no longer a continent-wide problem. It is limited to a few rearguard sectors.

The example of the Zapatista Army in Chiapas demonstrates the new meaning of guerrilla struggle: it is not a war movement, but a maneuver to attract media attention, and thereby have an impact on Washington. The new revolutionaries recognize that it no longer makes sense to try to conquer the national government; everything is decided in Washington. You have to act within society in the United States, and that has been shown to be quite feasible. In a world run by TV, penetrating into the mind of the citizens and leaders of the United States is not beyond the realm of possibility.

The problem of violence is different today, namely, the violence of the city: violence by young people with no future, violence of organized crime, and of drug traffickers who can move into this mass of unemployed and untrained young people, the violence of the police whose connections with the mobs and organized crime are growing, and the violence of ordinary citizens, who become tired of suffering violence and react in the same fashion.

An atmosphere of violence is thus created. Significantly, most city dwellers favor the death penalty, agree to the killing of teenaged thieves, and support a police force that kills over a thousand persons a year in São Paulo—fifteen times as many as are killed in New York, which has one of the worst reputations. Most reject activity to defend human rights, and accuse Cardinal Arns of having more sympathy for young thieves than for their victims. The atmosphere emerging is a call to violence. In such an atmosphere anything can happen. Provocateurs can lead gangs of young people to loot supermarkets or malls, set stores on fire, or destroy electric systems, water distribution systems, and so forth, all in order to legitimize an action aimed at wiping out the undesirables.

A culture of violence has arisen. The problem thereby arises: how struggle against this culture of violence? In the first place: how are we to struggle against this culture of violence within our own selves?

The ruling classes have chosen to flee, going off to live away from the cities, and that trend can only spread. The problem is for those who remain behind, and for the church that remains behind or sets itself up in the midst of violence.

In a new culture where many persons do not have a defined status, everyone is afraid of everyone else. Individuals seek refuge in a small family circle (brothers and sisters, cousins, and so forth). Even so, a problem of culture remains. There is an education for peace as there is an education for violence. Christians will be called to contribute with others to create a culture of peace.

"Culture of peace" means the capability of controlling oneself and resisting the instincts of a violent response to violent assaults. There does exist a culture of non-violence, which consists of learning to not react with violence to a violent act. Just as athletes learn to discipline their reflexes and control their movements, so also citizens can learn to discipline their spontaneous reactions. It used to be said that the police received special training to remain calm and not react with violence to provocations. Today, they sometimes seem to be trained for the opposite. Even so, such special training to always remain calm would be more useful than ever for them as well.

Violence is contagious. It is like a flame that spreads and causes a fire—hence the need for training. Only non-violent persons will be able to step in at those times when the masses begin to get out of control.

The lack of remedies for the ills of large cities makes it more than likely that there will be outbreaks of violence in the twenty-first century. Are the churches preparing to step in before the worst happens? Freeing people from their own violence will be a new—unexpected but unavoidable—challenge.

Today the church is facing its strongest competitors in the area of personal salvation. Many "saviors" are rushing in to offer their prescriptions and their remedies to our contemporaries. They have already won a good portion of the terrain: pentecostals, spiritists, Afro-American religions, Asian religions, new religions such as New Age, occult sects, esoteric theories and wisdoms, medicines, normal and paranormal psychologies, theosophy, and so forth. We can presume that a true Christian wisdom would make it possible to dispense with so many remedies, so many paths to individual salvation. There lies the challenge.

The Subject of History

Thirty years ago, in liberation theology circles subjectivity was not a problem: each person was called to be the subject of history. At least there was room for workers in the countryside and the city to be the subject of history, along with organic intellectuals, the class called to accompany the proletariat, and often even for a supposed "national bourgeoisie."

The very notion of the subject of history was itself subordinated to the idea of history, and the latter was very much influenced by nineteenth-century ideologies of history. History was understood as a necessary, single, irreversible process leading from one kind of society to another by virtue of forces acting in society independently of individual wills. This concept was common to liberalism, socialism, and positivism. Of course, in the twentieth century, Marxism was the most prominent such ideology, especially because a good portion of the European intelligentsia took it up, especially between 1945 and 1975 (Sartre: "Is Marxism unsurpassable?").

Recent events have made it clear that this concept of history must be made more flexible. History is not a single or unified process, but is made up of the interactions of many developments which are not even parallel or simultaneous. History is diversity: diversity of forces and diversity imposed by geography and the past.

When history was conceived as a unified movement there was a homogeneous subject: all those not ruled out were combining their forces to make up a single force of history. Under those conditions, the proportion of real persons actually operating in specific movements did not matter much in historic "praxis." Because there was only a single movement, those who were not participating would in fact some day come to participate. What mattered was that there be a conscious and active minority which would be the vanguard; it validly represented the historic subject.

Obviously, this concept of historic subject has to be loosened. There is no single subject; there is a variety of movements, more or less united, more or less parallel, in the midst of vast multitudes of the indifferent who are uninterested or who are busy pursuing other things. An association of forces can be created, but not a historic subject. There are many historic subjects but they do not make up a single grand subject.[21]

Once we take into account the diversity of subjects, we can and must take into account what has really happened, and what is happening, with Latin American peoples. First, activists are in retreat: their numbers, enthusiasm, and dedication have declined. The phenomenon of the withdrawal from activism, which took place in Europe and the United States in the seventies, is reaching Latin America. One can claim that insofar as problems have actually gotten worse, such a decline of activist consciousness is not justified, but it is a reality. That seems to indicate that activism is a response not only to the urgency of problems, but comes from broader forces connected to the movement of Western society as a whole. Even while they want to free themselves from the West, activists apparently tend to follow the rhythms and evolution of Western society.

Secondly, base communities, both Catholic and Protestant, are stagnating. While charismatic and pentecostal movements, Afro-Brazilian and other religions are growing astonishingly, CEBs are not growing and perhaps are beginning to move backward in some places, for example, where a bishop with a different line is appointed.

Third, most of the population never supported the revolutionary movements. The vast majority of people not only rejected the guerrillas and all armed movements, but have even inclined toward right-wing parties: El Salvador, Nicaragua, Brazil, Chile, Argentina, Colombia, Peru, Mexico, and so forth. Seldom do left-wing parties get more than 25% of the votes.

This means that the majority of popular masses are behind other projects; their minds are on something else and they have not been persuaded by discourse on transforming society. Is this just a problem of communication, culture, or lack of opportunity?

It seems likely, based on the testimony of so many people in popular circles, that in the popular imagination, the left is associated with violence and people are extremely fearful of violence. What can be done to purify this image and dissociate social change from violence? If such a dissociation is not achieved, the popular masses will continue to be mistrustful.

Nevertheless, social problems have not simply remained, but they are even more serious than they were thirty years ago. Why are not stronger subjects emerging now to take on a history that is more challenging and more complex?

One can no longer work with the illusion of a single subject. There will be a vast variety of popular movements and they will have to be pulled together for the sake of common projects.

For the peoples who are excluded now as the century ends, the narcissism of the ruling classes offers nothing but indifference. The dominant culture no longer offers anything and society is falling apart. The poor are going to have to act with far less protection than before, because they will be less integrated into the overall society. The ruling classes think everything is solved with more police or with speeches at international conferences.

The challenge is to reconstitute a praxis of liberation, to arouse subjects who will dedicate themselves to the liberation of their people, even if they have little time to devote to their own personal problems. Although this may be slow in coming, it is the way for it to be achieved. This slowness, however, should not make people think that they have been used in the service of sheer utopia, mere dreams with no future.

The church can again perform a decisive task in the preparation of these multiple subjects of a multiple history that we cannot guide, but that constitutes the field of our activity, the place where charity is put into practice.

True Liberation of the Person

Everything that has been said in this chapter on personal liberation expresses how our contemporaries see their own persons and their personal problems. Yet none of this gets at the real problem, namely, attaining the true self in the Christian sense.

The greatest reproach that can be made against liberation theology is that it has not devoted enough attention to the true drama of human persons, to their destiny, to their vocation, and consequently to the ground of the issue of freedom. This does not mean that in their own life or in their action as persons the theologians have not paid enough attention to it, but it does not come out clearly enough in their writings. This lack has made it possible for their followers or hasty activists to spread a superficial notion of Christianity that reduces it to a strategy of political or social struggle. One effect has been that prayer has often been superficial and has come to be confused with practicing consciousness-raising.

The new spiritualisms, with their recipes for happiness and joy are even more superficial: they throw out every element of suffering in life, all personal drama, and turn religion into a great entertainment in order to keep the Christian message forgotten. Religious enthusiasm, the search for knowledge and psychological exercises may have a therapeutic effect, but they distance people from the reality of life.

The revelation of the Christian subject is found in St. Paul, who is the author who presents the message of Jesus as seen from the side of the subject. That is where the true self is revealed. The first eight chapters of the epistle to the Romans constitute the most extensive and most systematic exposition on this point.[22]

It is the true self that experiences the contest between sin and grace, feels pulled by the two opposing movements, and struggles all life long because it never reaches a state of tranquillity. Many do not know what is going on because their whole life unfolds on a superficial level. Especially today one can experience so many forms of entertainment that one can spend the entire time without ever thinking about life, like an unconscious object moving here and there without asking why. Many people today are incapable of reaching the level of sin. They act, but none of their acts is theirs. Everything is produced by the impulses coming from society. They never choose. They don't live; they "are lived." They carry out a program already set by society which prescribes the food, sleep, activities, games, leisure, feelings, sex, and psychological crises. Everything is programmed.

Even so, there are moments of truth, times of real crisis and doubts. In most cases, however, these crises are treated as though they were superficial psychological problems and the person is offered new distractions in order to escape from them.

But the question is out there; one cannot continue indefinitely in evasion. The problem of what people are doing with their lives and what they are dedicated to must be resolved. There are unavoidably two paths, and only two, although a person can hesitate throughout life or go from one to another.

There is a moment when the person stands before a total and definitive decision in which he or she is evaluating not simply his or her professional, athletic, matrimonial, family, or political life, but life as a whole, and asks what his or her life is actually worth. For those who believe, the one judging is God. For others, it may not have a name, but it is the absolute benchmark from which the person makes the important decisions of his or her life. Specifically, what Paul calls sin or the flesh can appear in many guises. Deep down it is always fear, flight from a call, fear of loving or fear of giving, fear of committing oneself, of surrendering, fear vis-à-vis faith, vis-à-vis hope.

And yet, there is faith, self-surrender, hope and openness to the future, abandonment of any selfishness and of being closed in on oneself, and the rejection of fear.

Today it is very difficult to know where people place themselves, because these things are very deeply personal, and all people hide their deepest reserves. Moreover, we do not have many words for saying these things. We need the help of poets, playwrights, or writers, who know how to express the human dramas, and who sometimes reach the deep level of the true reality of human life.

Ultimately, it is always a choice between refusal to love and loving action. It is well to state immediately that this is not an academic choice, but life forces one to choose, and many choose without being aware, almost by instinct.

Paul presents the choice as a struggle. The pull downward is very strong, instinctive, unconscious. We occupy a great deal of our thinking in rationalizing our sin, convincing ourselves that it was not sin but something normal. Paul does not speak about particular acts; they are symptoms of the presence of the enveloping sin, of resistance to God's call. He seems to assume that the attraction of sin is almost irresistible—hence, the problem of salvation.

However, the problem lies not in sin but in liberation from sin. A thousand years of instilling guilt and "Augustinianism" have created a fixation around sin. The true problem is the deep desire to be other, to create something else, to be human beyond routines, and beyond the weight of customs, traditions, instincts, and innate selfishness. The moderns thought that the problem was social and that it was society that corrupted the individual. That does not help explain anything. Why does the individual settle so easily for this society and why does this society exist? Where does this society come from?

We know today that the human species has a long prehistory and bears all this prehistory bodily, from the initial explosion of matter to the history of the animal species that have gone before us. The human calling goes further, surpassing what these animal species have done, that is constituted their own life. How can a being emerging from this evolution of the material world be capable of exercising freedom? How can it learn to love, when the animal species survive by devouring one another, competing with their neighbors to assure their portion of food?

What is costly is the pull upward, the feeling of a higher calling which is found in all cultures and all civilizations, but which the life of Jesus and the entire Judeo-Christian history bring to an extreme state of tension. What is strange is not that there is so much sin—the strange thing is that human beings become resigned in the face of sin, and do not begin again indefinitely the struggle to overcome it, to go beyond their limits. The strange thing is not that there is injustice, domination, slaughter; the strange thing is that human beings should become resigned to this situation and cease having the ambition to rise higher. This ambition is God's grace.

When human beings seek to overcome their limits, overcome their past, basic liberation is taking place. This has also taken place in the fact that the human being has conceived a God-love, whom it seeks to imitate.

Only men and women who accept this vocation will be able to authentically assume the tasks of liberation. It matters little whether they visibly belong to the Body of Christ or not. What does matter is that they be involved because they have heard the call and have had faith. Indeed, any particular project can be vitiated by what has been done in the past: by the desire to live, no matter what, at the expense of others, by the will to power, by the will to possess (property, sex, prestige, and so forth). The history of the twentieth century offers an extensive display of the various ways in which projects of personal or social liberation have been coopted or reabsorbed by what Paul called the "old man."

Poverty is the visible sign of the failure of the human dream, the failure of utopia. It displays how great the distance is between aspirations and reality. If the elites are now fleeing far from the cities, it is probably so that they will not have to behold with their own eyes the spectacle of poverty; for that is the sign that they have failed and that their entire privileged life as consumers and property owners is a lie, an illusion, a way of running away from themselves. Between reality and their own life they try to raise a veil of so many things, so many objects, so many immediate concerns, but it is no use—poverty calls into question both the person and the entire society, even if they don't want to see it.[23]

Moreover, poverty is the most natural thing in the world if we consider the genesis of humankind. Why shouldn't human beings use their intelligence to exploit their neighbor? Why shouldn't the struggle for life leave victors and vanquished? The strange thing is that there is something in the human heart that protests and does not allow the voice of rebellion and of discomfort over these issues to be snuffed out. All societies have adapted to a kind (or various kinds) of poverty that naturally enters into the social fabric, but there is a latent protest, generally repressed, which now and again breaks out in cries, cries that are calls to a higher conscience.

Poverty is the most visible challenge. How is poverty to be overcome? That means asking: how reverse the entire history of five billion years, from the burst of the primordial atom to our own days? Nevertheless, the challenge is there. Attempts at revolution have been made in all civilizations—and the challenge remains.

The great illusion of modernity was to have imagined that it was enough to make some changes in the way society was organized. Or that abundance brought by technology would ultimately be enough. Even Marxism imagined that the abundance of material production would bring about a new society without poverty. How superficial intellectuals are!

The battle is much more serious—and permanent. It has been going on for two thousand years in christendom, and it is ever reappearing. In the *ancien regime* the church had taken on care for the poor. It did a lot, many works, many hospitals, many homes for the homeless, many schools for poor children—much more than now. And yet, after so many efforts there was always some other kind of poverty left over.

What the church did not manage to do in 1800 years—end poverty—the ideologies promised to do in one generation. Liberals, positivists, and socialists all promised to do better than the church. So now where do we stand? They have also done a lot. They have done things that the church had not seen or did not want to do, but the challenge remains. We now know that a social revolution is not enough to overcome the problem. The task is huge because it has to do with creating something new: a people of persons who place the good of all above their individual good. No animal species does that (except bees and ants out of sheer instinct).

The struggle against poverty can become sheer rhetoric, when moral indignation is not embodied in real services to real poor people, and is lost in the wind. There can be a prophetic passion which turns back on itself and does not produce anything. That simply amounts to rejecting the existing world. That has been the danger envisioned by the apocalypses throughout history— paralleling Christian history, there has always run an apocalyptic strain, which completely rejects the present world and grants it no value, but is waiting for it to be destroyed and for a new world to arrive through a miracle of God (there is a secularized apocalypse which expects the advent of the new world from a miracle of history).

The struggle against poverty can be confused with a conscious or unconscious struggle to attain power. Those who defend this perspective want power in order to save society, but all those who have ever sought power throughout human history have thought this way. How can it be known whether they want or even can realize their intentions? The boundless scepticism with which the poor masses always—or almost always—welcome politicians of any stripe is comprehensible.

The best thing about what the church in Latin America has done during the past thirty years has been that it has set itself up in the midst of the poor, sharing directly in their everyday life, in the midst of great struggles to be able to live more humanly despite everything. Animals can experience hunger and thirst, but they do not know humiliation and dire poverty. In order to live with dignity under such conditions people have to overcome the limits of normal human possibilities: there stands the grace of God. Christians (whether conscious or unconscious) who decide to share in this grace have entered into the struggle for liberation. Without real, material, ongoing solidarity, without a physical presence in the midst of the poor, how can it be known whether rhetoric is grounded in a real disposition of the person?

That is why the question of poverty stands at the center of the human drama of sin and God's grace; that is why all purely spiritual movements are suspect. On a continent with vast poverty, such a spiritual approach is even more suspect—although it is understandable. Many feel impotent if they are not doing anything and would rather flee. Nevertheless, no one is responsible for overcoming poverty alone. For many it suffices to stand alongside the poor to give them encouragement.

The drama of the liberation of the self that is captive to the sin of the world, of a sin that goes back to the beginning and is the signal of a magnificent calling, is not separate from the real and material world: it is right in the middle of it.

There would be no sin if there were no call to freedom, a call for the human being to really be human, a call for some to serve others, as St. Paul said.

This true liberation of the "self" lies at the very heart of all specific liberation struggles. If this has not been seen clearly enough, it should be made plain. It may be that during the recent period it was not clear enough. At that time "politics" was culturally so important. Newspapers and the media could only speak of liberation theology in political terms, and hence a myth was created in public opinion. "Liberation theology" became a label for designating a moment in history, similar to terms in the past like "progressivism" in France, "Christian socialism" in Germany, or "liberal Catholicism," or "ultramontanism," and so forth. History goes on; new names may appear, but the problems remain the same. Liberation cannot be removed from the Christian lexicon, because it is as biblical as freedom.

9

THE TASKS AHEAD

Some have spoken of a crisis of liberation theology. A crisis occurs when new circumstances question an institution or a process and the latter clearly fails to respond to the expectations of the new times. That is not the case of liberation theology; it has not been shaken by the events of the past decade. Some thought that the fall of socialism would lead to a breakdown in liberation theology, but socialism was never a basic component of it. All the major positions of liberation theology are still in place, regardless of the fate of socialist societies.

Liberation theology is at a standstill, first of all, because Catholic theology and Christian theology in general are at a standstill; nothing new is coming out. What is most new about the churches, now at the end of the century, is that there is no more interest in theology. What arouses interest is religious experience, and the new pietisms as they are manifested in pentecostal churches and in the Catholic charismatic movement.

Intellectual life is at a standstill. The postmodern generation is moving away from philosophy and from any kind of system of thought. It values what is of the moment, immediate sensation, passing experience. The new Catholic generation is no different. We are in a period when reason is being overshadowed. Under such conditions it is no wonder that no original theology is being produced.

Latin American theology is also quiet. There are thousands of theology teachers in Latin America but what they produce is infinitesimal. The generation of the founders of liberation theology is now over fifty years old, a number are over sixty, and some even over seventy. When will the new generation come along? How can anyone know?

In any case, the situations and problems that caused the first reflections starting in the sixties have not changed; they have become more serious and it is even more urgent that answers be found. There is no lack of material for a theology of liberation. It is obvious that the problems of that period have not been solved by the new period; they have become even more serious. But need alone does not create a bodily organ: even if theological reflection is needed, it does not follow that it will be done; that depends on people, and on whether anyone is still concerned about theology at a time when the prevailing tendency is toward sheer prayer of praise.

What is the current context of a Latin American theology, and what are the new challenges it must face as it extends the thinking of previous years?

The Rise and Fall of Neoliberalism

Neoliberalism catapulted to prominence in the United States in the seventies. It was Margaret Thatcher's official doctrine in Great Britain for ten years and that of Presidents Reagan and Bush in the United States for twelve years. Bush's electoral defeat in 1992 represented a shift. Since then neoliberalism has been somewhat discredited in the First World. Although it began to have doubts around 1993 and 1994, the IMF (International Monetary Fund) continues to impose this doctrine on third-world nations.

In Latin America, economic instability, inflation, and the lack of future prospects, aggravated by the need to pay the foreign debt, created the conditions for a new generation of economists to present neoliberalism as the miracle solution. Because politicians had no solutions and were awaiting a miracle themselves, the neoliberals were welcomed.

In Chile, Hernán Büchi had already set up a radical neoliberalism under the iron tutelage of Pinochet. The new democracy did not dare to change the model. Chile might be a special case, but when Carlos Salinas de Gortari assumed the presidency in Mexico in 1988, he quickly turned into a mythic figure: he was the miracle worker. Another economic wizard soon appeared, this time the minister of the economy in Argentina, Domingo Cavallo. Both applied the neoliberal prescriptions radically: open up to imports, attract international speculative capital, engage in privatization, maintain a strong currency tied to the dollar, cut social costs in order to balance the government budget, and dismiss government employees. Bolivia and Uruguay went down the same path, and Venezuela, under Carlos Andres Perez, paid a very high price, as did Peru with Fujimori. Only Brazil has been hesitant, and seems to be remaining so, having gone half way.

This looked like a triumphal march, but then Mexico was hit by a terrible shock in January 1995. At one stroke the dream ended and neoliberalism came tumbling down; it was all an illusion. It postponed problems, but new problems arose, caused by increased imports. The problems of the nation were still there, but now they were even more serious. The gap between rich and poor was wider and indices of social welfare were worse. This showed that a miracle solution is no longer possible; there is no magician-economist who can change lead into gold.

There is no longer any dogma that can justify the neoliberal idea that economic growth is the absolute priority. Nor is there any magic formula for economic growth. In each particular case people would have to be discerning about using dependence theory or free-trade theory. No theory is always valid.

Neoliberalism made the market a quasi-idol. Now people are discovering that there is no such thing as a free market. If it is not organized in accordance with the common good of the nation, the market is handed over to uncontrollable forces. The fantastic maneuvering of speculators has opened the eyes of the more naive defenders of the so-called free market, that is, the market handed over to the most powerful multinational conglomerates. Neoliberalism has fallen faster than it rose; at least the horizons have now been made more clear: a smokescreen has been blown away.

Social Exclusion

The 1995 Brotherhood Campaign in Brazil came along at a propitious time for condemning a situation that the bishops conference in Santo Domingo in 1992 did not highlight: the social exclusion of the majority of the population in Latin America. The modernization of the economy and the migration from the countryside to the city have produced a mass of people who have taken refuge in the large cities but do not have anything to do there. They are redundant; they are made to feel that they are a disturbance; there is no room for these people in the economy.

The traditional social gap has finally led to a situation of "social apartheid." This is the main challenge today. The pace of society is such that everything that happens, everything that is done, all the changes introduced to solve the problem, end up making the gap wider. Every effort to deal with apartheid ends up deepening it. What we have is a kind of exclusion-producing machine that no one can stop. With every passing year, the rich earn more and the poor less, despite so many speeches and good intentions.

No one is succeeding in dealing with the problem, inasmuch as political leaders no longer have large designs or goals; their goal is to prepare for the next election. Corporations are making money and pushing their executives ever further ahead, and have no reason to be concerned about the future. The ruling classes build their paradises in modern "Alphavilles." The middle classes are worried and try to preserve their dream of living in the First World. Everyone else struggles to survive. No one is concerned about the future. Everyone has foreboding that this can all end very badly, but feels powerless. Ultimately, the powerful of this world are watching the formation of the clouds that portend the coming storms, but they prefer not to act. The leaders of the Group of Seven are captives of economic necessities and political necessities. They have lost all freedom; they are prisoners of the system.

The church can still speak; it can tear away the veils that conceal the truth of the world today. But, since redemocratization, nothing like that is happening. The church seems to be content with the world as it is out there, and is tending to withdraw into its own quiet quarters, far from the turmoil of this world.

The Welfare State

For twenty years the neoliberals have engaged in a relentless offensive against the welfare state. The media, especially TV and the major newspapers, have demolished it with their criticisms to the point where socialist governments (France, under Mitterand, and Spain) have had to retreat. They have blamed the welfare state for all economic problems. The poor were blamed for all economic problems, because they cost the state too much: they receive free schooling, free health care, free retirement payments, aid to indigent families, aid in the event of unemployment. The poor were sinners, and the wealthy their victims.

These critics have taken advantage of the third industrial revolution: a weakened working class, systematic unemployment, retreat of labor unions, despair among youth, and the decline of popular movements. Capitalists feel stronger and they have managed to convince the public that the solution is to allow those who have money to make even more, and thus assure the growth of the economy—all this presented with the support of well-mounted advertising. The world of ordinary people has no way of struggling against television. Even so, in Europe and the United States, despite so many campaigns, the essence of the welfare state still remains, albeit discredited, because those in power do not dare to aggressively provoke organized labor.

In Latin America, workers have always been less organized and weaker. Things have never reached the point where a true welfare state was set up, despite the principles laid down in constitutions. The ruling classes have also been enthusiastic over the propaganda against the welfare state. They think the time has come to do away with the limited fragments of it that, with considerable effort, have been made part of the social and political structure. Propaganda against the welfare state enjoys support in television and radio networks and the main newspapers. Thus they have managed to convince what there is of "public opinion" that the welfare state itself was an aberration and that "readjustment" was the solution. They are convinced that any government involvement is harmful and that the solution to social problems lies in the free market, that is, in complete freedom for capital.

We must stand up to this propaganda: first, by being aware that this is very skillfully prepared propaganda; second, by defending the poor fragments of the welfare state; and third, by working for the creation of a true welfare state.

The fact that any social reform entails a redistribution of the production of the nation, particularly of growth, should not be concealed. Injustice cannot be corrected without touching the privileges of the very wealthy, without preventing growing revenues from always going to the same hands. How succeed in pressuring the privileged classes in such a way that they accept sacrificing a portion of their privileges and give up their dreams of unlimited wealth? That is the political problem and it is not the role of the church to resolve it. But what is indeed the church's responsibility is to insist on the need for change. Technical conditions for making changes exist; what is lacking is the will on the part of those who wield power. Of course, it is not so easy to voluntarily give up one's own privileges. Yet all can realize that it is preferable to voluntarily divide up a portion of what one has rather than risk a civil war.

Today "socialism" means nothing more than a utopia with no concrete content. No one can provide the word with economic, social, or political content; it remains a utopia. What is actually possible is a welfare state—just what is so attacked by the neoliberal campaign. It will plainly not be built, however, without long harsh struggles.

Cuba has shown by example that it is possible to achieve the goals proposed, even in an underdeveloped country—and in such a fashion that social apartheid is really ended. It can be done by placing priority on schooling, health care, employment, pensions, and basic services. Such reforms do not require structural socialism as in Cuba, much less a Marxist ideology.

The Mission of the State

In neoliberal preaching the state is blamed for all evils. The solution is said to be to privatize and to reduce the role of the government to police functions. The media repeat this message endlessly. Yet there is no case in which the state has not been the fundamental factor in economic development—this has been true even in England and the United States. The example of the Asian tigers, both old and new, is particularly revealing. Despite errors, abuses, and administrative bureaucracy, the state is absolutely necessary for promoting and guiding the economy.

Whether the state should or should not have its own enterprises and what the status of government enterprises should be, and so forth, are technical questions. Sometimes the state loses control over its enterprises; in other instances, government companies provide monopolies for distributing exorbitant privileges to its employees. But these are isolated cases of corruption that do not affect the principle.

If the effect of privatization is that what has been built with public money is distributed almost free to corporations, it is robbery. If privatization turns a government monopoly into a private monopoly it is not justified. These are all technical problems, however.

A strong state is one capable of asserting a country's rights in the concert of nations. Today national states are very much weakened vis-à-vis economic powers. National states are going to have to react and organize international society.

The neoliberal sorcerer's apprentices are now shocked at the sight of 13 trillion dollars dancing around the world seeking the most advantageous opportunity for speculation. This is a vast sum of capital that is not invested and is unproductive, while the world needs huge investments so that the majority of humankind can emerge from its misery. A trillion dollars moves each day from one country to another taking advantage of exchange rate variations: it threatens currency stability and nullifies policies set by governments. But what can a weak state do about the way worldwide capital is organized?

A strong state is one that actually collects taxes, particularly from those who have money. In Latin America there is no strong state in this sense, and the very wealthy do not pay taxes. Legislation is prepared in such a way that loopholes always remain. Governments are afraid of capital flight. Only strong states can negotiate the international agreements needed to prohibit tax havens and capital flight to other countries.

That is why preparing people for politics is more necessary than ever. Serving the nation is now a lost vocation. Many look at public service as a ticket to reach more lucrative positions in the higher reaches of multinational corporations. Politics has ceased being an end; it has become a way to confiscate state secrets in order to supply them to large corporations for an exorbitant remuneration.

The churches can play a role in preparing a new political generation that will be at the service of the nation.

Cultural Action

In a society where most people are reduced to being mere consumers of culture—limited to watching the show, unable to participate—any cultural action is positive. There is no point in preparing a specific program in advance. Anything that helps is useful—especially for young people who need to emerge from their passivity.

Humankind has never faced such a huge task: to create a culture for billions of people cut off from their past and their traditions and handed over to the spectacle of a culture that does not belong to them and is lived by others. We can presume that a millennium will be needed for this, just as a millennium was needed to prepare the West as it is. As of now, we must begin, or better, keep going without losing heart because the results thus far have been modest.

Activists often used to be rigid in their criteria for cultural action; they were unsparing in their condemnations of alienation. Today, there is no point in seeking to inculcate a particular type of awareness; there is no point in preparing a theory. We must go right to what is most urgent, namely the capacity to act. What is most urgent is a collaboration by all kinds of organizations or associations, whatever their ideology, religion, or academic level might be, in order to save the new generation from sheer consumerism. Everything else will come later. After all, they will not be able to emerge from apartheid if they become accustomed to passivity.

The ideology with which an activity is carried out does not matter much and has little influence on what the action is about. What matters is the action itself. We have had the experience of people who have assimilated an ideology perfectly well, but have not done anything, and of others whose ideology has been conservative but who in practice have become agents of change.

The Priority of the City

Rapid urbanization shows clearly that the problem is the city. To the poor, high-level politics seems to be something far removed. They do not understand it, and are confused by demagogues. High-level economics is incomprehensible. National society is an abstraction and international society even more so. What is real is the city. Where are the poor going to learn political practice except in their city, their neighborhood, their shantytown? The city is the politics of the concrete.

In dealing with the problems of the city, people can go through an apprenticeship in their own situation as citizens and active members of the community. Hence, we are going to need to give priority to the problems of the city. People often used to get into politics by way of ideology. For the mass of the poor that is the wrong road. They are unable to assimilate ideology sufficiently to make it a principle of action. Instead they substitute talking about action for action. They talk about praxis and think that the word takes the place of activity or is activity. That was what happened to activists from the popular classes.

The right path is to tackle the immediate problems of the city which force them to organize the neighborhood and form pressure and action groups. Politics is learned not in meetings but rather in the street and its challenges. At one time there used to be lots of meetings. The church itself thought that acting meant having meetings. But the meetings had no impact, and many became discouraged because they concluded that politics did not accomplish anything.

Practice has shown that candidates from the popular classes can win more easily in municipal elections and show their leadership and management ability. In municipal politics results may be more limited, but they are quicker and they prepare leaders for the national level.

Likewise, municipal politics has to be decentralized. Most of the really useful actions to serve the majority come from the citizens themselves. The municipality ought to accompany, aid, and provide financing when necessary, but not plan beforehand or bypass the popular forces. A municipality will never have enough funds to respond to all the needs. The primary power will come from the endless volunteer and free work done by the citizens themselves.

The neighborhood is the place for popular culture. Today only a few carefully chosen and artificially reconstructed stars reach the national level, make it into television, or participate in the festivals and expositions mentioned in the mass media. The popular culture taking shape is situated somewhere else. Popular culture will be against the star-system or it will not exist. The big corporations in the culture industry are moving about and taking from the people all the material that they need. They attract people who fit their criteria and withdraw them from contact with the real people. Popular culture must deliberately refuse to compete with the major stars. There is room for a type of local expression that can offer salvation from the invasion of the culture industry.

Intellectuals

Intellectuals are in low spirits and in retreat. In Europe they have been in retreat for twenty years, and the same thing is now happening in Latin America. They are no longer a driving force in society; they have been replaced by economists who claim the rank of scientists. We can assume that the retreat of intellectuals is only temporary, however.

In Latin America, intellectuals have been at the head of all changes since Independence, and there is no sign that things are going to change soon. The national bourgeoisie is weak. The truly powerful live in closed circles and do not like to appear in public life. Furthermore, they are on the defensive, and cannot draw too much attention. The popular organizations are still rather weak and only become significant when they are led by intellectuals. That is the case of the Workers Party in Brazil, but also more generally of left movements elsewhere.

Intellectuals are disarmed, and without much power. They shift around, and are sensitive to changes in intellectual fashions in the First World, even while striving to be nationalistic. Yet they are the only ones who can formulate a proposal for the future and devote themselves to achieving it.

Given the poor schooling of the people, intellectuals are still going to be absolutely necessary for giving guidance to popular movements for many years. They have the capacity to conceive of an overall action and to plan, express things, and coordinate actions. They have an overall vision of the nation, of the forces in contention, and of the ongoing political context.

Nevertheless, intellectuals will have to change how they act among the people. They are not expected to teach the people a confining ideology—that would be a completely useless thinking. With such an ideology simple people come to think that they know something, whereas they simply learn to recite some words that have absolutely no effect. They do not learn to prepare for action.

What intellectuals are expected to do is to make available to the people their professional or technical capabilities: the art of thinking, coordinating, planning, evaluating, and so forth. This demands a great deal of patience, given the need for true inculturation, because the people's way of thinking is quite different from the way thinking is done in schools, and their language is also different. Two distinct types of logic are involved. Intellectuals will have to give up their illusion of universality: university language is not universal, but simply the particular language of the university world and nothing more.

Thus, it will be from the class of intellectuals, with all their weaknesses, that movements for change will emerge. We do not have the illusion of thinking that most university students and graduates want change. Most simply want to be integrated into the existing society, but a portion will be capable of seeking something new. It is that portion with which we are concerned, and they are important for the church as well.

Spiritualizing Trends

Spiritualistic religion—pentecostalism, charismatic renewal, new movements, esoteric movements of all kinds—is enjoying great success. Spiritualism has always been a problem for the church, because spiritualistic movements seem to be more religious and more faithful than the institutional church.

Besides the traditional problems they have always raised, spiritualistic movements have a specific character in Latin America. They squarely oppose any allusion to social situations; for them the social is a taboo. Or they refuse to look at the situation out of hand, or deny that there are challenges for Christians, or deny that the Christian has to take a stand vis-à-vis the world and society. They react the way whites in the United States and South Africa reacted to the issue of black people. This in fact tends to confirm that we are in a true apartheid situation. Spiritualistic movements do not question the taboos of the dominant society. To invoke political or social responsibilities is regarded as something of the devil and communism; it is subversion and atheism.

Under such conditions, dialogue becomes difficult, because the spirituals insist more on what is within, on the sacred, and on specifically religious activities. No dialogue is possible because it is blocked. Moreover, most active members, that is, those who take part in the celebrations or other religious acts, are seeking there a refuge of peace and tranquillity. In the midst of the problems and anxieties of daily life or public life, churches become, as it were, a bit of paradise on earth, a presence of heaven on earth. Anyone not seeking that does not go to worship.

It was a mistake to introduce political consciousness-raising into the liturgy. For those present that meant touching on a taboo, and hence creating a climate of anxiety. For many it amounted to imposing the kind of ideas from which they wanted to be delivered. They said, "We're here to forget our everyday anxieties, and to look for peace and love. But they only talk to us about struggles, they only show us our miseries; we're all too familiar with them, and that is just what we want to forget for a few moments."

Religious and liturgical acts are of a specific nature and should be respected. Worship cannot be turned into a means for something else, like political consciousness-raising. That is how many people were alienated from liberation movements. An attempt was made to force the movements on people at the wrong time. The people who come to worship—on the whole no more than 5% of the baptized, and, on the outskirts of the cities, 1% or

2%—are the very people who are least likely to accept a political discourse in that setting. That is why CEBs have stagnated and only bring together a minority of practicing Catholics. One can only bring political rationality into worship with people who are already convinced. Participants had to be found among the non-practicing.

Social and political consciousness-raising can be done elsewhere. Mixing worship and public life is completely out of place; few people accept it. Leaving aside the fact that activists may be taking part in worship for reasons of consciousness-raising and not for prayer, it annoys those who have come to pray.

There is no point in provoking spiritualistic movements that have resistances to being involved socially. They can be asked to take on services of practical charity in the community, neighborhood, and city. It will be wiser to avoid any ideological type of discourse, or any hasty reflection on the social or political scope of such services. Let contact with the real situation, with the everyday anxieties of the poor, prompt the questions. Dom Helder used to say, "Our greatest ally is the real situation of Latin America." Many are unaware of it. Giving them a chance to become familiar with it will be the best way to prepare future alliances.

The Liberation of Theology

From early on, theologians saw that the theology of liberation would not be possible without the liberation of theology. Juan Luis Segundo was the one who best spelled out this question, devoting several very important works to it.

Such a liberation of theology has been carried out by northern European theologians, in close connection with Protestant, particularly Lutheran, theology, since the end of the nineteenth century. The work of these theologians ultimately led to Vatican II which incorporated it, albeit partially and somewhat ambiguously, because it did not want to break with previous theology. This northern European theology, as opposed to the southern European theology of Italy, Spain, and especially Rome, was a theology of the liberation of the person.

Scholastic theology was a theology of the object: it was Christianity viewed not from the standpoint of Christians living it, but from the standpoint of the clergy teaching it and—given the reality of christendom—imposing it. When faced with the awakening of subjectivity, scholastic theology, further reinforced in its objectivity by the Council of Trent, reached the point where lay people could not assimilate it. Theological literature was completely hermetic, incomprehensible to lay people, and utterly alien to the intellectual thrust of the West. A liberation of theology from a lay standpoint arose. Priests and religious took it on because lay people had no way of getting access to theological terminology. Certain priests acted as bridges; they learned the language of the modern intellectual world and sought to express Christianity from the angle of the Christian people. This task remains unfinished, but it has still been mostly the work of first-world theologians.

Something similar has emerged in Latin America since Vatican II, prompted by the example of European theologians and in connection with them. In this instance, Latin Americans are starting with the subject understood as the people, oppressed and exploited, as the Latin American people are. The lay people envisioned by the new European theology are primarily lay people with a university education, that is, intellectuals. The new theology is being worked out in dialogue with the intellectuals of Western society. Yet, even though intellectuals can easily imagine that they are a universal conscience, they are no more than a particular group, and they are by no means representative of the people as a whole.

The new Latin American theology starts from the Christianity lived by the victims, the oppressed, the underside of history. This Christianity of the poor stands in continuity with early Christianity, and yet it has been a perspective that has been consciously or unconsciously rejected—especially since the condemnations of the spiritual Franciscans in the fourteenth century. There have always been some exceptional figures. Latin American liberation theologians like to present Bartolomé de Las Casas as their founder, but Las Casas was an outcast. In the nineteenth century there were timid expressions of "Christian socialism," but these efforts were harshly rejected by the churches.

There was an attempt at religious socialism in Germany after World War I, and it had some ties with Karl Barth's dialectical theology. In Catholicism, there were pastoral movements to come close to the working class, but there was no effort to reformulate theology out of the oppressed Christian people. Moreover, in France, the working class was not a Christian people needing a theology, but rather a pagan people who needed a new mission, as the apostles of that time insisted.

Starting from the Christianity of the poor makes it clear that everything has to be reinterpreted. It becomes clear that the Christian concepts of traditional theology have been distorted by the situation under christendom: the imperialism of Roman law, the domination of the feudal system, the restoration of the priestly system of the Old Testament, and so forth. Everything has to be reexamined and reinterpreted—from the idea of God, to the theology of Christ, the church, grace and sin, the sacraments, and so forth. What is entailed is a true liberation of theology.

It is clear that European and North American theologians have often gone only half way and have not returned to the fullness of the biblical message. Theologians and exegetes have been influenced unconsciously by contemporary philosophies: their interlocutors have been these very philosophies. Latin American theologians have chosen the poor of Latin America as their privileged interlocutors.

At least that was their intention. As in the case of European theology, the authors of the new Latin American theology have been priests (in some cases ex-priests, which doesn't make much difference). That was inevitable. Lay people were not initiates, and were not familiar with theological terminology—

and that was all the more the case with lay people from the popular classes. It was inconceivable that a theology should be written by men and women of the people. Some priests have taken on a bridge function, seeking to state in theological language something of what was being experienced far from such language. Inevitably, they were not always on the mark. Most of them had received part of their training in Europe in contact with theologies for intellectuals and in contact with European philosophies.

Even so, on the whole the works of liberation theology reflect something quite different from European philosophies, and something not found in the new northern European theologies. They translated a viewpoint of the poor and rediscovered a fundamental perspective of the biblical message and the message of early Christianity.

This is where the much discussed issue of Marxism comes in. The accusations made were unjust. When one examines where they came from, it becomes clear that they were largely the product of personal enmities. It was other Latin Americans who persecuted the liberation theologians (born in Latin America or living there), until they had gotten them condemned.

Those who were involved in social movements in Latin America regarded Marxist movements as historic allies which were seeking the same immediate objective. They thought that they could work together. They thought that Christians or Marxists by themselves could never manage to change society. There was nothing wrong with this alliance, except that it happened to conflict with the strategy of the United States and NATO, and the Vatican as well.

The mistake was not to have stated publicly the criticisms of the policies of the former Soviet Union, China, Cuba, and so forth, that were made privately. Silence seemed to indicate approval. By this silence they wanted to prevent it from being said that they were giving weapons to their adversaries; they did not want to weaken the socialist front. In the short run, silence seemed more advantageous; over the long run, it turned out to be disastrous. Indeed, the condemnations of liberation theology very much weakened the anticapitalist struggle. For this silence helped create the impression that the fall of communism included the fall of liberation theology, which was also regarded as defeated. Publishing the criticisms would have avoided that problem.

What was borrowed from Marxism was its critique of capitalism—which anyone can borrow without being a Marxist. Indeed, this critique does not lose its value with the fall of communism, and will continue to be communicated and taught in the twenty-first century. Liberation theology in the Latin American sense has barely begun. It is going to be a long slow work that will require the collaboration of many people.

Some may be puzzled that there are no references here to indigenous theology, black theology, or feminist theology. However, as I understand it, these are very different things. Liberation theology is one thing. Indigenous, black or feminist theology is not part of liberation theology. They cannot be stand-ins for one another. In the 1980s, it was sometimes said that liberation theology had taken on the form of indigenous theology, black theology, or feminist theology. As a rule, the indigenous, blacks, and women have been unwilling to be thus assimilated—and they are quite right.

The theology of the indigenous and black theology have parallels in Asian and African theologies. Their problem is inculturation, the distance between the culture of Western christendom and their own culture, as well as colonialism, which imposed a specific Christian culture along with Western ways.

The starting point of feminist theology is a questioning of almost the entire history of humankind, within which Christianity is seen as one phenomenon. Patriarchy is so old and so deeply rooted that all civilizations have practiced it. Feminism questions culture and civilization as a whole. Its standpoint is different from the standpoint of a particular culture or of liberation in the Latin American sense.

The problem of liberation theology does not come from the clash between Christianity and some other outside human reality—a culture, the feminist world, etc. The problem is internal to Christianity: what was early Christianity? Why did Christianity change? How to return to the roots of Christianity? The poor do not question the church from outside, as do the indigenous or blacks. The poor are within the church, and by every right, are the church. So why are they not in fact what they are by right?

For women the problem is more radical. It is not enough to return to early Christianity; the solution will not be found there. And it is not very likely that the issue of women will be resolved through a theology, because it has much deeper roots which go beyond the domain of Christianity.

Is It Possible to See Ahead?

What future awaits us? Is it possible to see ahead?

In principle, there are three possibilities.

The first is that "nothing is going to happen; everything is going to go on as it is." This is the working assumption of those governing today. They are managing crises. They think that time will solve everything, or that they cannot do anything anyway. They are leaving everything as it is to see how it comes out. That is what first-world leaders are doing: they are not offering any solution to unemployment, ecology, or demoralized young people. They are not offering any solution to the political breakdown of the Soviet empire or Yugoslavia. The leaders of the Latin American republics are doing the same thing. After a few years of neoliberal enthusiasm, they no longer have a solution. They are holding on to see if they can win the next election.

If everything continues in this direction, we will have an ever more dualistic society, an ever richer bourgeoisie withdrawn into its artificial Edens while the cities will be ever more violent, unlivable, neurotic, and ever more ready to provide combustible material for explosions of irrational violence. This possibility cannot be ruled out, because it seems to be the one preferred by the ruling classes.

A second possibility is more optimistic. A large reform movement gets underway, one made up of an alliance of all the classes that are the victims of the way things are going. A strong leadership succeeds in mobilizing the multitudes to support fundamental reforms (all those that everyone claims to want but does not really want). A radical redistribution of national revenue succeeds in reducing the gap between the very rich and the very poor. Current tendencies begin to be reversed thanks to the power of a state that has become effective, and the privileged class is willing to accept it to avoid something worse. The biggest difficulty would be reaching an agreement with the United States and the IMF, but that cannot be ruled out, if the alliance remains strongly cohesive. Can we anticipate this second possibility?

The third possibility is the common fallback in Latin American history: the advent of a new populism. If nothing changes, ten or twenty years from now, democracy will be discredited; it will be the image of inefficiency. No one will remember the military dictatorships anymore. The new generations will be impatient. At that point a new savior will emerge. If he succeeds in winning over TV, he will be anointed dictator and applauded by the masses because he promises to act—something that democracy fails to do. The new leader will promise much, although he will then do little—but, even so, more than the gridlocked democracy. He will satisfy some of the demands of the people, but will not break with the traditional classes who will secretly support him, because they see in him a guarantee of order. Should this happen, the new populism will last ten or twenty years and then the whole cycle will begin again.

Populism is dangerous, because everyone knows that the best way to bring the nation together is war; and Latin American enthusiasm easily gets worked up over war, as in the recent conflict between Peru and Ecuador. People will go to war over some acreage in the jungle, a barren island, or a beach, and no one objects. That is the greatest danger. Such wars amount to slaughter for a few symbols that do nothing to improve peoples' lives.

The pessimist fears that the first possibility is the one that will take place; the optimist hopes it will be the second; the realist perhaps thinks that the third is most likely.

Can Christians take refuge in a spiritual fortress allowing the world to go on its way while the reign of God is triumphant in some parallel and purely spiritual world? That is what people used to say. Faced by great social upheavals, the nineteenth-century apologists used to argue that in the midst of so much confusion the church ought to remain undisturbed, ever the same, completely unchangeable, absolutely unshaken.

Since then we have had Vatican II and Medellín. We now have different guidelines: "The joys and the hopes, the griefs and the anxieties of people of this age, especially those who are poor or in any way afflicted, these too are the joys and hopes, the griefs and anxieties of the followers of Christ. Indeed nothing genuinely human fails to raise an echo in their hearts. . . . That is why this community realizes that it is truly and intimately linked with humankind and its history" (GS 1).

Are Christians willing to accept such a challenge? If so, let's roll up our sleeves! No single, all-encompassing solution exists, nor is any planning infallible. A great variety of actions is needed, but there is no way to rationally bring them all together. Within all this vast diversity, we need not wait for the bishops or the clergy to propose some unrealizable program. Lay people have no need to wait for guidance that is not forthcoming; they have to find in their faith the necessary inspiration and courage.

The times are not propitious for spectacular achievements. We are in a maturation period for minorities that are still hidden away. Previous programs are now exhausted. With the new realities in mind, it is time to begin to work like ants on a new and poorly known social terrain. There is not going to be any new Medellín in the near future. Nor will there be any new Vatican II in the near future; it would not have anything new to say because the church is not ready to receive a new impulse.

The social movement that led to social reform and to the welfare state started around 1870. Vatican II came ninety years later. A new social movement to respond to the new wave of economic revolution has barely begun. Now is the time to begin to work out new responses to the new challenges.

NOTES

Translator's Foreword

1. Essay in José Comblin, José González Faus and Jon Sobrino, eds., *Cambio Social y Pensamiento Cristiano en América Latina* (Madrid: Trotta, 1993).
2. *Théologie de la Paix* (2 vols. 1960, 1963); *Théologie de la Ville* (1968); *Théologie de la Révolution* (1970); *Théologie de la Pratique Révolutionnaire* (1974) all published by Editions Universitaires, Paris; *Educação e Fé* (São Paulo: Herder, 1962); *Nação e Nacionalismo* (São Paulo: Duas Cidades, 1965).
3. *Os Sinais dos Tempos e a Evangelização* (São Paulo: Duas Cidades, 1968); *O Futuro dos Ministérios na América Latina* (Petrópolis: Vozes, 1969); *La Résurrection* (1959) and *Echec de l'Action Catholique?* (1961) both published by Éditions Universitaires, Paris; *História da Teologia Católica* (São Paulo: Herder, 1969), *Mitos e Realidades da Secularização* (São Paulo: Herder, 1970).
4. *O Provisório e o Definitivo* (São Paulo: Herder, 1968). Two of my favorites are works done in the 1980s, *O Tempo da Açao* (1982) and *A Força da Palavra* (1986), both published by Vozes. The first examines the work of the Spirit in history and the second that of the word of God. Each is a kind of reflection on successive periods of the history of the church from the encounter with Hellenism, through christendom, the Reformation, and so forth. These are not treated as airtight chronological periods but as exemplifying ongoing trends and tensions in the life of the church. Thus, the issues around the Reformation arose before 1517 and have continued to the present. In each such moment, Comblin finds pluses and minuses. Contrary to many theologians who castigate Constantinian "christendom" and advocate a return to "pure" scriptural Christianity (which would be a utopian illusion) Comblin finds both fidelity and shortcomings in Christendom, and its survivals to the present. These works are not historical scholarship for its own sake—historians might find his lack of nuance exasperating—but theological essays intended to shed light on the present of the church by reflecting on its past, recent and remote.

Preface

1. Gustavo Gutiérrez, "La teología: una función eclesial," in *Páginas* (Lima), vol. XIX, n° 130, Dec. 1994, p. 15, English in *Gustavo Gutiérrez: Essential Writings*, James B. Nickoloff, ed. (Maryknoll, NY: Orbis Books, 1996), p. 274 (translation modified here).
2. This is the new fact highlighted by Hugo Assmann, "Teologia da Solidariedade e da Cidadania" in *Notas* (São Bernardo do Campo) year 1, N° 2, 1994, p. 4. For him the "major fact" today is exclusion. See also Hugo Assmann, *Crítica à*

Lógica da Exclusão (Paulus: São Paulo, 1994). It is significant that exclusion was the theme for the 1995 Brotherhood Campaign in Brazil.

3. A very suggestive critical analysis is found in the article by Hugo Assmann, "Teologia da Solidariedade e da Cidadania," pp. 2–9. Another is the Gutiérrez article cited. Another article by Hugo Assmann is, "Teología de la liberación: mirando hacia el frente," in *Pasos* (San José) n° 55, 1994, pp. 1–9. Somewhat older and less critical: Pablo Richard, "La teología de la liberación en la nueva coyuntura. Temas y desafíos nuevos para la década de los noventa," in *Pasos* n° 34, 1991, pp. 1–8; Fernando Castillo L., "Teología y liberación en los '90. Un análisis de la coyuntura latino-americana," in *Tópicos* (Santiago, Chile), n° 3, 1991, pp. 145–72 (Centro Diego de Medellín); a little older still and prior to the recent changes in the world, F. Taborda, "Métodos de Teologia da libertação na América Latina," in *Perspectivas Teológicas* (Belo Horizonte) t. 29, n° 49, pp. 293–319; Clodovis Boff, "Retrato de 15 anos de teologia da libertação," in *Revista Eclesiástica Brasileira*, t. 46, n° 182, 1986, pp. 263–271; Mário de França Miranda, "A situação da teologia no Brasil hoje," in *Perspectiva teológica*, t. 19, n° 49, 1987, pp. 367–376. More historical overview than critical analysis, João Batista Libânio, "Panorama da Teologia de América Latina nos últimos 20 anos," in João Batista Libânio and Alberto Antoniazzi, *20 Anos de Teologia na América Latina e no Brasil* (Petrópolis: Vozes, 1994), pp. 9–95. In the same book, Alberto Antoniazzi, "Enfoques teólogicos e pastorais no Brasil hoje," pp. 97–160. A broader explanation in Roberto Oliveros, "History of the Theology of Liberation," in Ignacio Ellacuría, S.J., and Jon Sobrino, S.J., eds., *Mysterium Liberationis: Fundamental Concepts of Liberation Theology* (Maryknoll, NY: Orbis Books, 1993), pp. 3–56.

Introduction

1. The number of works devoted to this event are beyond counting. Suffice it to recall that Pope John Paul II devotes an entire chapter of his encyclical *Centesimus Annus* to the events of 1989 (nos. 22-29). "The events of 1989 took place principally in the countries of Eastern and Central Europe. However, they have worldwide importance because they have positive and negative consequences which concern the whole human family" (*Centesimus Annus*, no. 26).

2. Jorge Castañeda says, "For the left, the fall of socialism in the Soviet Union and Eastern Europe represents the end of a stirring, effective, nearly century-old utopia." Jorge Castañeda, *Utopia Unarmed: The Latin American Left after the Cold War* (New York: Alfred A. Knopf, 1993, p. 241). Characteristic expressions of the loss of utopia are, for example, the debate, *Adeus ao socialismo* in *Novos Estudos* (CEBRAP) July 1991, n° 30, pp. 7–42; Franz Hinkelhammert, "O cativeiro da Utopia. As utopias conservadoras do capitalismo atual e o espaço para alternativas," in *REB*, vol. 54, n° 216 (1994), pp. 787–819; Frei Betto, *O Paraíso Perdido: Nos Bastidores do Socialismo* (São Paulo: Ed. Geração, 1993).

3. Typical reactions of the left: Robin Blackburn, ed., *After the Fall* (London: Verso, 1991), with articles by Norberto Bobbio, Ralph Milibrand, E. P. Thompson, Jürgen Habermas, Hans M. Ensenberger, Fred Halliday, Eric Hobsbawn, Robin Blackburn, Fredric Jameson, André Gorz, and Diane Elson; Atílio A. Boron, *Estado, Capitalismo e Democracia na América Latina* (São Paulo: Paz e Terra, 1994).

4. A huge publicity campaign has succeeded in deeply discrediting the state and politics. In the United States, it succeeded in putting Ronald Reagan and George Bush

into office and they became its greatest promoters. In Great Britain the Thatcher government performed the same work for ten years. During the 1980s, the state was blamed for all of society's ills. Ideological postmodernity has completely marginalized the state as though it were something that could be dispensed with. Neoliberalism has been primarily a campaign to weaken national states and thereby make way for the movement of international capital, especially for speculation.

5. The same publicity campaign created the myth first of Chile, then, Mexico, and then Argentina, as examples of "denationalization" or "de-statization." The myths came tumbling down in January 1995, with the financial crisis in Mexico, but there is still a widespread mistrust toward the state, although throughout the Third World the state is still very weak—or rather, does not even manage to establish a true state. Cf. Bertrand Badie, *L'Etat Importé* (Paris: Fayard, 1992); Georges Corm, *Le Nouveau Désordre Économique Mondial* (Paris: La Découverte, 1993).

6. Sociologists, philosophers, and theologians are still hesitant and do not know what to make of the new resurgence of the phenomenon of religion, which is so far removed from the practices and doctrines of traditional religions, and especially of institutionalized Christianity. Cf. P. Valadier, *La Iglesia en Proceso: Catolicismo y Sociedad Moderna* (Santander: Sal Terrae, 1990) (translation of French, 1987), pp. 63–97; Danièle Hervieu-Léger, "Les Manifestation Contemporaines du Christianisme et la Modernité" in Centre Thomas More, *Christianisme et Modernité* (Paris: Cerf, 1990), pp. 295–316.

7. We should not be deceived by the new citizenship movements, which are very tiny. Far more prevalent in Latin America, especially in the cities, are identity movements with symbolic differences (soccer clubs, kinds of music, etc.).

8. Cf. Alvin Toffler, *Powershift* (New York: Bantam Books, 1990); Paul Kennedy, *Preparing for the Twenty-First Century* (London: Fontana Press, 1993); Peter F. Drucker, *Post-Capitalist Society* (New York: HarperBusiness, 1993) and *The New Realities: In Government and Politics/ in Economics and Business/ in Society and World View* (New York: Harper & Row, 1989).

9. The working class has declined in number, is being diversified into many different functions, and is being isolated from the body of workers through outsourcing or breaking up of companies. The globalization of the economy furthermore makes it possible to quickly transfer a production unit from one country to another, or from southern to northern Brazil, where labor is weaker.

10. Cf. Hugo Assmann, "Brasil/1985: Sigue incierto el rumbo de la 'nueva república,'" in *Pasos* (San José) n° 2, 1985, pp. 1–11. Disenchantment with the new democracy is manifested in growing indifference toward election campaigns.

1. The Church Context

1. Cf. Michel Schooyans, "Centesimus Annus et la sève généreuse de Rerum Novarum," in Conseil Pontifical "Justice et Paix," *De "Rerum Novarum" à "Centesimus Annus"* (Vatican, 1991), pp. 27–72. The continuity of the church's social doctrine over a century is there made clear.

2. Cf. R. Aubert, "L'encyclique Rerum Novarum, point d'aboutissement d'un lente maturation," in *"De Rerum Novarum" à "Centesimus Annus,"* pp. 5–26.

3. Pope John Paul II has this comment on Leo XIII's encyclical: "To teach and to spread her social doctrine pertains to the church's evangelizing mission and is an essential part of the Christian message . . ." (*Centesimus Annus,* n° 5).

4. For many years liberation theologians were very cool to the church's social doctrine. They regarded it as "reformist," and the result of a historic development that had taken place in Western Europe. Moreover, Christian Democratic parties pointed to it as their theoretical basis, for example, in Chile, Venezuela, and Central America, and Christian Democrats began on the left and ended up on the right. Most of all, there was a difference of epistemological status between liberation theology and the church's social teaching. Liberation theology sought to begin from the social praxis of liberation of the Latin American people and so practiced an inductive method. By contrast, the church's social teaching had the appearance of a complete body of doctrine from which Catholics could draw concrete applications. Indeed, the social teaching of the church never explained its foundations or epistemological status. The social encyclicals are known to be the fruit of many theoretical studies, which themselves have been preceded by the practices of concrete movements. However, this entire labor of preparation remains hidden, as though the Christian people had to believe that the pope receives this social teaching in finished form, whether by divine revelation or by personal intuition. This method is alien to the theological practice that came to prevail in Latin America. That accounts for a distancing stance that naturally increased Rome's mistrust. That is how mutual suspicion arose. Even so, there have been various efforts to bring them together. Cf. R. Antoncich, *Ensino Social da Igreja* (Petrópolis: Vozes, 1986); *Christians in the Face of Injustice: A Latin American Reading of Catholic Social Teaching* (Maryknoll, NY: Orbis Books, 1987; Original, 1980); Francisco Ivern and Maria Clara Luchetti Bingemer, eds., *Doctrina Social da Igreja e Teologia da Libertação* (São Paulo: Loyola, 1994).

5. Eds. note: The Sillon was a lay apostolic movement in France aimed at reconciling the principles of Catholicism with democracy and social justice. Cf. É. Poulat, *Catholicisme, Démocratie et Socialisme* (Tournai: Casterman, 1977). On this same turn in history he had previously published, *Histoire, Dogme et Critique dans la Crise Moderniste* (Casterman, 1962); *Integrisme et Catholicisme Intégral* (Casterman, 1969).

6. Cf. R. Aubert, *Nova História da Igreja* Vol. V/III (Petrópolis: Vozes, 1976), pp. 133–138.

7. In Latin America specialized Catholic Action (of the Belgian and French type) made a major contribution to opening the way for Catholic movements to change society. Cf. Thomas Bruneau, *The Political Transformation of the Brazilian Church* (New York: Cambridge University Press, 1974). On the JUC (Young Christian University Students) cf. José Oscar Beozzo, *Cristãos na Universidade e na Política* (Petrópolis: Vozes, 1984), pp. 35–104.

8. The movement of JUC university students toward Ação Popular was typical. Cf. Haroldo Lima and Aldo Arantes, *História da Ação Popular: Da JUC ao PC do B* (São Paulo: Alfa-Omega, 1984); J.O. Beozzo, *Cristãos na Universidade e na Política*, pp. 104–132.

9. On the worker-priests, cf. Fr. Leprieur, *Quand Rome Condamne: Dominicains et Prêtres-Ouvriers* (Paris: Plon-Cerf, 1989); É. Poulat, *Une Église Ébranlée* (Tournai: Casterman, 1980), pp. 119–213.

10. Cf. Raymond Winling, *La Théologie Contemporaine (1945–1980)* (Paris: Le Centurion, 1983), pp. 92–100.

11. There is a vast literature on CEBs. Let us mention particularly, Marcello Azevedo, *Basic Ecclesial Communities in Brazil* (Washington: Georgetown University Press, 1987); Faustino Luiz Couto Teixeira, *Comunidades Eclesias de Base* (Petrópolis:

Vozes, 1988); Sergio Torres, ed., *The Challenge of Basic Christian Communities* (Maryknoll, NY: Orbis Books, 1981); Leonardo Boff, *Ecclesiogenesis: The Base Communities Reinvent the Church* (Maryknoll, NY: Orbis Books, 1986).

12. The aim of rebuilding a christendom is not that of John Paul II alone. It is the continuation of what all popes since Leo XIII and most bishops have aimed at. Vatican II did not break this continuity despite the new topics that it proposes. For Vatican II does not establish any new structure or lay the groundwork for a new model. Cf. É. Poulat, "Jean Paul II et l'Europe Chrétienne," in *Le Religieux dans le Politique* (Paris: Seuil, 1991), pp. 59-68.

13. Cf. Patrick Michel, "Y a-t-il un modèle polonais?" in *Le Retour des Certitudes* (Paris: Le Centurion, 1987), pp. 142–160. On the new evangelization, cf. René Luneau, ed., *La Rêve de Compostelle: Vers la Restauration d'un Europe Chrétienne?* (Paris: Le Centurion, 1989).

14. See the explicit statement by Cardinal Ratzinger in Joseph Ratzinger and Vittorio Messori, *The Ratzinger Report: An Exclusive Interview on the State of the Church* (San Francisco: Ignatius Press, 1986). This was the high point of the current pontificate.

15. The church retains a great deal of social and political prestige. What is the reason for that prestige? And yet, Catholics go looking for religious answers in other religions. The prestige of the Catholic church is more political than religious. Why?

16. The Santo Domingo document (1992) criticizes the fact that "a certain clerical mentality persists in many pastoral agents—clerical and even many lay people devote themselves to tasks within the church and do not have an adequate formation, they are unable to respond effectively to the challenges of society today" (96). It goes on to say that "further development of the laity must be an ongoing process free of any clericalism, and it must not be reduced to matters within the Church" (97).

17. There are many examinations of the "restoration" of the present papacy. Cf. Giancarlo Zizola, *La Restauración del Papa Wojtyla* (Madrid: Cristiandad, 1985), translated from Italian.

18. Cf. Michel Mollat, *Les Pauvres au Moyen-Âge* (Paris: Hachette, 1978).

19. Cf. Gordon Leff, *Heresy in the Later Middle Ages* (New York: Manchester University Press, 1967) vol.1, pp. 139–166. See the condemnation of John XXII in the bull *Cum inter nonnullos* of 1323 in DS 930.

20. Since then, the church has continued to care for the poor, but the church no longer defines itself as poor. Poverty ceases being a characteristic of the church. Moreover, during the Middle Ages reality emphatically contradicted principles. Even so, prophets of poverty reminded the church of its origins.

21. For the Catholic church the emergence of the working class was an especially painful drama. For the first time, the poor rose up against the church and against Christian charity and were denouncing them as forces of oppression. Certain priests and lay apostles endured martyrdom because they wanted to reconcile belonging to the church and solidarity with the working class. They were persecuted on both sides, for the church appeared to be part of the bourgeois world but not part of the popular world. Cf. Pierre Pierrard, *L'Eglise et les Ouvriers en France (1840–1940)* (Paris: Hachette, 1984).

22. *Rerum Novarum* takes up the defense of the rights of workers and thereby reintroduces poverty into the Christian message. It is not simply about the practice of aid, but about the content of Christian teaching. Nevertheless, until Vatican II the social doctrine of the popes always has two sides: one of them is the defense

of the workers and the other is the condemnation of errors, mainly of socialism. The Catholic bourgeoisie accepts the latter and either rejects the former or keeps silent about it.

23. How far the church was from placing the issue of poverty at the center of its concerns can be seen, for example, in Claudia Fuser, *A Economia dos Bispos* (São Paulo: Bienal, 1987); Sergio Miceli, *A Elite Eclesiástica Brasileira* (Rio de Janeiro: Bertrand Brasil, 1988).

24. Even in the nineteenth century and especially in the early twentieth century, there was a vigorous movement of priests and Catholic lay people in the direction of a Christian Socialism. However, Pius X wrapped it all up in the wave of modernism, condemning and destroying the movement, which remained utterly underground, and arose only after World War I but under very strict control. Cf. É. Poulat, *Catholicisme, Démocratie et Socialisme*, pp. 71–171. In Brazil there was the lonely voice of Father Júlio Maria. No one paid any attention to him, let alone looked to him for inspiration. Cf. *O Catolicismo no Brasil* (Rio de Janeiro: Agir, 1950).

25. John XXIII was the one who put forth the expression "church of the poor" even before Vatican II, as though he wanted to propose a basic issue for the Council's assembly. He was the first who spoke of "shaking off the imperial dust that has been deposited on the throne of St. Peter since Constantine." Cf. Yves Congar, *Pour une Église Servante et Pauvre* (Paris: Cerf, 1963), p. 119.

26. Cf. P. Gauthier, *Jesus, l'Église des Pauvres: Réflexions Nazaréennes pour le Concile* (Paris: Edit. Universitaires, 1962); "Consolez mon Peuple": Le Concile et "l'Église des Pauvres" (Cerf, 1965). This book was written at the request of a group of bishops who were part of the "church of the poor." Cf. also Y. Congar, *Pour une Église Servante et Pauvre*.

27. On September 7, 1962, encouraged by Pope John XXIII himself, Cardinal Lercaro, the archbishop of Bologna, "the red cardinal," made a thrilling appeal to the Council fathers, asking that the mystery of Christ in the poor be at the center of the church's doctrine. He received a great deal of applause but nothing happened. This matter was not in the minds of most bishops, nor was it among the Catholic people. See P. Gauthier, *"Consolez mon Peuple,"* pp. 198–203.

28. See the list of bishops in ibid., p. 11.

29. Latin American theologians of the new generation immediately picked up the Medellín theme to safeguard its full sense. The poor in the gospel, the poor in Medellín are the poor as a social category, the material poor, they are the "Lazaruses" of St. Luke. Cf. the observations of Gustavo Gutiérrez, *A Theology of Liberation* (Maryknoll, NY: Orbis Books, 1988); *The Power of the Poor in History* (Maryknoll, NY: Orbis Books, 1983); *Evangelización y Opción por los Pobres* (Buenos Aires: Editora Paulinas, 1987); "Option for the Poor," in Jon Sobrino and Ignacio Ellacuría, eds., *Systematic Theology: Perspectives from Liberation Theology* (Maryknoll, NY: Orbis Books, 1996), pp. 22–37. See also George Pixley and Clódovis Boff, *The Bible, the Church, and the Poor* (Maryknoll, NY: Orbis Books, 1989).

30. The reception of Medellín varied. Cf. Enrique Dussel, *De Medellín a Puebla: Una Década de Sangre y Esperanza: 1968–1979* (Mexico City: Edicol, 1979); José Marins, *De Medellín a Puebla: A Práxis dos Padres da América Latina* (São Paulo: Paulinas, 1979).

31. The first reaction seeking to empty the Medellín idea was to spiritualize what poverty was about. Thus everyone fits into the category of the poor and the

option vanishes because all are equal. The second reaction was to multiply preferential options, as happened at Puebla (1979), which added the option for youth. In Santo Domingo (1992) there were so many priorities that everything was a priority. The option for the poor thereby ceases being a threat for Catholics who belong to the privileged and do not want to give up their privileges.

32. Under the impulse of Michael Novak and Peter Berger there has arisen a theology that makes capitalism the way to embody the option for the poor. Cf. Amy L. Sherman, *Preferential Option: A Christian and Neoliberal Strategy for Latin America's Poor* (Grand Rapids: Eerdmans, 1992). Since 1990 the World Bank and the International Monetary Fund have adopted the terminology of the option for the poor. Cf. World Bank, *Assistance Strategies to Reduce Poverty* (1990); *Making Adjustment Work for the Poor* (1990); cf. Michel Chossudovski, "Les ruineux entêtements du Fonds Monétaire International," in *Le Monde Diplomatique* (Sept. 1992), pp. 28–29.

33. The abrupt notion of truth expressed in the encyclical *Veritatis Splendor* poses an absolute rejection of all demands of the human mind at least since the Renaissance. It turns truth into pure objectivity and there is no way of knowing where this "object" of absolute value comes from. But believing blindly is no longer believing, because it is an act of sheer will with no intelligence. It is submission of the will but it is not conviction of reason and hence it is not faith. In our age it will be very difficult to attract our contemporaries with such objectivity because they stand at the very opposite extreme, in pure subjectivity. Under such conditions and with such means the reconquest of culture sought by L. Giussani and Communione e Liberazione can only be an illusion.

34. Under the impulse of integralist movements like Communione e Liberazione, the prevailing trend in the 1980s was an aggressive proclamation of the objective teaching of the church, no matter how abrupt it might be. At the end of the decade it cannot be said to have accomplished much. Catholics continue to go toward other religions, and especially to esoteric beliefs, while there remains a small group of fanatics who, like the Opus Dei young people, go along with the pope on all his travels to give him feverish acclaim.

35. The need for a new evangelization appeared in the papacy of Leo XIII and Catholics—Christians in general—felt the need for deep changes if they were to be able to evangelize. Today the new evangelization looks like a fixation on the past, as if the content of the new Catechism were obvious.

36. It was around Puebla in particular that a theology of popular religion was developed. Conservatives saw in it a bulwark against liberation theology, and liberation theologians saw it as a support for liberation movements. Today its decline is so great that the topic is losing its relevance.

37. Significantly the most valuable studies on popular religion are the work of pastors working with indigenous people. Among indigenous people many customs of the Catholic church still operate as symbols of indigenous culture. Of course, this is all the more true of devotion to the Virgin of Guadalupe.

38. There is a general silence about popular devotions during the past century (1860–1960).

39. The Brazilian Bishops Conference (CNBB) recently published a very thorough statement on the charismatic renewal in Brazil. However, there remains the problem of a de facto parallelism. Parallelism will not be solved through administrative measures because these are not voluntary decisions. There exists a de facto dualism between two religions or two expressions of Christianity. The question

is therefore raised: are we going to witness a new episode of parallelism between parish religion and the religion of religious orders, as has existed from the thirteenth century to the twentieth? Can there be a reconciliation, a fusion, an inculturation, to the point where the charismatic movement and the parish are a single thing?

40. Typical of the conflict between humanism and the Catholic counter-reformation, M. Mataillon, *Erasmo y España* (Mexico City: Fondo de Cultura Económica, 1950).

41. A variety of movements are active in the nineteenth and twentieth centuries: Catholic liberalism, social Catholicism, Christian democracy. There is some continuity among them in the sense that all of them seek to evangelize the world, that is, carry out a new evangelization of the West, essentially through commitment in the world through politics in the broad sense of the word. They were all more tolerated than supported by the hierarchy, and underwent periods of condemnation from which they reemerged.

2. The Gospel of Freedom

1. In Catholic circles the contemporary exegete who has placed the question of freedom back at the center of the Pauline gospel was the Jesuit S. Lyonnet. He published an early article in the review *Christus* v. 4, 1954, pp. 6–27, which was included in the collection edited by I. de la Potterie and Lyonnet, *La Vie selon l'Esprit* (Paris: Cerf, 1965).

2. Cf. Ernst Käsemann, *Der Ruf der Freiheit* (Tübingen: Mohn, 1968).

3. J.-M. Aubert, "La Moral Catholique est-elle évangelique?" in C. Yannaras, R. Mehl, J.-M. Aubertt, *La Loi e la Liberté: Evangile et Morale* (Tours: Mame, 1972), pp. 119–158.

4. Cf. J. L. Segundo, *El Caso Mateo: Los Comienzos de una Ética Judeocristiana* (Santander: Sal Terrae, 1994), pp. 11–18.

5. Cf. J. L. Segundo, *¿Qué Mundo? ¿Qué Hombre? ¿Qué Dios?* (Santander: Sal Terrae, 1993), pp. 42–54, 77–85; *El Hombre de Hoy ante Jesús de Nazaret* II/2 (Madrid: Cristiandad, 1982), pp. 625–670.

6. Cf. J. L. Segundo, *El Caso Mateo* (1994), pp. 18–21.

7. Cf. J. Jeremias, *Teologia do Novo Testamento* (São Paulo: Paulus, 1980), pp. 176–189.

8. Cf. Juan Mateos-Juan Barreto, *O Evangelho de São João* (São Paulo: Paulus, 1989), pp. 388–391.

9. J. L. Segundo, *The Liberation of Theology* (Maryknoll, NY: Orbis Books, 1976).

10. Cf. J. L. Segundo, "El Dios Creador y el Hombre Libre," in *¿Qué Mundo? ¿Qué Hombre? ¿Qué Dios?*, pp. 385–404; P. Chaunu, *Liberté* (Paris: Fayard, 1987).

11. Hence, in scholasticism, freedom is a quality of the human act; it is means rather than end. For the Greeks it is a lack rather than a value. Christian theologians have to give it a positive meaning. However, freedom remains subordinated to order. Freedom is accordingly the capacity to obey God. It is valuable because of obedience, not in itself, and obedience to the order established by God will then be the supreme value.

12. Modernity has experienced a continual conflict over freedom. On the one hand, the sciences all tend to affirm a universal determinism. Each science seemed to destroy one more aspect of freedom. Until the twentieth century the sciences were determinist and have been a continual challenge to the aspiration for freedom.

Cf. Jeanne Parian-Vial, *La Liberté et les Sciences de l'Homme* (Paris: Privat, 1973). At the same time, modern philosophy was exalting the pursuit of freedom. Cf. Mariano Grondona, *Los Pensadores de la Libertad: De John Locke a Robert Nozick* (Buenos Aires: Ed. Sudamericana, 1986). Today, the conflict between determinism and freedom seems to have been overcome. Contemporary sciences tend to be "historical" and portray the human being as part of a universe which as a whole is tending toward freedom. Cf. Jean-François Kahn, *Tout Change parce que Rien de Change: Introduction à un Théorie de l'Evolution Sociale* (Paris: Fayard, 1994); J. L. Segundo, *¿Qué Mundo? ¿Qué Hombre? ¿Qué Dios?*, pp. 137–175.

13. Cf. Pierre Chaunu, "Construire la Liberté," in *La Liberté*, pp. 25–110.

14. Cf. P. Ganne, *Appelés à la Liberté* (Paris: Cerf, 1974); K. Rahner, *Freedom in Grace* (London: 1969).

15. Cf. José Maria Gonzalez Ruiz, *Epístola de San Pablo a los Gálatas* (Madrid: Max-Marova, 1971, 2nd ed.), pp. 230–242; S. Lyonnet, *Libertad y Ley Nueva* (Salamanca: Sígueme, 1967), pp. 93–104.

16. This inculturation of charity-love is already clearly present in the so-called family codes in the deutero-Pauline epistles, Colossians 3:18-4:1; Ephesians 5:22-6:9.

17. Classics on modern individualism: Louis Dumont, *O Individualismo: Uma Perspectiva Antropológica da Ideologia Moderna* (Rio de Janeiro: Rocco, 1985); Werner Sombart, *El Burgués* (Madrid: Alianza Universal, 1972); Marshall Berman, *All That Is Solid Melts into the Air* (New York: Viking, 1988); Allan Bloom, *The Closing of the American Mind* (New York: Simon and Schuster, 1988).

18. For the importance of the Other, we are much indebted to E. Levinas (Cf. *Totalité et Infini* [1961]; *La Trace de l'Autre* [1963]. In Latin America the theme was raised by E. Dussel and Daniel E. Guillot, *Liberación Latinoamericana y Emmanuel Levinas* (Buenos Aires: Bonum, 1975); see also E. Dussel, *Para una Ética de la Liberación Latinoamericana* v. 1 (Buenos Aires: Siglo XXI, 1973), pp. 97–192.

19. The Christian philosopher who has most highlighted the radical depth of freedom as the true essence of the human being was Nicolai Berdyaev, cf. *Freedom and the Spirit* (New York: Scribners', 1935).

20. Curiously, the passage from St. John says exactly the opposite: it does not say that freedom depends on truth, but rather that truth depends on freedom, for the end of truth is freedom, which is the means for arriving at that end, freedom.

21. Scholastic theology reduced freedom to free will, that is, free will to a quality of the will, and was incapable of making it the supreme reality of the human person. Cf. Nicolai Berdyaev, *Freedom and the Spirit*; J.L. Segundo, *¿Qué Mundo? ¿Qué Hombre? ¿Qué Dios?*, pp. 217–324.

3. Freedom and Liberation

1. Cf. E. Dussel, *Ethics and Community* (Maryknoll, NY: Orbis Books, 1988), pp. 205–218.

2. Cf. G. Gutiérrez, *A Theology of Liberation* (Maryknoll, NY: Orbis Books, 1988, rev. ed.; first ed. in Spanish, 1971), Chapter 9, "Liberation and Salvation," pp. 83–105; I. Ellacuría, "Historicity of Christian Salvation," in I. Ellacuría and Jon Sobrino, eds., *Mysterium Liberationis: Fundamental Concepts of Liberation Theology* (Maryknoll, NY: Orbis Books, 1993), pp. 251–289; *Conversión de la Iglesia al Reino de Dios* (Santander: Sal Terrae, 1984). Before Vatican II, the issue

of the natural and the supernatural had been proposed by the school of Rahner as well as by the *nouvelle théologie* and had prompted condemnations and silencings on the part of Rome.

3. Cf. C. Boff, *Theology and Praxis: Epistemological Foundations* (Maryknoll, NY: Orbis Books, 1987), pp. xxviii–xxix. See the vigorous response by I. Ellacuría, "Historicity of Christian Salvation," in *Mysterium Liberationis*, pp. 252–256.

4. At that time the phenomenon of critique of the churches and of "declericalization" was interpreted as a phenomenon of the secularization of Western society. That is how sociologists of religion at that time interpreted events, and there arose a "theology of secularization" whose first and best known representative was Fr. Gogarten. Cf. J. Comblin, *Mitos e Realidades da Secularização* (São Paulo: Herder, 1970).

5. The retreat of liberation theology is part of a broader movement, namely the retreat of theology itself in the Christian churches. Indeed, spiritualistic movements have no need for theology. They mistrust it and fear that the effect of any theological reflection will be a cooling religious fervor.

6. "One of the worst things that happened to liberation theology was that—because of accolades and especially because of attacks—it was led to talk about itself too much." H. Assmann, "Teologia da Solidariedade e da Cidadania," in *Notas* (São Bernardo do Campo), 1 n° 2, p. 2.

7. It is noteworthy that the most aggressive condemnations have come from Latin America and that the entire press and most of the media engaged in a systematic campaign to obtain condemnation from Rome and finally obtained it.

8. For example, a liberation theology can only be discredited by a statement such as this, "It is the first theology in the churches that seeks to be built up from the standpoint of the victims," for "never in the history of Christianity have the poor been the epistemological locus, that is, the place from which the idea of God, Christ, grace, and history is conceived." Leonardo Boff, in Hugo Assmann, ed., *René Girard com Teólogos da Libertação: Um Diálogo sobre Ídolos e Sacrifícios* (Petrópolis: Vozes, 1991), p. 40. Moreover the statement is not true. It is surprising that the author, who was a Franciscan for so many years and proud of his order, should forget Franciscan theology, both the thirteenth-century theology and the sixteenth-century theology that guided the missionaries sent to the Americas.

9. That is why the great work of Gustavo Gutiérrez on Bartolomé de Las Casas is to be so commended. Cf. *Las Casas: In Search of the Poor of Jesus Christ* (Maryknoll, NY: Orbis Books, 1993). For it is absolutely essential to show that liberation theology is not completely new but that it stands in a historic continuity. It is true that only a minority of theologies have taken the poor as their standard and they were not adopted by the organized church as a guide for their activity. Even on this point liberation theology is not new; it is a theology that has always been that of a minority. Cf. H. Assmann, "Teologia da Solidariedade e da Cidadania," p. 7, "Liberation theology has been mistaken in thinking that the option for the poor was the only solution for church and society."

10. Liberation exegesis has not been exempt from concordisms when it sought in the biblical texts analogies with present situations. The fact is that in order to be accessible to the people exegesis cannot avoid concordisms, since the popular masses have no sense of historicity. Exegetes, however, may be victims of their own concordistic practice.

11. On the importance of the thought of Fernando Henrique Cardoso at that time,

cf. Rolando Ames Cobián, "Factores Económicos y Fuerzas Políticas en el Proceso de Liberación," in *Fe Cristiana y Cambio Social en América Latina* (Salamanca: Sígueme, 1973), pp. 33–63.

12. Cf. P. Richard, "La Teología de la Liberación en la Nueva Coyuntura: Temas y Desafíos para la Década de los Noventa," in *Pasos* n° 32, 1991, pp. 6–8.

13. For example, the theology that was taught in the seminary in Olinda between its foundation in 1800 and its closing in 1817 as the result of the 1817 revolution, which was called the "priests' revolution" precisely because it was inspired by the Olinda seminary and the priests trained there.

14. See the issue presented by Juan Luis Segundo in the article, "Libertad y Liberación," in Ellacuría and Sobrino, eds., *Mysterium Liberationis* (Madrid: Trotta, 1990) Vol. I, pp. 373–391. By not making explicit the roots of freedom and liberation in the Bible and tradition, theologians have opened the way to exaggerating the importance of the social sciences or of philosophical Marxism in their work.

4. Social Liberation

1. Cf. Fatles, *Camilo Torres: Revolutionary Writings* (New York: Harper & Row, 1969), p. 265.

2. Ibid., p. 315.

3. On Sunday, April 23, 1995, the *Folha de São Paulo* published a list of the twenty biggest selling books in Brazil that week. Seventeen of the twenty were in some fashion presentations of contemporary esotericism. If they were not formally part of New Age, they belong to the same cultural domain.

4. Cf. H. Assmann, *Theology for a Newer Church* (Maryknoll, NY: Orbis Books, 1976), p. 99.

5. The main proponent of this idea is Cristovam Buarque, *O Que É Apartação: O Apartheid Social no Brasil* (São Paulo: Brasiliense, 1993); *A Revolução nas Prioridades: Da Modernidade Técnica à Modernidade Ética* (São Paulo: Paz e Terra, 1993), pp. 78–96.

6. Another topic that has entered into everyday speech today is that of exclusion. All around the world a dual society is being built where one part of the population, a majority or minority depending on the case, is excluded from development and participation in society, either in consumption or in production. Pope John Paul II condemns this situation in *Centesimus Annus*: "The fact is that many people, perhaps the majority today, do not have the means which would enable them to take their place in an effective and humanly dignified way within a productive system in which work is truly central. . . . Thus, if not actually exploited, they are to a great extent marginalized; economic development takes place over their heads, so to speak . . ." (CA 33).

7. On this new class, Robert B. Reich, *The Work of Nations: Preparing Ourselves for 21st-Century Capitalism* (New York: Vintage Books, 1992), pp. 177 ff. The author was President Clinton's Secretary of Labor in the first administration; Peter Drucker, *The New Realities: In Government and Politics / in Economics and Business / in Society and World View* (New York: Harper & Row, 1989), pp. 207 ff.; *Post-Capitalist Society* (New York, HarperCollins, 1993), pp. 181ff.; Alvin Toffler, *Powershift* (New York: Bantam Books, 1990), pp. 159–234.

8. The portion of revenues going to executives is ever increasing while the portion for wages and capital is declining. Cf. Reich, *The Work of Nations*, pp. 204–205.

9. Ibid., p. 7.
10. Ibid., pp. 177 ff. The new elite is made up of "symbolic analysts," those who know how to work with symbols and language, which is the main factor in the economy.
11. Ibid., pp. 208 ff.
12. Ibid., pp. 269 ff.; see also the suggestive evocation of J. K. Galbraith, *The Culture of Contentment* (Boston: Houghton Mifflin, 1992).
13. Reich, *The Work of Nations*, pp. 271 ff.
14. Cf. Christopher Lasch, *The Culture of Narcissism: American Life in an Age of Diminishing Expectations* (New York: Norton, 1991).
15. In Europe descriptions of postmodernity generally ignore the economic and social condition underlying the new mindset. This is probably because in Europe philosophers and sociologists are further removed from business and are less attuned to developments in business.
16. In Brazil the Catholic church has invested a great deal in struggles for an agrarian reform that has not taken place and will not take place. Today there is no more point in winning the land. The peasants who want land want to be able to sell in order to have a small bit of capital that will make it easier for them to move to the city. How many plots of land won with great effort have now been sold or abandoned by their new owners! The very struggle for the land amounts to a training that helps the peasant move to the city.
17. Reich, *The Work of Nations*, pp. 213 ff.; P. Drucker, *Post-Capitalist Society*, pp. 72 ff.
18. The new elite class demands tax cuts. It was able to get the IMF and the World Bank to include among the conditions of a "readjustment" lower public investment (education, health, infrastructure). That was what the Reagan and Bush administrations did in the United States and it is what is being imposed on the Latin American countries that have adopted the neoliberal model. Cf. Reich, *The Work of Nations*, pp. 253 ff.
19. Cf. Jorge Castañeda, *Utopia Unarmed: The Latin American Left after the Cold War* (New York: Alfred A. Knopf, 1993), pp. 198 ff.
20. Cf. ibid., pp. 177 ff.
21. It is true that for the moment the clergy is withdrawing from political struggle. That situation can only be temporary because it runs counter to all of Latin American history.
22. Cf. G. Gutiérrez, "Option for the Poor," in *Mysterium Liberationis*, pp. 235–250.
23. Puebla document, 1137.
24. Castañeda notes the paradox: by reason of its Marxist origins the left stresses *class* whereas the term *people* has a greater impact. See *Utopia Unarmed*, pp. 235 f.
25. "The Marxian dilemma for years . . . had been that the working class in fact rebelled and won—if just partial victories—only when it acted 'as if it were the people.'" Ibid., p. 235.
26. Cf. Hugo Assmann, "Teologia da Solidariedade e da Cidadania," in *Notas*, year 1, no. 2, p. 6.
27. Castañeda, *Utopia Unarmed*, pp. 40 ff.
28. Ibid., pp. 51 ff.
29. The popular forces were overestimated. Why did this mistaken judgement of forces take place? Jorge Castañeda says, "Catholic influence, the Marxist notion of progress, and the despair of intellectuals facing a permanently dramatic status quo converged in the current of contemporary left thinking: the future included

redemption, the vengeance of a last judgement when good would triumph over evil, the poor over the rich, the indigenous over the foreign." *Utopia Desarmada: Intrigas, Dilemas e Promessas da Esquerda Latino-Americana* (São Paulo: Companhia das Letras, 1994), p. 207.

30. The conciliar ecclesiology was marked by a return to the Bible and the ancient tradition of the church. With the Bible and the patristic tradition the conciliar bishops and theologians sought to at least partly overturn, or at least balance medieval and modern scholastic theology. Not much help was sought from the social sciences, and so the conciliar ecclesiology often gives the impression of being archaic. It offers an archaic, even fundamentalist, vision of the church. That is also why it did not come to be applied in practice. The real church did not change because no way was found to reintroduce structures that had not existed for 1,500 years or more. That explains how many can deceive themselves and under the cover of the Council propose as a pastoral program a community utopia from the early days of the church.

31. Cf. L. Boff, *Ecclesiogenesis* (Maryknoll, NY: Orbis Books, 1986). Boff understood the renewal of the church to be a meeting and merging of the hierarchical institution and the movement of the CEBs arising from the grassroots. The CEBs would thus completely renew the church without any break. Cf. L. Boff, "Theological Characteristics of a Grassroots Church," in S. Torres and John Eagleson, eds., *The Challenge of Basic Christian Communities* (Maryknoll, NY: Orbis Books, 1981), pp. 124–144.

32. It has sometimes been thought that the CEBs could provide the basis for a "popular subject" charged with bringing about structural reform in Latin American society. In this view CEBs are the praxis of the Christian people, a transforming praxis. Cf. João Carlos Petrini, *CEBs: Um Novo Sujeito Popular* (São Paulo: Paz e Terra, 1984).

33. Hence the sociologist Pedro A. Ribeiro de Oliveira proposes that the CEBs should be a structure parallel to the parish structure, cf. "Estruturas da Igreja e conflitos religiosos," in ISER, *Catolicismo, Modernidade e Tradição*, Pierre Sanchis, ed. (Loyola, 1992), p. 61: "a single local church with a twofold structure, the parish on the one hand and the CEBs on the other."

34. It is not merely by chance that the topic of citizenship has spread in the last few years. However, the most important thing is going to be the application of citizenship to its most obvious point of insertion, the city.

35. On Brasilia, cf. James Holston, *The Modernist City* (Chicago: University of Chicago Press, 1989).

36. Cf. Cândido Procópio Ferreira Camargo et al., *São Paulo, Crecimiento e Pobreza* (São Paulo: Loyola, 1976); Paul Singer et al., *São Paulo: O Povo em Movimiento* (Petrópolis: Vozes, 1980); Lucia M. Bogus and Luis Eduardo W. Wanderley, *A Luta pela Cidade em São Paulo* (São Paulo: Cortez, 1992).

37. Cf. Larissa A. de Lomnitz, *Cómo Sobreviven los Marginalos* (Mexico: Siglo XXI, 1975, 1991).

38. Cf. Susan Eckstein, *The Poverty of Revolution: The State & the Urban Poor in Mexico* (Princeton: Princeton University Press, 1977).

39. On popular movements, cf. Jorge Castañeda, *Utopia Unarmed*, pp. 203 ff.; Ana Maria Doimo, "Igreja e Movimientos Sociais Pós-70 no Brazil," in Pierre Sanchis ed., *Catolicismo: Cotidiano e Movimientos* (São Paulo: Loyola, 1992), pp. 275–308.

40. Those in government themselves are increasingly aware of the limits of the capacity

of governments to solve the people's problems. Hence the need for the state to unload government services through contracts with private companies. Cf. a best seller, David Osborne and Ted Gabler, *Reinventing Government* (New York: Addison Wesley, 1992).

41. Cf. Robert Reich, *The Work of Nations*, pp. 301 ff. The author held a cabinet post and his position represents the mindset of the United States government. However, the U.S. Congress resists any imposition on the rich. The Congress is in the hands of the wealthiest people in the nation, as is the case today in practically all industrialized countries. Where will change come from? That is what we can never foresee.

5. Economic Liberation

1. Theologians adopted dependency theory without reservation: everything seemed so simple; cf. G. Gutiérrez, *A Theology of Liberation*, pp. 49–57.
2. Cf. Peter F. Drucker, *Post-Capitalist Society* (New York: HarperCollins, 1993), pp. 27 ff.
3. Ibid., 33 ff.
4. The idea of a third industrial or economic revolution has become a commonplace and is very widely accepted. Among those writing on it, there is a broad consensus on how it is to be described. Cf. Robert Reich, *The Work of Nations*; Peter Drucker, *Post-Capitalist Society*; Alvin Toffler, *Powershift*.
5. During the early phase the goal was production and a large volume of products that were all alike. Henceforth, production will pursue products that are diversified, few in number, and of high value. That is where profit is to be found. Cf. Reich, *The Work of Nations*, pp. 63–68.
6. On the decentralization of production and the formation of very complicated networks of companies, cf. ibid., pp. 87 ff.
7. On the globalization of production, cf. ibid., pp. 119 ff. There is no such thing as a "national" product because everything is made up of parts or components that come from many nations. Cf. ibid., pp. 87 ff.
8. Cf. Peter Drucker, *Post-Capitalist Society*, pp. 68 ff.
9. Cf. Alvin Toffler, *Powershift*, pp. 202–212; Peter Drucker, *The New Realities*, pp. 207 ff.
10. It is now calculated that fourteen trillion dollars circulate through the world, besides the trillion dollars that crosses national borders, disrupting national currencies and stock exchanges. Cf. Ibrahim Warde, "La Dérive des Nouveaux Produits Financiers," in *Le Monde Diplomatique*, July 1994, pp. 26–27. In 1950, financial monetary operations were twice as large as operations related to trade in goods; today they have become fifty times as large. Cf. Michel Béaud, "La Basculement do Monde," in *Le Monde Diplomatique*, October 1994, pp. 8–9. Money is concealed in tax havens. Gibraltar has 42,000 companies devoted to financial operations. Luxemburg has 8,000 holding companies. Cf. Theirry Lambert, "Paradis Fiscaux, la Filière Européenne," in *Le Monde Diplomatique*, October 1994, pp. 8–9. We are not even mentioning here cases like the Bahamas, the Caribbean islands, and the like.
11. On neoliberal ideology, cf. Hugo Assmann and Franz J. Hinkelhammert, "La Política del Mercado Total, su Teologización y Nuestra Respuesta," in *Pasos* n° 1, 1985, pp. 2–7.
12. Cf. F. Hinkelhammert, "Del Mercado Total al Imperio Totalitario," in *Pasos* n° 6, pp. 9–19.

13. Cf. Reich, *The Work of Nations*, pp. 13–77, showing that the total market is an illusion.
14. Propaganda for the total market actually serves the interests of speculators. Cf. ibid., pp. 183–193.
15. On the ambitions of this new class without solidarity, cf. Christopher Lasch, *The Revolt of the Elites and the Betrayal of Democracy* (New York: Norton, 1995). Speaking of the "free market," Pope John Paul II says that it "must be appropriately controlled by the forces of society and by the state, so as to guarantee that the basic needs of the whole of society are satisfied" (*Centesimus Annus* 35).
16. Cf. Cristovam Buarque, *A Revolução nas Prioridades: Da Modernidade Técnica à Modernidade Ética*, pp. 19–28.
17. This mistake has been common in the Third World. Cf. G. Corm, *Le Nouveau Désordre Économique Mondial* (Paris: La Découverte, 1993), pp. 59–65.
18. Hence the problem of so-called "modernization." Cf. Juan Carlos Casas, *Nuevos Políticos y Nuevas Políticas en America Latina* (Buenos Aires: Atlántida, 1991).
19. Cf. Franz Hinkelhammert, "Capitalismo sin alternativa? Sobre la sociedad que sostiene que no hay alternativa para ella," in *Pasos* n° 37, 1991, pp. 11–24, and idem., "Capitalismo y socialism: la posibilidad de alternativas," in *Pasos* n° 48 (1993), pp. 10–15.
20. The most radical critique is found in Robert Kurz, *O Colapso da Modernização* (São Paulo: Paz e Terra, 1993). But see also G. Corm, *Le Nouveau Désordre Économique Mondial*, pp. 21–33. Or, for Brazil, Cristovam Buarque, *A Desordem do Progresso* (São Paulo: Paz e Terra, 1991). The pope himself criticizes the worsening of the situation: "Moreover one must denounce the existence of economic, financial, and social *mechanisms* which, although they are manipulated by people, often function almost automatically, thus accentuating the situation of wealth for some and poverty for the rest. These mechanisms, which are maneuvered directly or indirectly by the more developed countries, by their very functioning favor the interests of the people manipulating them. But in the end they suffocate or condition the economies of the less developed countries" (*Sollicitudo Rei Socialis*, 16).
21. On the repercussions of the fall of socialism on the Latin American left, cf. Jorge Castañeda, *Utopia Unarmed*, pp. 237 ff.
22. Cf. Hélio Gallardo, *Crisis del Socialismo Histórico: Ideologías y Desafíos* (San José: DEI, 1991); Frei Betto, "Vigencia de las Utopías in América Latina," in *Pasos* n° 55 (1994), pp. 10–14; Franz Hinkelhammert, "El cautiverio de la utopía," in *Christus* (Mexico) vol. LIX, n° 679–680, Oct. 1994, pp. 56–69; J.-Y. Calvez, "Quel avenir pour le marxisme?" in *Études* (Paris), n° 373 (1990), pp. 475–485.
23. Cf. Carlos Bravo, "¿Qué ha pasado en Chiapas? Los hechos y las perspectivas," in *Christus* vol. LIX, n° 679–680, October 1994, pp. 43–47.
24. "We have seen that it is unacceptable to say that the defeat of so-called 'Real Socialism' leaves capitalism as the only model of economic organization" (*Centesimus Annus*, 35).
25. Even previously, the heads of the International Monetary Fund and the World Bank had to recognize that the policies they had imposed were having catastrophic social results and that they had not anticipated them. Cf. Walden Bello and Shea Cunningham, "De l'ajustement structurel en ses implacables desseins," in *Le Monde Diplomatique* (September 1994), pp. 8–9. Enrique Iglesias, the president of the IDB, admitted that the gains made from the 1950s to the 1970s have been lost as a result of the policy of readjustment imposed on Latin America:

Reflections on Economic Development: Toward a Latin American Consensus (Washington: IDB, 1992), p. 103.

26. Cf. Hugo Assmann and Franz Hinkelhammert, *A Idolatria do Mercado: Ensaio sobre Economia e Teologia* (1989); H. Assmann, ed., *René Girard com Teólogos da Libertação: Um Diálogo sobre Ídolos e Sacrifícios* (Petrópolis: Vozes, 1991); Franz Hinkelhammert, *Sacrificios Humanos y Sociedad Occidental* (San José: DEI, 1991).

27. Cf. Santo Domingo document n° 170, pp. 194–199. Cf. Roberto Oliveros, "Visão da Pessoa Humana e da Sociedade," in *Santo Domingo: Ensaios Teológico-Pastorais* (Petrópolis: Vozes, 1993), pp. 242–248. There was no cry of alarm proportional to the seriousness of the situation. The condemnation of neoliberalism is lost among a hundred other matters.

28. Cf. Jorge Castañeda, *Utopia Unarmed*, pp. 427 ff.

29. Ibid., pp. 441 ff.

30. Ibid., pp. 457 ff., also pp. 133 ff.; P. Vuskovic, "Economía y Crisis," in Pedro Vuskovic et al., *América Latina Hoy* (Mexico: Siglo XXI, 1990), pp. 19–63; José Márcio Camargo, "Distribuir para Crescer: Propostas para um Governo Popular e Democrático," in César Benjamin et al., ed., *1994: Idéias para uma Alternativa de Esquerda à Crise Brasileira* (Rio de Janeiro: Dumará, 1993), pp. 103–121.

31. Critiques of the welfare state and of all government involvement have been taken up by those who defend the "theology of capitalism" and who present the market as the only route for the preferential option for the poor, especially Michael Novak and Peter Berger. Cf. Amy L. Sherman, *Preferential Option: A Christian and Neoliberal Strategy for Latin America's Poor* (Grand Rapids: Eerdmans, 1992).

32. The criticisms have to do primarily with the direct administration of social services by the state. That cannot be a reason for inferring that the state should not be involved. The state need not manage but it must govern, that is, impose conditions on the initiatives of private companies. Moreover, in the Third World in most cases private initiative is completely lacking.

33. Most nations in the Third World use the state to provide conditions for a parasitical life. The new wealthy are parasites who live under the protection of a corrupt state: speculators, drug traffickers, and construction companies. The state sells public positions and thereby grants the right to plunder the people. Cf. G. Corm, *Le Nouveau Désordre Économique Mondial*, pp. 26–29; 44–47; 69–84. The abuses of the state actually result from its weakness. Abuses are committed by the privileged who take the state hostage and commit all kinds of crime with impunity. The remedy is not "less government" but building a true state.

34. The problem of the foreign debt remains intact after over a decade of debates. Cf. Franz Hinkelhammert, *La Deuda Externa de América Latin* (San José: DEI, 1988); Franz Hinkelhammert, "Enfoque Teológico de la Deuda Externa," in *Pasos* n° 17 (1988), pp. 11–19.

35. Cf. Castañeda, *Utopia Unarmed*, pp. 452 ff. There is an extraordinarily strong campaign in the United States against taxes on wealth. Nevertheless, there is no other way. Without contributions from wealth, that is, without redistribution, society will never be able to make the social investments that are absolutely necessary. For a hundred years the ruling elites of the Western world have accepted high taxes. The fact is that no government in the First World is going to radically dismantle the welfare state. The welfare state is something from the past whose essence no one is challenging. What is most discussed are its problems. In the

Third World, however, the welfare state would actually be something new. If all its negative features are discussed before it is even set up, the welfare state will never emerge and the dual society will become entrenched. Poverty will be the fundamental structure of third-world societies.

36. Ibid., p. 454.

37. Ibid., pp. 463 ff.

6. Political Liberation

1. The rejection of politics in the First World, and especially in the United States, is a long-range phenomenon resulting from a real cultural change. The new ruling class in the United States has seceded. It has silently condemned the "national pact" that was the basis for national identity. More critical observers see clearly that this is not a passing phenomenon. It is tied up with the movement of the economy, but also with changes in culture and in the means of culture. In Latin America the elites are taking on an attitude copied from the elites in the North; culturally, they live in Miami. It would be risky to fail to recognize this fact. Because they have just recovered democracy, Latin Americans are afraid to examine the fact that politics has fallen out of favor, but ignorance of the facts can only aggravate the problem.

2. There is no proportion whatsoever between the reality of armed revolutionary movements in Latin America between 1956 and 1990 and what they stirred up in the minds of young people and also among many adults. A few thousand became involved in guerrilla struggle, but many millions felt identified with those few. Repeated failures did not diminish the fervor but rather heightened it, until the guerrillas themselves became convinced that they no longer had a future. Cf. Jorge Castañeda, *Utopia Unarmed*, pp. 51–128. All the literature from that era treats guerrilla struggle and liberation as the same thing. Sometimes that identification was a trap. Liberation theology was condemned because in people's minds it was mixed up with guerrilla warfare. All protestations and all denials were in vain.

3. Cf. Peter Drucker, *Post-Capitalist Society*, pp. 142 ff.; Paul Kennedy, *Preparing for the Twenty-First Century* (London: Fontana, 1993), pp. 128–132; Ibrahim Warde, "La Dérive des Nouveau Produits Financiers," in *Le Monde Diplomatique* (July 1984), pp. 26–27; Michel Bréaud, "La Basculement du Monde," in *Le Monde Diplomatique* (October 1994), pp. 16–17.

4. Robert Reich, *The Work of Nations*, pp. 119 ff.

5. Cf. Michel Chossudovski, "Les ruineux entêtements du Fonde Monétaire Internacional," in *Le Monde Diplomatique* (September 1992), pp. 28–29. The World Bank itself is concerned about poverty but has not gotten to the point of changing strategy. Cf. *Assistance Strategies to Reduce Poverty* (1990); *Making Adjustment Work for the Poor* (1990).

6. Cf. Bertrand Badie, *L'État Importé* (Paris: Fayard, 1992), pp. 116–121.

7. The military governments proclaimed their intention to form the nation. However, they wanted to form it on the basis of large economic projects that did not involve the masses of Brazilians. The huge projects did not form the nation. That is why in Third World countries no "national pact" is possible at this time. Cf. Reich, *The Work of Nations*, pp. 301 ff.; Jorge Castañeda urges a "national agreement" for Latin American nations, pp. 471 ff. That the nation is still Latin America under construction, can be seen in Castañeda, *Utopia Unarmed*, pp. 297 ff.

8. Cf. José Ricardio Tauile, "Estado e desenvolvimento capitalista: Propostas para um projeto contemporâneo," in *Alternativa de Esquerda à Crise Brasileira*, pp. 171–195.

9. Cf. *Le Monde Diplomatique*, "Manières de voir," "Europe, l'Utopie Blesśee," nº 22 (May 1994).

10. The problem is how to reduce the chasm between rich and poor, but that cannot be done without progressive taxation. The problems of the welfare state are the result of the secession of the ruling class. Cf. Reich, *The Work of Nations*, pp. 282 ff.

11. In the Third World, elites have always wanted a weak state so that they could plunder it at will. Cf. G. Corm, *Le Nouveau Désordre Économique Mondial*, pp. 69–84.

12. What was discovered was that the state cannot do everything. It cannot provide a solution to all problems. That was what the crisis of socialism showed. There comes a time when excessive state intervention paralyzes the economy. Cf. Peter Drucker, *The New Realities*, pp. 143 ff.

13. The globalization of the economy very much limits the state's ability to intervene in the economy. A great deal of economic life is beyond the control of the state.

14. Cf. Cristovam Buarque, *A Revolução Na Esquerda e a Invenção do Brasil* (São Paulo: Paz e Terra, 1992), pp. 39–82; Pablo González Casanova, "El Estado y la política," in *América Latina Hoy*, pp. 64–122.

15. Cf. Guillermo O'Donnell, "Sobre o Estado, a democratização e alguns problemas conceituais," in *Novos Estudos* (CEBRAP), nº 35, pp. 123–145.

16. Cf. Roger-Gérard Schwarzenberg, *L État Spectacle: Essai sur et contre le Star System en Politique* (Paris: Flammarion, 1977).

17. Cf. Graciela Ducatenzeiler, Philippe Faucher, Julian Castro Rea, "A democracia incerta: Argentina, Brasil, Mexico, Peru," in *Novos Estudos* (CEBRAP), nº 34 (1992), pp. 165–197.

18. Cf. Vilmar Faria, "A conjuntura social brasileira: Dilemas e perspectivas," in *Novos Estudos* (CEBRAP), nº 33 (1992), pp. 103–114.

19. Cf. Bertrand Badie, *L'État Importé*, pp. 177–226.

20. "The national-popular current is so deeply rooted in Latin American history and tradition" (Jorge Castañeda, *Utopia Desarmada*, [Portuguese version] p. 54). Between the theory of development and the theory of dependence which have been in vogue in America (the former in the 1950s and 1980s, and the latter in the 1960s and part of the 1970s), there is a third theory which could be called a typically Latin American model, namely corporativism in which the state is the driving force of change and controls organizations of both business and workers. Cf. Javier Elgua, *Las Teorías del Desarrallo Social en América Latina* (El Colegio de México, 1989), pp. 97–100. Cf. also Edward Littwak, "¿Por que o fascismo é a onda do futuro?" in *Novos Estudos* (CEBRAP), nº 40 (1994), pp. 145–151.

21. Cf. Herberto de Souza, "As ONGs Na década de 90," in *Comunicações do ISER* (year 10) nº 41 (1991), pp. 5–10.

22. "Terceira arena, capaz de proporcionar à sociedade instrumentos de defesa contra processos de mercantilização das relações sociais" (Leonardo Avritzer, "Além da dicotomia Estado/mercado," in *Novos Estudos* (CEBRAP), nº 36 (1993), p. 214.

23. There is a tendency to exaggerate the power of popular movements of the 1970s and 1980s. See for example, Jorge Castañeda, *Utopia Unarmed*, pp. 203–236;

Daniel Camacho, "Los movimientos populares," in *América Latina Hoy*, pp. 123–165. Such exaggeration is especially relevant with regard to church based movements. We should keep in mind the following remarks by Bernardo Sorj in "Crises e horizontes das ciências socias Na America Latina," in *Novos Estudos* (CEBRAP), n° 23 (1989), pp. 154–162: "When the relative importance of certain things is exaggerated, such as the new social movements or the formation of a citizenship awareness, whether by exaggerating the importance of the processes taking place or by failing to acknowledge contrary facts, social sciences run the risk of collapsing out of irrelevance" (p. 158).

24. Here is what Lula has to say about the PT (Workers Party), "Look, I'm going to tell you something I've already said, not just now but since 1991. I think the PT is becoming an elite party insofar as it suitably represents the organized portions of society. We do a wonderful job of representing the Volkswagen worker, who already has thirty strikes under his belt or the Ford or Sofunge worker; students at the University of São Paulo and the Catholic university, the Brazilian middle class—the PT can fight over this sector with any other party, it may be the party with most credibility in this group. The fact is that there is another half of Brazil that doesn't read the paper, doesn't go to the movies, doesn't go to the theater, that is not a union member, and doesn't participate in anything" (Interview, *Novos Estudos*, CEBRAP, n° 36 [1993], p. 73).

25. The popular movements that carried out redemocratization, and others since then, are demanding that the laws be applied, they are not even striving to win new rights. Cf. Paul Monteiro, "Questões para a etnografia numa sociedade mundial," in *Novos Estudos* (CEBRAP), n° 36 (1993), p. 171.

26. We are confronting the "Washington Consensus." The phrase was coined in 1990 by an Englishman living in the United States, John Williamson, at a seminar promoted by the United States government. The Washington Consensus is the program that by common agreement the IMF, the World Bank, and the United States government are seeking to impose on the rest of the world: opening to the world market, fiscal equilibrium, and privatization. In a word, open door to United States capital and multinationals. National governments have very limited powers for dealing with such concentrated power, and civil society cannot do any more than the national government.

27. If democracy does not restore a minimum of national community, populism is powerful. Cf. Norbert Lechner, "A la búsqueda de la comunidad perdida," in Luis Abala-Bertrand, ed., *Cultura y Gobernabilidad Democrática: América Latina en el Umbral del Tercer Milenio* (Montevideo: UNESCO, 1992), pp. 53–57.

28. Cf. L. Kowarick-A. Singer, "A experiência do Partido dos Trabalhadores na prefeitura de São Paulo," in *Novos Estudos* (CEBRAP), n° 35, (1993), pp. 195–216.

7. Cultural Liberation

1. What St.-Simon eloquently stated in his book *Le Nouveau Christianisme* (Paris: Ed. du Seuil, 1969) is an aspiration that is at least three centuries old. It is the entire spirit of modernity.

2. The church's social doctrine continually issues oracles announcing or proclaiming the failure of both socialism and liberalism. Unfortunately, the intellectual world still remembers how things used to be, when all powers were under the church.

3. That nostalgia for christendom can be great is attested by the book of Pedro Morandé, *Cultura y Modernización en América Latina* (Santiago de Chile: PUC, 1984).

4. As a radical demand for freedom, postmodernity is actually a radicalization of modernity, albeit taking the individualistic line to the extreme. Cf. Sergio Paulo Rouanet, *As Razões do Iluminismo* (São Paulo: Companhia das Letras, 1989), pp. 229–276.

5. On the scientific method, cf. Thomas S. Kuhn, *The Structure of Scientific Revolutions* (Chicago: University of Chicago Press, 1970).

6. On the current scientific vision of the world, cf. a very short summary by Ilya Prigogine, in *Idéias contemporâneas* (Paris: Le Monde, 1984), pp. 51–59.

7. All the works cited that offer a comprehensive view of the way the world is moving today highlight the fact that science is becoming the primary factor in production, more important than labor or capital: Robert Reich, Alvin Toffler, Peter Drucker, Paul Kennedy. The Frankfurt School has emphasized the relationship between science and power as though it were something unusual, unforeseen, or shocking. Actually, from the outset scientists have sought to engage in an activity in the world, that is, to exert power.

8. Neoliberalism presents itself as a science: it is the most recent ideology. As an example of scientific analysis of the economy, cf. Javier Elguea, *Las Teorías del Desarrollo Social en América Latina: Una Reconstrucción Racional* (Mexico: El Colegio de México, 1989). It makes clear the distance between science and ideology.

9. Cf. Jean Baudrillard, *Le Miroir de la Production* (Paris: Ed. Galilée, 1985).

10. It is in the United States itself that the most severe critiques of American culture have emerged. Cf. Allan Bloom, *The Closing of the American Mind*. The desperate struggle of the French at the Uruguay Round to salvage something of French culture will be in vain. No one can compete!

11. We cite only one significant work: the worldwide best seller, Daniel J. Boorstin, *The Discoverers* (New York: Penguin, 1983).

12. The fact that a third of American scientists and engineers work in the war industry does arouse some fears. In Paul Kennedy's view, excessive militarization is a hindrance in the competition with the other great blocks of humankind. Cf. Paul Kennedy, *The Rise and Fall of the Great Powers* (New York: Fontana Press, 1988); *Preparing for the Twenty-First Century* (New York: Fontana Press, 1994), pp. 290–324.

13. Ecology has now become a primary concern around the world. The literature is already significant and vast. We merely cite the book of the Vice President of the United States, Al Gore, *Earth in the Balance* (Boston: Houghton-Mifflin, 1992).

14. See a vision of the history of political economics in G. Corm, *Le Nouveau Désordre Économique Mondial*, pp. 9–93. The aim of political economy was always the problem of how to overcome poverty. It changed after World War II, when it became the science of development, that is, of production.

15. Classic works on bourgeois morality: B. Broethuysen, *Origines de l'Esprit Bourgeois en France* (1927); Werner Sombart, *Der Bourgeois*; and we should not forget Max Weber who connects bourgeois ethics to Puritanism.

16. That is why Christopher Lasch's book, *The Revolt of the Elites and the Betrayal of Democracy* (1995), caused such a stir. In Europe people tend to speak more of postmodernity. Postmodernity is a radical critique of the bourgeois ethic with regard to both work and nation.

17. In Latin America human rights have been invoked as the basis for challenging

military regimes, but not very effectively. Governments paid no attention. To this day human rights are invoked in struggles for the rights of the poor, likewise without practical results. The reason is that human rights were expressed in the claims of the bourgeoisie against the power of an absolute monarchy. The bourgeoisie, however, has economic power, while the poor have no power on which to base their rights. The bourgeoisie is unlikely to make concessions to the poor in the name of human rights. Human rights need an ethics much deeper than the ethics of human rights, i.e., an ethics of solidarity. Such an ethics is absent from today's social elites.

18. The title of Cristovam Buarque's book is suggestive: *A Revolução nas Prioridades: Da Modernidade Técnica à Modernidade Ética.* The problem is that technical rationality is rooted in culture, and the new ethics spoken of is to this day nothing but a word with no roots in culture. Pope John Paul II has tirelessly repeated appeals for an ethics of solidarity. Indeed, only such an ethics can provide support for the aspirations of the poor, and a content for the rights of the poor. Cf. *Sollicitudo Rei Socialis,* n° 38–39.

19. Cf. Richard Bergeron et al., *A Nova Era em Questão* (São Paulo: Paulus, 1995).

20. On Central America, cf. Phillip Berryman, *Stubborn Hope: Religion, Politics, and Revolution in Central America* (Maryknoll, NY: Orbis Books, 1994), pp. 144–158.

21. That Protestant pentecostalism is experienced as cultural liberation is demonstrated by Carlos Rodrigues Brandão in "Creença e Identidade," in Pierre Sanchis, ed., ISER, *Catolicismo no Brasil Atual* Vol 3, *Catolicismo: Unidade Religiosa e Pluralismo Cultural* (São Paulo: Loyola, 1992), pp. 7–74. "Pentecostalism is today everywhere the legitimate possibility for persons of the popular classes to create and advance their own churches as churches" (p. 33).

22. On the charismatic renewal: "Pedro Ribeiro de Oliveira, in interpreting the renewal as it is experienced by the urban middle classes, states that it seeks to stand up to the religious domination exercised by the clergy. The believer, who is in charge of his or her life in other spheres, also wants to guide his or her own religious life," Nair Costa Muls and Telma de Souze Birchal, in ISER, *Catolicismo no Brasil - 3: Campesinato: Modernização e Catolicismo* (1992), p. 88.

23. It is the church's function to provide "readjustment" with a human face. Cf. "Adjustment with a Human Face," in Amy Sherman, *Preferential Option: A Christian and Neoliberal Strategy for Latin America's Poor,* pp. 107–129.

8. Personal Liberation

1. Cf. Paulo Fernando Carneiro de Andrade, "Militância e crise de subjetividade," in *Cadernos Fé e Política* (Petrópolis: Vozes) n° 5, p. 5.

2. Ibid., p. 10.

3. Cf. Gordon Leff, *Heresy in the Later Middle Ages* (New York: Barnes & Noble, 1967) Vol. 1, pp. 314–321 and on the movement of Beghards and Beguines, pp. 321–407.

4. Obviously there is an immense literature on this world of semi-underground spiritualism. If one wants a good sampling of this parallel world one may read Umberto Eco's novel, *Foucault's Pendulum* (New York: Harcourt Brace, 1992).

5. Thomas Kuhn explains how scientific hypotheses little by little break away from the fantasies of traditional representations and thus gradually free themselves from esotericism. Cf. Kuhn, *The Structure of Scientific Revolutions* (Chicago, 1970).

6. Hence, it is possible to discuss endlessly whether postmodernity is the end of modernity or its radicalization. It may be the end of those ideologies that sought to discipline modernity with the structure of an equivalent of christendom, and of an imposed and rationalized social order. But the deepest yearnings of modernity, which are yearnings for autonomy, remain and become more acute in postmodernity.

7. Cf. Nicolás Casullo, ed., *El Debade Modernidad-Pos-Modernidad* (Buenos Aires: Puntosur, Buenos Aires, 1989); Sergio Paulo Rouanet, *As Razões do Iluminismo* (São Paulo: Companhia das Letras, 1989), pp. 229–277; Manfredo Araujo de Oliveira, "A Modernidade da America Latina," in the essay collection *Vida, Clamor e Esperança* (São Paulo: Loyola, 1992), pp. 77–86.

8. Here Foucault is extremely influential in Latin America among intellectuals precisely because of his radically anti-institutional stance.

9. In the sense of Christopher Lasch, *The Culture of Narcissism* (1991).

10. Cf. Jean-Louis Schlegel, "Néo-ésoterisme et Modernité," in Centre Thomas More, *Christianisme et Modernité* (Paris: Cerf, 1990), pp. 273–293.

11. Cf. Richard Bergeron, Alain Bouchard, Pierre Pelletier, *A Nova Era em Questão* (São Paulo: Paulus, 1994).

12. This must be the primary reason for the triumphal success of the Catholic charismatic renewal (which can only be compared with the success of pentecostal Protestantism). Cf. Pedro R. de Oliveira, *Renovação Carismática Católica* (Petrópolis: Vozes, 1978), pp. 119–175.

13. Actual experience of personal contact with persons who still belong to the world of christendom shows that there always are and certainly always have been exceptions, persons who have had spiritual experiences almost by instinct. These were and still are the anonymous mystics. Nevertheless the usual case has been that of a faith that is accepted in inculturated form. Such a faith is not lacking in depth. However, it enters into crisis when it must confront the new religious experiences, which are much more conscious and personalized. The traditional Christian feels tiny when confronting religious activity that is much more militant.

14. Cf. Phillip Berryman, *Stubborn Hope: Religion, Politics, and Revolution in Central America* (Maryknoll, NY: Orbis Books, 1994), pp. 144–158.

15. Cf. J. B. Libânio, "Religião e Catolicismo do Povo," in C. Brandão et al., *Igreja que Nasce da Religião do Povo* (São Paulo: Ave Maria, 1978), pp. 119–175; Pedro R. de Oliveira, "Religiosidad Popular na América Latina," in *REB*, vol. 32 (1972), pp. 354–364; "Catolicismo Popular e Romanização do Catolicismo Brasileiro," in *REB*, vol. 36 (1976), pp. 131–141.

16. On the challenge of the experience of God, cf. Leonardo Boff and Frei Betto, *Mística e Espirtualidade* (Rio de Janeiro: Rocco, 1994).

17. In the sense of J. K. Galbraith, *The Culture of Contentment*.

18. For centuries the church has instilled guilt and it grounded a good portion of its pastoral work in instilling guilt. Perhaps historians can shed some light on the question of to what extent the church instilled guilt in the people of the West or, to the contrary, was imbued with a feeling of guilt that was intrinsic to the environment. On the history of sin and of instilling blame in the West, we have the magisterial works of Jean Delumeau, *La Peur en Occident: XIVe-XVIIIe Siècles* (Paris: Fayard, 1978); *Le Péché el la Peur: La Culpabilisation en Occident. XIIIe-XVIIIe Siècles* (Paris: Fayard, 1983). After centuries of deeply instilled guilt, the twentieth century came along like a huge catharsis which has given the impression of a huge psychological liberation: liberation from the feeling of sin. Now

the new generations have not even heard sin mentioned, while the generation of their parents exorcise and ridicule it because they have shed their fear. Sin has become something to joke about.

19. For centuries the church's precept of annual confession was torture for countless Christians. St. Alfonsus Ligouri complained about the large number of sacrilegious confessions, that is, deceitful or incomplete confessions. The precept of annual confession was a major factor in instilling guilt. In Brazil, and Latin America in general, the revolt against confession is not so strong because most Catholics never went to confession, and a huge number of baptized people do not even know what it is. Fortunate ignorance that avoids the sin of rebellion!

20. Cf. Lasch, *The Culture of Narcissism*, pp. 71–99.

21. Cf. the remaking of the subject after modernity, Alain Touraine, *Critique de la Modernité* (Paris: Fayard, 1992).

22. The best exposition of this part of Paul's message in the Latin American context is that of Juan Luis Segundo, *La Historia Perdida y Recuperada de Jesús de Nazaret: De los Sinópticos a Pablo* (Santander: Sal Terrae, 1991), pp. 371–634.

23. On this mystical meaning of poverty as the great revealer, see the testimonies gathered by José Ignacio González Faus, *Vicarios de Cristo: Los Pobres en la Teología y Espiritualidad Cristianas* (Madrid: Trotta, 1991).

INDEX

decline in moral conscience in, 164; retirees in, 71; sense of guilt among various groups in, 192; service jobs in, 71; social apartheid in, 65; working class in, 70

Brazilian bishops, 51, 225n.39

Brotherhood Campaign (Brazil), 205, 219n.2

Büchi, Hernán, 110, 133, 204

Buddhism, 152–53, 183

Bultmann, Rudolf, 31

Bush, George, 68, 106, 124, 204, 220–21n.4, 230n.18

Camara, Dom Helder, 212

capital: computers and, 103–4; current state of flow of, 101–2; international speculation and, 161. *See also* capitalism; economics; market, the

capitalism: current amorphous state of, 101–2; current expansion of, 99; dangers of neoliberal, in Latin America, 113–16; John Paul II on the fall of socialism and, 233n.24; liberation theology and the Marxist critique of, 214; opening of socialism to, 112; as opposed to civil society, 134; the popular masses' acceptance of, 112–13; poverty created by, 107; production and, 145; science and, 156; a theology of the poor and, 225n.32. *See also* economics; market, the

Cardoso, Fernando Henrique, 133, 228n.11

Caribbean, the, 169

carnival, 164

Castañeda, Jorge, 115–18, 220n.2, 230n.24, 230–31n.29, 236n.20

Catechism for the Catholic Church, 10, 11, 34, 225n.35

Catholic Action, 3–4, 6, 52, 222n.7

Catholic Charismatic Renewal. *See* charismatic renewal

Catholic church: the bourgeoisie and, 165; on the failure of socialism, 237n.2; as folklore, 150; guilt caused by, 191–93; history of personal liberation vis-à-vis, 173–84; land reform and, 230n.16; liberalism and socialism on the failures of, 139–40;

medieval culture of, prior to Vatican II, 138; modernity and, 138–39, 153–54; needing to condemn neoliberal capitalism, 113–16; the new evangelization of, 1–7, 9–18; obstacles to evangelization by, 169–70; overemphasis on sin, 30; the pentecostal churches and, 169; personal freedom and, 185–90; the poor and, 7–9, 167, 200, 201, 223n.20, 224n.27; and resistance to global culture, 153; science and, 142; subjectivity as a challenge to, 171–73; the working class and, 223n.21

Cavallo, Domingo, 110, 133, 204

Centesimus Annus, 229n.6, 233n.15

charismatic renewal: in Brazil, 225–26n.39; and the current sources of interest in religion, 203; methods of, 169; as a North American phenomenon, 55; reasons for success of, 15, 211, 240n.12; relation to the clergy, 239n.22

Chicago school, 104

Chile: the church and the poor in, 75; democracy in, 131; the import substitution model and, 110; inclination of people toward right-wing politics in, 196; industrial workers in, 74; neoliberalism in, 111, 112, 204; ``No'' campaign in, 120; populism in, 77; privatization in, 124; Protestantism in, 169

christendom: arbitrary notions of God of, 190; attempts to replace, 178; attitude toward the poor, 75; as a basis of solidarity, 38–39; the Congregation for the Doctrine of the Faith's continuing belief in, 35; the individual in, 173; modernity as emancipation from, 165; the new evangelization and, 19; Trent and, 176; view of evangelization presented by, 10–11

Christian base communities, 167; beginnings of, 84; Boff (L.) on, 231n.31; Catholic Action compared with, 6; current needs of, 90; discouragement and hope regarding,